ART OF THE WORLD

EUROPEAN CULTURES

THE HISTORICAL, SOCIOLOGICAL

AND RELIGIOUS BACKGROUNDS

THE ART OF GREECE: THE AGE OF HELLENISM

BY

T.B.L. WEBSTER

CROWN PUBLISHERS, INC., NEW YORK

Frontispiece: *A male and female centaur in a chariot driven by a winged Victory, Gnathia Krater from Egnazia, early 3rd century* B.C. *British Museum, cf. pp. 30, 69, 177.*

FIRST PUBLISHED IN 1966

LIBRARY OF CONGRESS CATALOG NUMBER 66-26188
PRINTED IN HOLLAND

In memoriam Andreae Rumpf

LIST OF COLOUR PLATES

LIST OF FIGURES

ACKNOWLEDGMENTS

The following museums kindly allowed reproduction of the plates on the pages listed below:

Athens, Agora Museum 61, 68, 78
Berlin, Staatliche Antikenabteilung 105
Cleveland, Cleveland Museum of Art 29
Florence, Museo Archeologico 175
Hamburg, Museum für Kunst und Gewerbe 121
Istanbul, Archaeological Museum 45, 46
London, British Museum 3, 22, 47, 52, 58, 63, 73, 113, 187, 190, 191
Munich, Staatliche Antikensammlung 27, 48
Naples, Museo Nazionale 39, 40, 42, 109, 117, 118
New York, Metropolitan Museum 81, 133, 135, 137
Paris, Musée du Louvre 34, 99, 151
Rome, Museo Capitolino 103
Rome, Vatican Library 138, 139
Rome, Terme Museum 111
Salonika, Archaeological Museum 21
Stanford, Stanford Museum 100
Thasos, Archaeological Museum 54

The colour plates on the following pages were kindly supplied by:

M. Chuzeville, Paris 34, 151
Fratelli Fabbri, Milan 160
S. R. Gnamm, Munich 27
Ionian and Popular Bank, Athens 65
R. Kammel, Neustadt 56
R. Kleinhempel, Hamburg 121
N. Kontos, Athens 21, 54, 61, 68, 78, 144, 147, 148, 155, 156
A. Pachos, Rhodos 84
J. Remmer, Munich 3, 22, 39, 40, 42, 47, 52, 58, 63, 73, 103, 109, 111, 113, 117, 118, 138, 139, 175, 179, 187, 190–1
Editions Rencontre, Paris 114, 158, 159
M. Seidel, Mittenwald 45, 48

The following museums kindly allowed reproduction of the black-and-white plates listed below:

Athens, Agora Museum 14–16
Athens, National Museum 2, 9, 18–21
Bardo, Musée National 12
Berlin, Pergamon Museum 7, 8, 10
Istanbul, Archaeological Museum 17, 26
Kavalla Museum 4
London, British Museum 6
New York, Walter C. Baker Collection 13
Paris, Louvre 3
Rome, Terme Museum 11
Rome, Vatican Museum 1
Rome, Vatican Museum, Braccio Nuovo 5
Syracuse, Museo Nazionale 23

The author wishes to express his gratitude to Dr Ann E. Keep for preparing the text for the press and for compiling the index.

CONTENTS

INTRODUCTION

Political history

The Hellenistic age is the link between classical Greece and Imperial Rome. It may be taken as beginning with the death of Alexander and the death of Aristotle and ending with the death of Julius Caesar. The political history is immensely complicated. Alexander had spread the boundaries of the Greek world eastward to India; his generals divided his inheritance between them and founded dynasties which had a more or less chequered career until they were conquered one after another by the Romans.

Within this ring of potentates the old Greek cities of the mainland, the islands, and the coast of Asia Minor continued as independent city-states, sometimes menaced and sometimes protected, until they too came under the Romans. In art and thought they were strongly conservative, clinging to a way of life which could not survive for long in the new world. The new Hellenistic courts were centres of art and literature, attracting artists and poets from the old Greek cities and in their turn influencing the old Greek cities by their products.

The old Greek cities of Sicily and South Italy were between the great military powers of Carthage and Rome. Rome conquered Carthage and by the end of the third century B.C. Sicily and South Italy were under Roman domination. But from early in the third century Rome was already a force to be reckoned with by the Hellenistic kings: Ptolemy II of Egypt sent an embassy to Rome before 270 B.C. and Attalos I of Pergamon was allied with Rome in the latter part of the third century.

Rome and Greek art

Horace's epigram 'captive Greece conquered its savage captor' is so well known that we are apt to think of Rome as unaware of Greek art before the middle of the second century. The truth was very different. Through the medium of Etruscan art, and to a smaller degree from direct imports, Romans had known Greek forms and Greek stories from the seventh century B.C.; from 338 B.C. the Greek cities of Campania had become Roman allies, and their art must have been well known to the Romans. From early in the third century Greek art started pouring into Rome, first from the nearer conquests in South Italy and Sicily and later from further afield.

Aristotle

If Alexander was the political father of the Hellenistic age, Aristotle was the intellectual father of the Hellenistic age. We are not concerned with his contributions to philosophy and natural science, but rather with his ideas and ideals in so far as they may have affected the history of art. Very simply they may be summarised as the establishment of biological categories, the establishment of a classical ideal, and the beginnings of scholarship. All three are clear enough in Aristotle's work on literature, and though we can only see traces of their adaptation to art, it is reasonable to suppose that contemporaries and successors went to Aristotle for inspiration and applied the same methods to art criticism as he applied to literary criticism. The parallelism of art and literature was well established as an idea before Aristotle wrote, and in the later fifth century the great artist as well as the great poet wrote on his technique.

Art theory

Thus we find Aristotle comparing Polygnotos to Sophokles and Zeuxis to later tragedians; and the two important biological notions, that a particular genre of literature like tragedy grew to perfection and then stopped, and that the beginning of a new genre was due to a unique and seemingly random reaction between human nature and environment, were as applicable to art as to literature. This second notion seems to be behind the story told by Douris of Samos, a pupil of Aristotle's successor, Theophrastos: the great fourth-century sculptor Lysippos was a smith in a bronze-foundry until one day he asked the painter Eupompos what earlier painter influenced him; Eupompos pointed to the crowd and said, 'Follow nature, not another artist'; this inspired Lysippos to start sculpture. The story may be true, but Douris clearly picks it because it fits the Aristotelian scheme.

The other biological notion, growth to perfection, is much more influential, and again we can see a critic of the early third century, Xenokrates, who was himself a sculptor, using it for the history of art: 'Pheidias first opened the way to the art of bronze-casting and Polykleitos perfected it'. This notion leads to the establishment of a classical ideal: Sophokles and Euripides in tragedy, Lysippos in sculpture, Apelles in painting. The Greeks had always admired the glories of the Mycenaean age; in fact, that memory had probably kept them alive through the dark centuries from Mykenai to Homer. But admiration for the more recent past only appears very occasionally in the late fifth century, rather more often in the fourth century, until it meets us continually in the Hellenistic age. The biological notion of growth to perfection provided an intellectual framework for this admiration.

Scholarship

If history is to be written on this scheme, scholarship must provide the materials. For literature Aristotle is the founder of scholarship both by making a record of dramatic productions from the beginning of the dramatic competitions and by insisting that difficult passages in ancient poets may have a historical explanation. In the Hellenistic age this kind of work was developed in the Mouseion of Alexandria; the initiative came from Demetrios of Phaleron, a pupil of Aristotle's successor Theophrastos, and here the work of collecting texts, cataloguing them, commenting on them, summarising them and writing biographies of archaic and classical authors was carried out by scholars, five of whom at least were leading poets of the day. Scholarship was exercised by poets and immediately influenced their poetry.

We know much less about the scholarship of art than about the scholarship of poetry, but Vitruvius in the late first century B.C. and Pliny in the first century A.D. give ample testimony to the amount of factual information that had been collected by their time to fill out the summary outlines of the growth to perfection theory. Some of the writers were themselves artists: Antigonos of Karystos, a sculptor who worked at Pergamon, is credibly supposed to have taken over Xenokrates' work and to have added much biographical fact; Pasiteles, sculptor and metal-worker of the first century B.C., wrote 'five volumes about notable works in the whole world'; Vitruvius was a practising architect. Scholarship influenced art as well as poetry.

Kallimachos

A certain amount is known also about the lists and descriptions in Hellenistic prose of works of art, but it is perhaps more interesting to look for a moment at the third-century Alexandrian poet Kallimachos. One poem of about sixty lines, partially preserved, is addressed to a friend who is sailing to Elis to see the temple of Zeus at Olympia, which contained the gold and ivory statue of Zeus by Pheidias. The poem gave the length, height, and width of the statue itself, of the throne on which the god sat, of his footstool, and of the pedestal which supported the whole; this is not great poetry but a remarkable testimony to the information of the poet and the interest of the reader in a great classical statue.

Another poem is a dialogue between the poet and a statue of Apollo made for the limestone temple of Apollo in Delos between 650 and 550 B.C. After a brief reference to an earlier aniconic statue the god describes himself as 27 cubits high, golden, clad only in a belt; he holds a bow in order to punish fools for their insolence, and to good men he stretches out his hand with the three Graces on it; the bow is in the left hand because he is slow to chastise and the Graces are on his right hand because he is always disposed to distribute pleasant things. The archaic sculptor probably had no such message in mind; the bow was Apollo's normal attribute; in Delos he was also given little figures of the three Graces standing on his right hand, because they had an important cult there. The Hellenistic poet has not only shown his interest in art history but has provided a religious interpretation of an archaic statue which is in line with contemporary ethics.

Collections

Parallel to the Hellenistic libraries which collected and edited texts were the art collections. In the middle of the third century Aratos, not the astronomical poet but the tyrant of Sikyon, was according to Plutarch 'a good judge of painting and collected works by the best artists, particularly Pamphilos and Melanthos'. Pamphilos and Melanthos were classical Sikyonian painters of the first half of the fourth century and therefore were Old Masters when Aratos collected them. Not only did he collect for himself but he sent a number of paintings to Ptolemy III of Egypt so that the story is evidence for a royal collection of Alexandria as well. In Pergamon the royal collection of sculpture included archaic statues of the Graces by Boupalos of Chios and other statues of the very early fifth century. Greeks had, of course, always been able to see early works of art dedicated in temples, and buildings like the Stoa Poikile of Athens were decorated with frescoes by the leading painters of the day when they were built. What is new in these royal collections is the conscious collection of old masterpieces, which were certainly on some festival days open to the public view. Greek temples were in fact collections of works of art because generations of dedicators had offered the most beautiful and costly things to the gods. It is questionable how much of the temple was open to visitors in earlier times and how much the visitors looked at earlier works of art. For the Hellenistic age we have the evidence of the poem by Herondas which describes two women visiting the temple of Asklepios at Kos and exclaiming at the sculptures outside and the paintings inside the temple. The women certainly treat the temple as an art gallery and this attitude is quite different from the religious attitude with which we suppose the contemporaries of Pheidias viewed the sculptures of the Parthenon or the dedicators themselves made the dedications. It would be interesting to know how the Romans regarded the numerous Greek works of art which they dedicated in Rome. Mummius in the middle of the second century after the sack of Corinth observed that Attalos II of Pergamon bought a fourth-century Theban painting for an enormous sum. Mummius therefore withdrew the picture from the sale and dedicated it in the temple of Ceres at Rome. Attalos undoubtedly was securing a piece for the royal collection; was Mummius primarily pleasing the goddess by a noble gift or enriching the temple collection? We do not know, but we know that in the next century Cicero's contemporaries regarded the temple of Athena at Syracuse as a picture gallery: they were charmed by the long series of portraits of Sicilian tyrants and kings, by the skill of the artists, and by the fact that they could see what these famous men looked like. *Temples*

For the royal library at Pergamon the king wanted a statue of Athena, as the patroness of Athens and of learning, and the most famous Athena was the gold and ivory statue of the Athena Parthenos made by Pheidias for the Parthenon; he had a free copy made on a reduced scale. This is one of the earliest instances we know of copying; his successor had the paintings of Polygnotos in Delphi copied and presumably the copies were added to the royal collection. *Copies* FIG. I

In the late second and early first centuries there was an immense demand for works of art from private collectors, particularly in Italy. The ancient cities of Greece were by now included in the provinces of Rome and so successive conquests were no longer a source of works

FIG. 1 – *Athena Parthenos. Marble. Copy of statue by Pheidias. Cf. p. 17 and below.*

of art. It became the practice to take mechanical copies of Greek statues and reliefs; a copy of Pheidias or Polykleitos was as acceptable or more acceptable than a contemporary work. Thus the Athena Parthenos in the royal library at Pergamon is a precursor of the later large-scale trade in copies, and at the same time as the king ordered his Athena, the ordinary householder could buy reduced copies in terracotta of fourth-century statues from the factory at Myrina.

Statues could be reproduced by mechanical copying, and moulds could be taken from silver ware to give accurate copies in metal or clay. The methods employed in copying paintings are not so clear. Large-scale copies made on the spot are probably the exception rather than the rule: a king of Pergamon could arrange this, or a Roman general might leave an accurate copy to replace an original which he had taken to Rome. The very fine tiny mosaics signed by Dioskourides of Samos seem to be late second-century copies of third-century originals probably painted in Pergamon: they were found in Pompeii and one of them is copied in a wall-painting from Stabiae. Here at least is one case where the transmission from Asia Minor to Italy can be illustrated.

PLATES PP. 117–18

Summary

The general picture of the Hellenistic age is something like this. Art production was divided between the old cities of Greece, Asia Minor, and Italy and the new courts of the Hellenistic dynasties. The old cities were very conscious of their pasts. The new dynasties were more adventurous, but also made their own claims to preserve and re-incarnate the Greek heritage. Rome, long aware of Greek art, plundered all the art she could as the Greek world fell beneath her sway, and in the last century of the Republic imported artists as well as works of art. All alike were conscious of classical Greece, and art historians, guide-books, collections, and copies all combined to remind artists and public of the summits achieved in sculpture and painting by the fifth and fourth centuries. Thus, by the side of great technical proficiency and in some directions great originality, erudition, formalism, classicism, and conservatism may always appear in Hellenistic art.

I. EARLY HELLENISTIC PERIOD

The Hellenistic period may be said to start with the death of Alexander and Aristotle, but several of the great artists lived over the break and the early Hellenistic period is dominated by them and their successors. The great sculptors of the third quarter of the fourth century were Lysippos of Sikyon, Praxiteles, Leochares, and Bryaxis of Athens, and Skopas of Paros. Of these Lysippos was succeeded by his pupils and Praxiteles by his sons. We cannot point to direct successors for the others; but the fleshy, leonine brows and deep sunk eyes of Skopas, the milder, more pathetic eyes of Bryaxis, and the dramatic poise of Leochares' statues live on in many Hellenistic figures. The great painters were Pausias of Sikyon, Euphranor of the Isthmos, Nikias of Athens, Apelles of Ephesos. Less is known about the pupils of the painters; but again the survival of distinctive styles can be shown, and Apelles himself lived on to work at the court of Ptolemy I in Alexandria.

HERITAGE OF LYSIPPOS AND PAUSIAS

Lysippos was a superb bronze-worker, who, besides being a naturalist in the treatment of detail, in one statue at least, the Apoxyomenos, realised a new concept of sculpture: the athlete stands with one arm stretched out towards the spectator and the other across the body so that no single view is satisfactory and the figure must be considered three-dimensionally. This method of composition survives in a number of striking groups in the Hellenistic period.

Tyche of Antioch

APPX. PL. I

One of the earliest is the group of Antioch on the Orontes made by Eutychidas of Sikyon, a pupil of Lysippos. Seleukos was one of Alexander's generals and the first of the Seleukid dynasty, and ruled much of Alexander's Eastern empire with an eastern capital on the Tigris and a western capital at Antioch on the Orontes. The statue is called Tyche, which in this context is better translated Success than Chance. She is the success of the new city. Her crown shows its walls. Her right hand holds the palm-leaves of victory. Her eyes look into the glorious future. She sits on her cliff above the river, and the river-god, swimming by, looks back in astonishment at the new goddess seated on his banks. The composition is a very accomplished construction of triangles set in different planes so that the spectator is forced to apprehend the volume of the group. The whole figure is neat, and the folds of the drapery are simple and their lines clear: the echo of the vertical lines of the veil by the folds falling over the rock is particularly successful. Com-

PLATE P. 63

parison with a Praxitelean figure shows that it is composition rather than style of drapery or proportion of the figures which distinguishes the successors of Lysippos from the successors of Praxiteles.

The goddess, seated on her cliff looking into the future and herself regarded by the swimming river-god, recalls the slightly later passage of the *Argonautika* of Apollonios Rhodios in which, when the Argo set sail, 'the Nymphs of Mount Pelion gazed in wonder on their highest peaks, as they saw the ship of Athena and the heroes themselves mastering their oars'. In classical Greek art places were normally represented by the figures of their nymphs; Eutychidas and Apollonios add this element to the personification – the nymphs are on their peaks, Tyche sits on her cliffs. Later the balance is changed and the figures are reduced to a minimum when the painter becomes interested in land-

PLATES PP. 138–9

scape for its own sake.

Dherveni krater

PLATE P. 21

The Tyche is only known to us from Roman copies. A magnificent original which has been reasonably attributed to the school of Lysippos is the bronze krater found in 1962 at Dherveni, ten kilometres north-east of Salonika. The name Asteiounios of Larisa, son of Anaxagoras, is inscribed on the vase; presumably he was a Thessalian who died in Macedonia, and his ashes were buried in the vase. The figures are in the neat athletic style of Lysippos. The decoration except for the frieze of animals on the neck is all connected with Dionysos: fruited ivy round the neck; figures of Dionysos, maenads, and satyr on the shoulder; round the body Dionysos and Ariadne and their thiasos of satyrs and maenads.

The krater is a mixing-bowl used at the symposion for mixing wine and water before it is dealt out in oinochoai to the cups of the drinkers. Dionysos is the god of wine so that it is appropriate that a krater should be decorated with the story of his wooing Ariadne in the company of his devoted band of satyrs and maenads; kraters had been so decorated since at least the early sixth century B.C. This scene is a modernised

PLATE 2 – Head of Aura (Breeze) rising from the middle of flowers and vine tendrils. Apulian vase. Mid-4th century B.C. *British Museum. Cf. pp. 25, 66, 186, 189.*

version, with exciting movement and drapery, of an old theme, and we shall meet it again and again in Hellenistic art. Ivy is also particularly associated with Dionysos; he himself and his satyrs and maenads frequently wear a wreath of ivy, and at the symposion the drinking often took place beneath long sprays of fruited ivy.

PLATE P. 21 But this krater, like the great painted clay kraters from Tarentum which provide the nearest parallel in shape, was found in a tomb and contained the cremated ashes of the dead man. The association of Dionysos with the dead is a difficult subject. He is the god of all life that rises in the spring, the sap in the trees and the semen in animals and men. By worshipping him men may hope to rise again after the

PLATE I – Bronze krater from Dherveni with figures of Dionysos, maenads and satyrs, inscribed with the name of Asteiounios of Larisa. *Circa* 320 B.C. *Height 73 cm. Archaeological Museum, Salonika. Cf. pp. 20ff., 24ff., 64.*

winter of death and to revel for ever with his thiasos in what Plato calls 'eternal intoxication'. This statement is, of course, oversimplified, but Asteiounios or his family must have believed something of this kind when his ashes were committed to this magnificent bronze krater with its Dionysiac decoration.

PLATE P. 65
Pella mosaics

Small neat Lysippan figures appear again on the mosaic signed by Gnosis, which was found in a rich house in the Macedonian capital of Pella, some thirty kilometres west of Salonika. The Athenian orator Demosthenes naturally liked to represent the Macedonians as barbarians, but already in the late fifth century Archelaos, king of Macedon, had summoned the tragic poet Euripides and the painter Zeuxis to his court, and the Early Hellenistic pebble mosaics found at Pella are magnificent. Mosaic was a comparatively new art then. The much simpler coarse pebble mosaics from Olynthos date from shortly before the middle of the fourth century; the full refinement of technique with carefully prepared stones belongs to the Middle Hellenistic period. But the mosaics at Pella show a considerable colour range in the pebbles, which are sometimes confined by inset strips of lead.

Mosaics are a floor decoration and in some houses were confined to the floor of the men's dining-room, where dinner was followed by the symposion. They were closely related in design to the elaborate textiles which wealthy Greeks hung on their dining-room walls. Painting, figured textiles, and mosaic run on parallel courses from the early fourth century through the Hellenistic age.

The Pella mosaics come from two houses of the late fourth or early third century. Their stylistic connexions are various, but the Dionysos and the lion hunt from one house are clearly influenced by Sikyonian painting; the lion hunt may indeed be an echo of the bronze group by Lysippos and Leochares, dedicated at Delphi by Krateros, who took part in the lion hunt and saved Alexander from the lion. The deer hunt signed by Gnosis is a well-balanced composition held together by the two diagonals which run from corner to corner. The treatment of space is the same in all the mosaics: a plain backdrop with a narrow shelf in front, which here represents rocky ground with a light stone in front of the hunter's foot on the right. The Sikyonian painter has none of the Sikyonian sculptor's desire to force the third dimension on the spectator. The modelling of the bodies and the foreshortening of the dog's hindquarters give us some understanding of the skill of Sikyonian painters in encaustic: Pausias painted a foreshortened ox, in which he attained a great effect of depth without highlights by modelling in different tones of black.

Floral decoration

Pausias also painted a 'great variety of flowers', and it must have been at him that the Athenian painter Nikias aimed his criticism: 'Choose big subjects and do not mince up your art into birds and flowers.' The beautiful floral border of the mosaic signed by Gnosis is, therefore, like the main picture, in the Sikyonian tradition. The whole recalls a Hellenistic epigram: 'Consider, all you spectators, whether Apelles painted this by genius or by art. Greetings also to the flower-painter; I do not know his name but he was a good painter.' The subject of this epigram was evidently a painting by Apelles set in a floral frame painted by another painter.

The floral borders of Pompeian mosaics are quite different from the Gnosis florals; they are composed of mixed flowers and fruits, often with masks hung on them. Their origin is clear: the dining-room might be decorated by such a long swag of mixed flowers or fruits with or without pendant masks (appropriate because Dionysos was the god of drama as well as of wine) or by painted copies of them, and the individual drinker could wear a wreath of mixed fruit or flowers on his head: the wreath of fruited ivy round the neck of the Dherveni krater is merely a simpler version. Pausias may well have painted pictures of these swags since he was said to have been in love with a garland-maker.

PLATE P. 21

The Gnosis florals do not belong to this symposion tradition. Gnosis has given us mixed flowers, leaves and tendrils growing out of a bunch of akanthos leaves: rose, crocus, lily and some kind of euphorbia can certainly be identified, and the tendrils suggest convolvulus. This is a never-never tree. It recalls first the contemporary decoration of the house at Vergina, thirty kilometres to the south-west, where one room has a mosaic completely given over to mixed floral decoration with a goddess in each corner rising from inverted akanthos-leaves. In Vergina also is a remarkable Hellenistic tomb which has an Ionic façade with an elaborate door leading to a vestibule inside the tomb. Under the

FIG. 2

FIG. 2 – *Mixed flowers, leaves and tendrils. Painted frieze on the façade of a Hellenistic tomb at Vergina. Circa 200 B.C. Cf. p. 24.*

pediment of the façade is a frieze of mixed flowers, leaves and tendrils attached to a single running stalk. The background is blue, the leaves green, the stalks white and the flowers white or red with yellow centres. The never-never tree is therefore as suitable for the tomb as for the dining-room.

Very similar decoration occurs in the West – in a tomb in Syracuse, probably decorated by a Tarentine artist, and on Tarentine vases. Again, as with the Dherveni krater, a close stylistic analogy can be seen between Tarentum and Macedonia; the common factor is the style of Sikyonian painting and metalwork; its influence can be traced back in Tarentum to the earliest years of the fourth century. A Tarentine vase in the British Museum, which dates about the middle of the fourth century, has a woman's head rising from a flower in the middle of mixed floral ornament, which certainly includes lilies, akanthos and vine tendrils. She is inscribed AURA, 'breeze'. The inscription is the one certain clue we have to interpretation. On these Tarentine vases, many of them certainly funerary, the mixed floral ornament constantly surrounds a woman's head (which sometimes has wings on either side) but this is the only vase that gives her name. It may not be wrong to think of Sokrates' picture of an ideal education: 'As if living in a healthy place, the young men may profit from everything, from all the fair works of which something impinges on their sight or hearing, like a Breeze bringing Health from noble places.' The 'noble places' might be the garden of the Hesperides or the islands of the

PLATE P. 21

Apulian vases

PLATE P. 22

Blest; in either place never-never trees could grow. The Breeze lives there and can bring Health to the banqueter in the palace or can take the dead back to live in eternal bliss. Olympos, the dwelling of the gods, also had such foliage, which explains the gold ornamental flower towards which the eagle carries Ganymede on his wing.

Eileithyia, the goddess of childbirth, has been suggested for the woman among the flowers, on the analogy of terracottas which have Eileithyia among flowers. In fact the connection of Breeze with childbirth is close. The chorus of Euripides' *Hippolytos* speak of the Breeze which blew through them at childbirth, and the winged woman carrying a formal flower, who appears on Attic wedding vases, may very well be a Breeze bringing the young wife a flower from Eileithyia's garden, a hope for successful childbearing in the future.

The neat Lysippan figures also appear in the work of the painters
PLATE P. 27 of the big Tarentine funerary kraters of the late fourth century. One
PLATE P. 21 in Munich has the same ornament on the lip as the Dherveni krater and the same leaves round the foot as occur on the mosaic in the Vergina palace. That this vase was intended for the dead is clear from the back which shows honours being paid to the tomb of a young man. The mythical scenes on the front are probably meant to associate him with the heroic dead. The main scene is inspired by a tragedy on the subject of Medeia, and these vases give us an insight into the theatrical life of Tarentum in the century before Livius Andronicus took Greek drama to Rome. The play is not Euripides' play but a play by a contemporary who was strongly influenced by Euripides.

The painter has a strong feeling for the architectural shape of the vase, which he emphasises by the perspective of the beams painted round the top of the neck. In the main scene on the body the shape of handles and neck is picked up by the two white columns at the top corners, by the central white building and by the chariot below.

He has divided his space into three levels. The top level is occupied by divine spectators: Herakles, Athena, the Dioskouroi, set between

PLATE 3 – Tarentine krater with extracts from a Medeia tragedy. Found at Canosa. *Circa* 330–320 B.C. *Staatliche Antikensammlung, Munich. Cf. pp. 26ff., 47, 80, 192.*

ΚΡΕΟΝΤΕΙΑ

two columns bearing tripods, which symbolise the victory of the producer and the poet in the tragic competition. The middle level, which curves upwards from the sides, chiefly illustrates the messenger speech of the tragedy: in the palace at Corinth, represented here by the white wooden Ionic building with perspective roof beams, which is itself a reminiscence of the central door of the theatre background, the enthroned princess, Jason's new wife, has collapsed under the influence of the poisoned wreath, which Medeia has sent her in the box now lying at the bottom of the steps. On the left the king, Kreon, is involved in his daughter's disaster; his wife Merope runs towards him. Beyond her is an old man, the tutor of Medeia's children, and a girl. To the right the princess' brother Hippotes runs up; an old woman, perhaps Medeia's nurse, runs away. On the extreme right an old man in royal tiara stands on a rock: he is labelled Ghost of Aetes (Medeia's father), and perhaps he spoke the prologue of this play.

The bottom level shows subsequent events: Medeia kills one of her children who has taken refuge on an altar (this again must have been narrated and not acted); to the left a youth saves another child (a variant from the Euripidean version). In the centre the snaky chariot of the sun-god, on which Medeia will make her escape, is occupied by Oistros, the mad jealousy which accounts for her action (possibly Oistros appeared in the play, like Lyssa – mad fury – in Euripides' *Herakles*). On the right Jason arrives too late to punish Medeia.

The painter has made an efficient composition which fills the space and bears some relation to the shape of the vase. Only the top row of gods are irrelevant; on other vases, however, though composed on the same scheme, the gods are closely connected with the action. In the strict sense the painter does not illustrate the play; he selects moments – prologue, two messenger speeches, final scene of Medeia's escape – for commentary. Medeia, Kreon, the old tutor and the ghost are in full stage costume with long red sleeves, as they would have appeared on the stage.

Gnathia vases

This red-figure painting has more colour than Attic red-figure, more white, more yellow, and the deep red of the sleeves. A parallel line of vases (known as Gnathia because many were found at Egnazia), probably painted in the same workshops, omits the reserved figures of

PLATE 4 – Gnathia oinochoe. Early 3rd century B.C. *Height 45.5 cm. John L. Severance Collection, Cleveland Museum of Art, Cleveland. Cf. pp. 30, 38, 46, 69.*

red-figure and has all its decoration in added colour. The earliest examples, about 350 B.C., are very informative about contemporary colour, and have been reasonably connected with Sikyonian painting. Early Hellenistic Gnathia has a restricted colour range but is still gay and interesting with the white contrasting with reds, yellows and golden brown. A krater in the British Museum has a male and female centaur in a chariot driven by a winged Victory. The painting is accomplished and the difficult foreshortening causes the artist no trouble. The vines with grapes on either side of the picture are a reminder of the symposion for which the mixing-bowl is intended. A mixed centaur pair is a new idea; Hellenistic artists and poets were interested in the private life of monsters. When the Argo sails, it is the centaur Cheiron's wife who holds up the little Achilles to wave good-bye to his father.

PLATE P. 3

PLATE P. 29

An oinochoe in Cleveland is much more gay and brings us to comedy within a generation of its transference to Rome. The moulded mask at the top of the handle is the mask worn by the young man about town, and the two masks on either side of the main picture belong to young prostitutes, the kind of girls whom in comedy the young man about town loves and rescues. They hang from a long vine-stem with leaves, tendrils and bunches of grapes such as might be suspended or painted on the walls of the dining-room; the hanging red scarves also belong to this kind of decoration. Between them a fat boy dances, while another plays the flute – entertainment during the drinking. The belly of this wine-jug is surrounded by a painted wreath of fruited ivy with white and red ribbon twisted round the stem, such a wreath as the drinkers might wear.

This is the kind of art which the Romans found when they captured Tarentum in 272 B.C. The Sikyonian heritage is strong. The town possessed two colossal bronzes by Lysippos himself, a Zeus in the Agora and a Herakles on the Acropolis, which was removed to Rome by Q. Fabius Maximus in 209 B.C.

HERITAGE OF NIKIAS AND EUPHRANOR

A quite different tradition inspires some other Early Hellenistic paintings, a tradition of large solemn figures, who sometimes look straight out of the frame at the spectator. This tradition comes rather from the Attic artist Nikias, whom we know best from the copy of his Perseus and Andromeda in Pompeii, and the Isthmian artist Euphranor, who painted in Athens and whose art is reflected in red-figure vases of the middle of the fourth century: his 'beef-fed' Theseus was contrasted with the Theseus 'fed on roses' of Parrhasios which was in the rich style of the latest fifth century.

Four very different examples show this tradition continuing in the *Centuripe vases* third century. The Sicilian town of Centuripe, which lies behind Catania, produced a unique series of vases in the third century. The commonest shapes are large, nearly cylindrical kraters with domed lids, and low dishes with conical lids. The artist conceives his vase as a piece of architecture, a round building with a roof, and contrasts the heavy mouldings which he uses for the knob on the top of the lid, in the handle zone, and on the lowest part of the body, with the smooth painted fields. On one of the dishes the handle zone shows a winged Breeze set in a mixed floral band, as on the necks of Tarentine vases, but here she and her flowers stand out from the dark blue background in low relief, coloured yellow. On another fragment the handle zone APPX. PL. 23 is conceived as the cornice supporting a roof: it is decorated with lion's heads, which would be spouts in a building, and with architectural mouldings. The painting is polychrome and the figures, as on the Pella mosaics, are set on a narrow shelf against a plain backdrop, PLATE P. 65 black in the earlier vases and mauve in the later ones like this. A flute-player stands on the left, looking across at the bride. The wreathed bridegroom reclines on the right. A chubby Eros makes the connexion between him and the bride seated on the right (she is known from a Roman painting which must go back to the same source as the vase). The modelling in light and shade is very accomplished. The little Eros appears constantly in Hellenistic art and literature: here he plays his proper part; elsewhere we shall find Erotes doing grown-up things and amusing because these are not their proper tasks. The pair may be Dionysos and Ariadne rather than ordinary mortals.

Further north this tradition shows itself again in the grand figures of *Etruria* the Tomba dell'Orco, and in the remarkable picture engraved by Novios Plautios at Rome on the bronze Ficoroni Cista. The Roman engraver seems to have copied fairly accurately a major Greek painting of the mid-fourth century, which showed the Argonauts landed from their ship to get water at a spring, after Polydeukes had defeated at boxing the brutal local king, Amykos. It is a competent, if uninteresting, assembly of tough young men, which illustrates the ancient judgment that Euphranor represented 'the dignity of heroes'.

Boscoreale Lastly this tradition can be seen in a fresco from the villa of P. Fannius Synistor near Boscoreale. The decoration has been dated as early as PLATE P. 40 50 B.C. and as late as A.D. 12. The fresco, however, which concerns us is a copy of an original of about 275–270 B.C. The big hall of the villa was decorated with nine big figured panels of which six survive. There is no reason to suppose that they were connected in subject or in style. Our picture has had many interpretations. In style this APPX. PL. 23 group of large quiet figures on a narrow shelf in front of a plain background recalls the Centuripe vases. An elderly man wearing cloak and sandals looks across at two massive seated women, one wearing a Macedonian military cap, holding a spear, and having a Macedonian shield in front of her, and the other wearing a folded kerchief on her head.

The distance between the man and the women and the monumentality of the women suggest that he is an ordinary mortal and that they are APPX. PL. 1 goddesses or at least personifications like the Tyche of Antioch. The woman with the Macedonian cap, spear and shield is a personification of Macedonia. The folded kerchief is worn by dancers associated with Kybele, Demeter and Dionysos. The woman wearing the kerchief has her hand to her chin, a gesture particularly used for those seeing a vision. The old man looks like the portraits of the poet Aratos.

If this identification is accepted, the picture can be explained. Aratos was one of the most famous poets of the Early Hellenistic age; he wrote a poem on the constellations, which was immediately accepted and had a success which endured into Roman times. This poem is said to have been commissioned by Antigonos Gonatas, the young king of Macedonia, although it was probably conceived and written in Athens. In 276 B.C. Antigonos married Phila, the sister of Antiochos I, king of Syria, and Aratos wrote her a congratulatory poem. About this time he went to live at Pella. Soon after this he moved to Syria to live at the court of Antiochos. If the folded kerchief may be associated with Kybele, the seated woman wearing it may personify Hellenised

Anatolia, or, more specifically, Antiochos' Syria, and the vision which she sees is the coming of Greek poetry and scholarship to Asia in the person of Aratos with the goodwill of Macedonia. This then is the official art of the Macedonian court roughly a generation after the Pella mosaics. The great-grandson of this Antiochos, Antiochos III, who reigned at the end of the third century has been recognised in a head in the Louvre (a Roman copy), which shows how this official style continued for the portraits of the great. PLATE P. 34

BRYAXIS AND THE SARAPIEION

Another sculptor of the mid-fourth century leads us to Alexandria and the early Ptolemies. Bryaxis is a disputed figure. There seems to me to be a genuine stylistic connexion between the Mausolos, other figures from the Mausoleum, some of the reliefs of the Mausoleum, the Demeter of Knidos, and the seated statue of Sarapis, which was certainly the work of Bryaxis. The style essentially belongs to the tradition of Euphranor but has a distinctive pathos in the treatment of brows and eyes. The story preserved by Clement of Alexandria that the people of Sinope in gratitude for help in a famine gave to Ptolemy II a statue of Plouton by Bryaxis, which he then consecrated in Alexandria as Sarapis, may be true or partly true. The Alexandrian Sarapis, which is known from copies, could well have been a fourth-century statue, and Sarapis, like Plouton, was a god of the underworld. The god sits at ease with one hand on the head of the hell-hound Kerberos and a sceptre in the other; he looks directly at the spectator, like the Demeter of Knidos. It is this direct communication between god and worshipper which recalls Euphranor; it separates these gods from the gods of Praxiteles, who never look at the spectator but are intent on their own beautiful but abstracted life. FIG. 3

The cult of Sarapis was the most successful attempt to Hellenise an Egyptian god, and the institution of the sacred place, the Sarapieion, in Alexandria may even go back beyond Ptolemy I to Alexander himself. It is possible, however, that the great statue was not installed until the time of Ptolemy II, and the Sarapieion was certainly rebuilt and enlarged under Ptolemy III.

FIG. 3 – *Sarapis. Marble. The god is enthroned, one hand resting upon the head of the hell-hound Kerberos. Copy from original, circa 330 B.C. Cf. above.*

The influence of the great statue can be traced both in literature and art. The poet Kallimachos must be recalling it when he describes the messenger-goddess Iris sitting beside the golden throne of Hera like a hunting dog. In art the seated Sarapis of Bryaxis was in the mind of the sculptor who made the seated statue of Homer for the Homereion built by Ptolemy IV. Homer also was seated at ease with a sceptre in one hand and a roll of papyrus in the other: instead of Kerberos, a personification of the *Iliad* knelt on one side of the throne and a personification of the *Odyssey* on the other. Round Homer were statues of the cities which claimed to be his birthplace. APPX. PL. 6

In this grouping also the Homereion had an ancestor in the Sarapieion. The Sarapieion at Memphis had a semicircular exedra, or lecture-hall, in which statues of poets and thinkers from Orpheus to Demetrios of Phaleron including Homer, Thales, Herakleitos, Protagoras, and Pindar were grouped round Sarapis. The exedra at Memphis was probably a copy of a similar exedra in the Sarapieion at Alexandria. The inclusion of Demetrios of Phaleron in the group probably dates the original composition early in the reign of Ptolemy II because Demetrios of Phaleron fell out of favour and committed suicide early in his reign. Demetrios of Phaleron was exiled from Athens and took refuge with Ptolemy I, who put him in charge of the library. He is said to have been cured from blindness by Sarapis, but in this assembly of poets and thinkers he owed his place to his librarianship and his political wisdom rather than to his special connection with Sarapis.

It is surprising to find poets and thinkers grouped round Sarapis; the reason is probably to be found in the suggestion that the Alexandrians felt that Sarapis was akin to Dionysos because both gods promised immortality to their initiates; and therefore, as Dionysos was also the god of drama, Sarapis could be surrounded by intellectuals. The *First Iambos* of Kallimachos is set in the Sarapieion: Hipponax, the satirical poet of the sixth century, returns from the dead and summons the scholar poets of Alexandria to the Sarapieion to hear the story of

PLATE 5 – Marble portrait bust of Antiochos III. Roman copy of a lost original from the end of the 3rd century B.C. *Louvre, Paris. Cf. pp. 33, 45.*

the Seven Sages; a gold cup was left to the best of the Seven Sages; it was given to Thales and he passed it to Bias; it went the rounds until it came back to Thales, who dedicated it to Apollo. The present quarrels of the Alexandrian scholar-poets, says Kallimachos, are due to jealousy; Hipponax, as a bitter satirist, is the perfect exponent of reconciliation, and he preaches his sermon in the presence of the statues of past and present thinkers and poets. The poem and the statues of the Sarapieion together demonstrate the Alexandrian feeling for the continuity of Greek poetry and thought; the Alexandrians were at once the heirs and the preservers of a tradition which goes back to Orpheus.

Portraits FIG. 4

Among the scholar-poets were Lykophron and Philikos, of both of whom we have portraits. Lykophron was brought from Chalkis to deal with the manuscripts of comedy in the library. But he was himself a writer of tragedies and satyr plays, and composed the *Alexandra*, an extraordinarily difficult and learned monologue, in which a slave reports to Priam the prophecy made by Kassandra on the day that Paris sailed from Troy for Sparta and Helen. He has been recognised on a Roman silver cup found at Berthouville in France. The poet is seated on the right, looking across at the standing Kassandra; between them a mask is suspended over a krater. The mask is the mask of a girl in tragedy with her hair cut short because she grieves, suitable for Kassandra; the krater is found in other scenes connected with prophecy. The artist therefore alludes to the poet's most famous work, the *Alexandra*.

On the other side of this cup the astronomical poet Aratos and the Muse of astronomy have been recognised, and a twin cup has the philosopher Menedemos of Eretria (who was put on the stage in a satyr play by Lykophron) and the pastoral poet Theokritos. This conjunction of four early Hellenistic writers suggests very much that the originals belonged to the early Hellenistic period. It is perfectly possible that the originals were themselves silver cups and that the surviving cups were the result of mechanical reproduction through a number of intermediaries. A set of plasters which belonged to a metal-worker of about the same date as these cups was discovered at Begram in Afghanistan: they probably came from Alexandria, and some of them certainly go back directly or through intermediaries to the Early

FIG. 4 – *Lykophron looking at mask of Kassandra. Found at Bernay-Berthouville. Adaptation from original, circa 270 B.C. Cabinet des Médailles, Paris. Cf. p. 36.*

Hellenistic period. On the other hand the Early Hellenistic originals of the cups may equally well have been paintings or reliefs, which the silversmith translated into his own medium.

A painting from Herculaneum or Pompeii in scale and conception has obvious analogies with the Lykophron. A man is seated with his hand to his chin contemplating a female tragic mask which is held by a second man. As the seated man is not wearing stage costume he must be a poet rather than an actor. The gesture, which is the same as that of the 'Syria' of the Boscoreale fresco, means that he has a vision of the character's life while he composes her part in the tragedy. The picture was probably completed by a further figure on the left, perhaps the Muse who inspires the poet, or perhaps the character whose part he is writing. Pliny says that Protogenes of Rhodes, a famous painter of the late fourth century, painted Philikos the tragic poet 'in meditation'. It is tempting to identify this as the original of the Campanian picture. Philikos wrote forty-two tragedies in Alexandria and was priest of Dionysos and a leading member of the Guild of Artists of Dionysos (poets, musicians and actors).

PLATE P. 39

PLATE P. 40

Another painting may also be tentatively connected with Alexandria. A very fine small picture from Herculaneum (it was cut out of another wall but is nevertheless presumably a copy rather than an original) shows a tragic actor resting after his performance. He is still wearing his costume, his purple cloak lies across his lap. His right hand holds a sceptre and his left hand a sword. On the right a woman writes a label under the young man's mask which the actor has taken off. She has been called Skene, a personification of the stage, but her small size

PLATE P. 42

perhaps makes this unlikely. The label presumably dedicates the mask to Dionysos. The mask is in a box, over which hang tainiai like the scarves on the Cleveland Gnathia oinochoe: they will be wound round the mask when it is dedicated. The man behind the box cannot be an actor as has been suggested because he wears ordinary clothes; from the position of his hands it looks as if he were picking up or putting down another tainia. A date in the late fourth or early third century is given by the likeness of the actor to the portraits of the comic poet Menander. The treatment of space in both these pictures recalls the Boscoreale fresco; the action still takes place on a narrow shelf in front of a backdrop, but in both of these pictures the backdrop is varied – by a pillar in one and by a doorway in the other.

PLATE P. 29

PLATE P. 40

A famous Athenian actor, called Gorgosthenes, had his picture painted by Apelles in Alexandria, and the picture from Herculaneum may be a copy of this; its quality suggests an original by a very great painter. It is sad that nothing can be associated certainly with Apelles, the most famous of all Greek painters. A recent suggestion derives the Alexander mosaic from a picture by Apelles; undoubtedly it too copies a very great original, but the scale and subject are so different that no cross-links can be discerned with the Herculaneum picture.

HERITAGE OF PRAXITELES

Alexander sarkophagos

The other large representation of Alexander battling with the Persians introduces another great tradition in Early Hellenistic art, the tradition of Praxiteles and his sons. The Alexander sarkophagos is not Praxitelean in the ordinary sense, but the style of heads, particularly the heads of the Greek participants, suggest that the sculptor was an Athenian of the post-Praxitelean school. The sarkophagos was found at Sidon and was evidently used for a royal burial. The king was probably Abdalonymos, who was installed on the throne by Alexander after his defeat of the Persians at Issos in 333 B.C. The lid of the marble sarkophagos is conceived of as the roof of a temple, rather as the upper parts of Apulian and Centuripe vases are treated as architectural members. The lid shows the marble tiles, ridge tiles, akroteria, antefixes, cornice

APPX. PL. 26

PLATES PP. 45, 46

APPX. PL. 23

PLATE 6 – Fresco of a tragic poet, from a villa in Herculaneum or Pompeii. Copy from original, *circa* 300–270 B.C. *Height 39 cm. Museo Nazionale, Naples. Cf. pp. 37, 46, 192.*

PLATE 7 – Fresco from a villa at Boscoreale, representing Macedonia with a shield and spear and Syria in meditation. Copy from original, *circa* 270 B.C. *Height 1.50 m. Museo Nazionale, Naples. Cf. pp. 37, 38, 64.*

with griffin spouts, pediments, and frieze of a temple. The frieze is in low relief decorated with vine-leaves growing from a winding stem. It is perhaps likely that the vine was chosen because of its connexion with Dionysos and was felt therefore to be some guarantee of immortality. The frieze has lost most of its colour, but the pediments and the sculptured scenes on the sides of the sarkophagos itself give us some idea of what we lose by seeing classical and Hellenistic sculpture without its colour. Praxiteles himself was said to have employed the great painter Nikias to colour his marble statues, and bronzes originally were the colour of sun-tanned flesh instead of the unrealistic and unpleasant green which is so highly prized today. The colours of the Alexander sarkophagos have, of course, faded, but much remains: the prevailing impression is of yellows and blues, but there are also reds and browns. Particularly effective are the variegated trousers of some of the Persians, the flying red cloaks of the Greeks, the blue shields with red rims, and above all the lively eyes with their pupils of darkest brown.

PLATE P. 45
PLATE P. 46

The scenes are presumably scenes in the life of the king. One long side is a wild battle between Greeks and Persians with Alexander recognisable on the extreme left. The other long side has a lion hunt, in which Greeks and Orientals take part, and the Oriental rider attacking the lion may well be Abdalonymos himself. The long sides are very competently balanced compositions of figures in violent movement. The individual figures of the short sides and of the pediments are equally successful, but the composition is not nearly so well adapted to the space available. One short side has a panther hunt; the other short side and the pediments have further battles.

Tanagra statuettes

Praxiteles and his sons worked in Asia Minor, and a sculptor trained by one of them may have made the Alexander sarkophagos. Their influence is also very strong in one of the most charming legacies of the ancient world, the Tanagra statuettes. These owe their name to the fact that numbers of them were discovered in the cemeteries of the small Boeotian town of Tanagra, but more recent excavations, particularly in the Agora of Athens, have shown that the models from which the moulds used in many other parts of the Greek world were taken, were made in Athens from the middle of the fourth century

PLATE 8 – Wall-painting from Herculaneum. Copy of an original, *circa* 310–300 B.C. *Height 36 cm. Museo Nazionale, Naples. Cf. pp.* 37, 46, 59, 60.

through the Early Hellenistic period. The stylistic affinities of these figures with the art of Praxiteles and his successors has always been clear. These figures, generally elegant, sometimes realistic but always charming, are the best illustrations of the sophisticated, disillusioned, sometimes realistic but always sympathetic comedy of Menander, the contemporary poet, whose statue in the theatre at Athens was made by the sons of Praxiteles.

A trio of statuettes from Tanagra in the British Museum gives an idea of the range of these figures and provides a starting point for pursuing three different lines of development. The first is an old nurse, the second a girl with a comic mask, and the third a girl with an ivy-wreath. The old nurse with her fat arms, hunched shoulders, sagging chin and big nose, has a realism which seems discordant with the girls, but this was a world which contained ugly people as well as elegant people and the artists record both. She reminds us of the realistic nurses of comedy, but she is a nurse of real life: her face has not the gaping mouth of a comic mask. She is an ancestor of what have been termed the Old Derelicts of Middle and Late Hellenistic art: the best known of them is deservedly the drunken old woman in Munich. She sits on the ground, looking blissfully to heaven with her wine-jug between her knees, her chiton slipping off her right shoulder and her himation sliding down her left arm. The forms of face and body show her age. The echoing folds round the base perhaps intentionally suggest waves of inebriation. Pliny ascribes a drunken old woman at Smyrna to the fifth-century sculptor Myron, but there was a later Myron who worked at Pergamon in the early second century: Pliny may have confused the two Myrons and the later Myron's drunken old woman may be the original of the Munich statue: the form of the wine-jug, a lagynos instead of an oinochoe, quite apart from the style, shows that the original was Hellenistic. The old woman would have approved (perhaps did approve) of the early third-century poem of Poseidippos of Pella: 'Attic lagynos, pour the dewy juice of Bacchos, pour. Let our bottle-party receive the dew. Silent be the wise swan of Zeno and the Muse of Kleanthes. Our care be bitter-sweet Love.'

Zeno and Kleanthes were contemporary philosophers of the pompous and puritanical Stoic school. Philosophers were another kind of Old

PLATES PP. 47, 52, 63

Realism

PLATE P. 48

FIG. 5

Derelict portrayed in Early Hellenistic art. The old man in Boston is Attic of the earliest third century. His himation is wrapped untidily round his body; he wears no chiton. He pushes his way along on his stick; his head is aggressively thrust forward, a head which clearly derives from portraits of Sokrates. This is not Sokrates but a contemporary who is felt to be in the Sokratic tradition, perhaps a Cynic. Again we are reminded of Menander, and here of the hero of the *Dyskolos*, the angry old man who lived and worked his large farm practically alone because he hated the mercenary ways of the world; he might look like this. The dignified Aratos of the Boscoreale fresco is very different.

In 280 B.C., forty years after his death, the Athenians set up a bronze APPX. PL. 5 statue of Demosthenes, the great statesman who had tried unsuccessfully to weld Greece into a unity capable of resisting the conquering power of Alexander's father, Philip of Macedon. The sculptor was an otherwise unknown Polyeuktos. The statue was placed in a conspicuous place in the Agora, near the Altar of the Twelve Gods. The epigram inscribed on the base was said to have been composed by Demosthenes himself: 'If your strength had equalled your resolution, Demosthenes, the Macedonian war-god would never have ruled the Greeks.' It is an official portrait of a great patriot, which lacks all the flattery expected then as now in an official portrait: Aristotle had said that the good portrait-painter renders the individual form but makes it more beautiful. The statesman naturally wears a more adequate himation than the street philosopher, but how simple and careless its draping compared with the rather earlier portrait of his pro-Macedonian rival Aischines. The interlaced hands, which Plutarch describes and which survive in the Copenhagen copy, the deep lines on cheeks and forehead, the untidy hair are all signs of nervous tension rather than strength; they make Aischines' description of Demosthenes' behaviour on the embassy to Philip of Macedon uncomfortably credible – his touchiness as a travelling companion, his boasting of his eloquence, his breakdown before Philip – and the statue is a perfect illustration of the epigram: 'If your strength had equalled your resolution . . .'

APPX. PL. 3 The realistic tradition lives on in the portrait of Chrysippos, the third head of the Stoic school, which must have been made late in the third century: a little man with spindly legs, a big head with high domed forehead and an enormous nose, emphasising his philosophical points by counting them off on his fingers. A rather complicated chain of argument has led to the identification of this statue: the body in the Louvre has been completed with a cast of the head in the British Museum. It is identified with Chrysippos by the likeness of the head to inscribed portraits, and Cicero describes the seated statue of Chrysippos in the Kerameikos as having his hand stretched out. A further step identifies this statue with 'the man counting on his fingers' ascribed in Pliny to the Athenian sculptor Euboulides. The difference from the contemporary official portrait of Antiochos III is startling. PLATE P. 34

Muses and drama

The second of the Tanagra statuettes from the British Museum is a PLATE P. 52

PLATE 9 – Sarkophagos of a ruler of Sidon with scenes from the life of Alexander the Great, known as the 'Alexander Sarkophagos'. From the necropolis at Sidon: detail of long side. *After* 330 B.C. *Height 1.95 m. Archaeological Museum, Istanbul. Cf. p. 38.*

PLATES PP. 27, 29, 39, 42

girl of great elegance in the purest Praxitelean tradition. She holds a comic mask in her hand and so leads us again to Menander and drama. Tragedy and comedy were both extremely popular in the Hellenistic period. We have seen pictures of the tragic Medeia and also comic masks on vases made in Tarentum, and we have noted tragic poets and a tragic actor in Alexandria. Any city of any importance in the Greek world had its theatre and its performances.

Thasos

The island of Thasos in the north provides notable outlying evidence for this interest in Greek drama. It was colonised from Paros in the

PLATE 10 – 'Alexander Sarkophagos'. Detail from the other long side (cf. p. 41). Marble with traces of the original colours. *After* 330 B.C. *Height 1.95 m. Archaeological Museum, Istanbul. Cf. p. 38.*

PLATE II – Old nurse. Terracotta statuette from the end of the 4th century B.C. *British Museum.* *Cf. p. 43.*

seventh century and the French excavations have produced a great deal of interesting architecture, sculpture, bronzes and pottery. In the fourth century the stamps on the wine amphorai (its wine was widely exported) were sometimes decorated with dramatic masks. The

PLATE 12 – Drunken old woman. Marble statuette, Roman copy of a lost original, possibly by Myron of Pergamon, from the early 2nd century B.C. *Height 92 cm. Staatliche Antikensammlung, Munich. Cf. p. 43.*

theatre is an extraordinarily beautiful ruin on the hillside above the town; in its present shape it goes back to the earliest third century. But the most interesting theatrical monument is a small building well below the theatre and attached to the precinct of Dionysos. It consists of a room, 10.90 metres square, of which one side is extended into a semicircular space with statues: the semicircular space was unroofed. The inscriptions of the preserved statues show that they celebrated a particular performance at which tragedy, comedy, and two different kinds of choral song (Dithyramb and Nykterinos) were performed in honour of Dionysos. It was therefore in part a monument set up by the choregos, the rich man who was entrusted with the production by the state, but the rectangular room was an addition to it and was probably used for banquets or drinking-parties by worshippers of Dionysos, particularly actors, musicians and other performers. There are analogous buildings in Alexandria and Pergamon, and we have already noticed the exedra in the Sarapieion at Alexandria and Memphis (see p. 35) where lectures were given under the statues of ancient and recent poets and thinkers. FIG. 6

Only half of the bases at Thasos have been preserved; the corresponding four on the other side of the central Dionysos have been lost. Dionysos was over life-size and young. The only well-preserved figure, Comedy, is life-size. The four bases have inscriptions: 1) Tragedy, Theodoros acted; 2) Comedy, Philemon acted; 3) Dithyrambos, Ariston of Miletos played the flute; 4) Nykterinos, Batalos played the flute. Theodoros and Philemon are known in Athens as actors of tragedy and comedy. The poets' names were not recorded, and this may mean that the plays were classical Athenian plays, e.g. by Euripides and Menander, instead of new local productions. Only one tragic actor and one comic actor are named because each would be responsible for engaging his two assistants. For the choral performances the accompanying flute-players were the important and expensive persons; the choirs would be composed of Thasians. PLATE P. 54

FIG. 5 – *Old man, possibly a philosopher. Terracotta statuette from Athens. 300–275 B.C. Height 12 cm. Museum of Fine Arts, Boston. Cf. p. 43.*

FIG. 6 – *The choregeion below the theatre at Thasos: reconstruction. It consists of a rectangular room, 10.90 metres square, of which one side is extended into a semicircular space with allegorical personifications of dramatic art. 300–275 B.C. Cf. p. 49.*

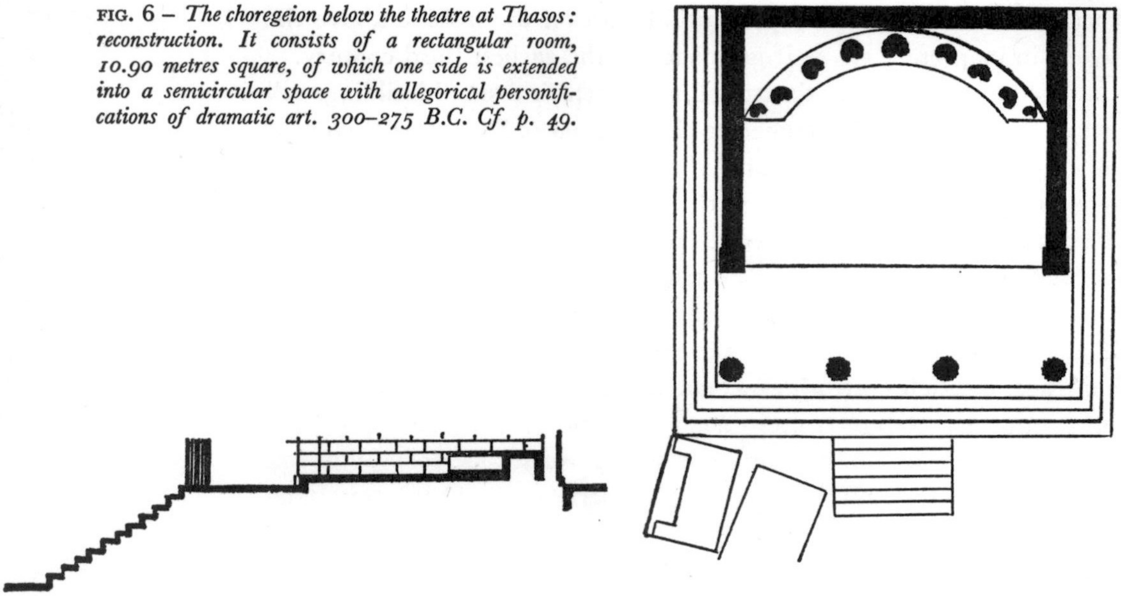

Theatres The Thasos performances show the double function of the Greek theatre; both plays and choral performances were produced there. In the old days the plays themselves, both tragedy and comedy, included a chorus as an integral part of the performance, and at times close intercommunication between chorus and actors was essential. All through the fifth century, therefore, the stage was at most a low platform, and this low platform, although extended sideways so that three doors could give on to it, was included in the rebuilding of the theatre at Athens about 330 B.C. Now, however, in new plays the chorus only sang interludes and took no part in the action and dialogue; for better seeing and hearing, therefore, the actors were put on a high stage, and the chorus were confined to the circular orchestra or dancing floor, which was also used for purely choral performances like the dithyramb. In the revivals of classical tragedy, on the rare occasions when intercommunication was essential, wooden ladders were apparently used to connect stage and orchestra.

PLATE P. 56 The theatre with the high stage appears in two different forms in different places in the third century. It is now established that the very beautiful theatre at Epidauros was designed and built in the third century with a high stage. The high stage was approached from each side by a ramp which started from one side of a double gateway: the other half led along the level into the orchestra. With this solution, the chorus would enter through either or both the inner gateways into the orchestra, and an actor representing a character who came from somewhere off-stage, country or town, would use one of the outer gateways to climb the ramp. He would be in view of at least part of the audience as he went up. This arrangement is found in several other theatres in the Peloponnese and Euboia. The alternative arrangement, which can be seen in the little theatre at Akrai (as also in other theatres, including Thasos, in Greece and in Greek Asia), has a similar projecting stage but no ramps; then entrances from off-stage were made at stage level, either round the side of the stage-building, or if, as at Athens, the stage-building had wings, from doors in the wings. In either case the actor could change costume and mask quickly in the stage-building and come on again; he did not have the considerable walk up or down the ramp and round the back. The ramp may have

FIG. 7

APPX. PL. 22

FIG. 7 – *Ground-plan of the theatre at Epidauros. Circa 300–250 B.C.*

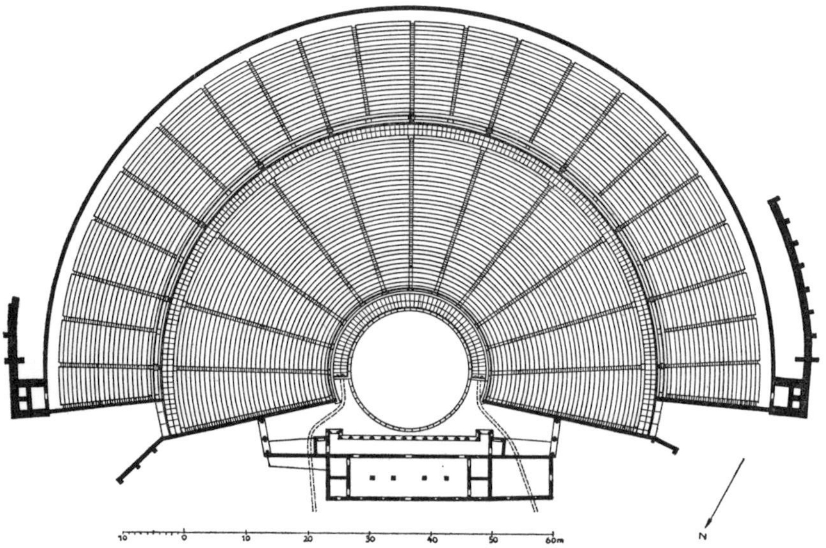

PLATE 13 – Muse with comic mask from Tanagra. Terracotta statuette of the late 4th or early 3rd century B.C. *British Museum. Cf. pp. 43, 45, 55, 62.*

been the first method devised for entering from off-stage, and it may have been preserved in some theatres for ceremonial entrances of civic dignitaries and the like, when the theatre was used for public meetings.

The architect of Epidauros has made beautiful use of a natural hollow in the mountain. The semicircular auditorium will seat more than 14,000 spectators. It has a passage running round the top, and a second wider horizontal passage runs round about a third of the way down. It is divided vertically by thirteen stairways rising from the orchestra, which are continued above the lower horizontal passage to the top, and there are twelve more stairways running up from the lower horizontal passage to the upper horizontal passage. The middle row of the block of seats below the lower horizontal passage is level with the top of the gateway and with the raised stage. The gateway thus ties the auditorium to the stage-building.

The front wall of the raised stage was decorated with half-columns. The stage-building presumably exhibited three doors and was probably also ornamented with columns between which panels with scenery for tragedy, satyr play and comedy could be fixed. It is unlikely that at any one time the theatre would have more than three sets, one for tragedy, one for comedy and one for satyr play; but the satyr play set could be borrowed for a tragedy or comedy set in the country. Even today, without the stage-building and without the high stage to assist the voice, the acoustics are wonderful, and it is noticeably more comfortable and more effective to speak from the line of the stage than from the middle of the orchestra.

The figure labelled Tragedy in the building at Thasos held an old man's mask in its hand, which has been preserved. It is a very remarkable head, bald, with wrinkled forehead, sunken cheeks, and deep pouches under blind eyes. The sculptor at this time (and there are parallels in terracotta) is thinking beyond the mask to the character; he carves a blind old man (like the Old Derelicts discussed on p. 43) rather than the mask of a blind old man. Perhaps his choice here was determined by the particular tragedy produced at the festival. This man cannot be Oidipous the king because he would have had a tower of hair over the forehead. He could be Teiresias, but Teiresias occurs in several plays. Oidipous in the *Phoinissai* of Euripides or the *Oidipous*

FIG. 8

PLATE 14 – Comedy. Life-sized marble statue from Thasos. *Circa* 300–270 B.C. *Height 1.70 m. Thasos Museum. Cf. pp. 49, 64.*

FIG. 8 – *Old man's mask from the choregeion at Thasos. Circa 300–275 B.C. Height 32 cm. Thasos Museum. Cf. p. 53.*

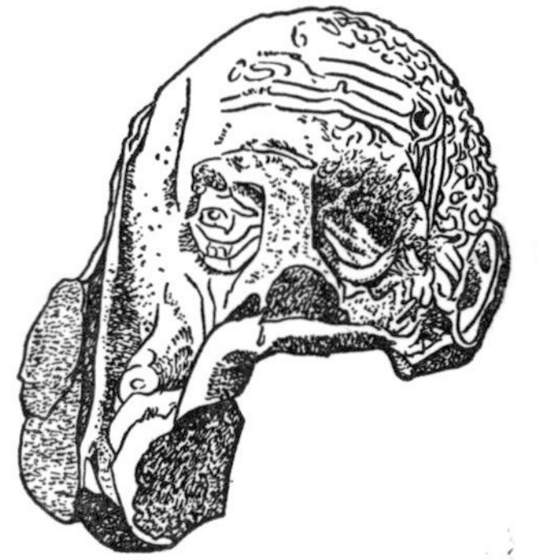

Koloneus of Sophokles or Phineus in his name-play by Sophokles could wear this mask. But the old man cannot be certainly identified: somewhere on the monument an inscription probably gave the titles and authors of the plays performed.

The figure holding the old man's mask is called Tragedy, and the corresponding figure is labelled Comedy. It would be interesting to know how Tragedy was dressed. In the fifth century both Tragedy and Comedy appear on red-figure vases as maenads in the train of Dionysos. This is easily intelligible: tragedy and comedy are the product of Dionysiac inspiration, and maenads are women inspired by Dionysos. In the second century Tragedy is represented in tragic costume wearing mask and thick-soled shoes, and Comedy looks like a woman in comedy. The Thasos figures are between the two chronologically. Neither the Thasos Comedy figure nor the British Museum terracotta holding the comic mask provide the answer. There is no way of determining what they are: maenads are much more elegantly dressed and more calm in disposition in the late fourth century, and these figures might possibly be maenads.

APPX. PL. 10

PLATE P. 54

PLATE P. 52

Muses

But the Thasos Comedy figure looks remarkably like a Muse. The cross-legged stance can be seen on a Gnathia Muse of about 340 B.C., and the elegant drapery is a development of the drapery on the Muses of the Praxitelean base from Mantineia. But there is a closer analogy: the Muse of Comedy on a Roman coin. Undoubtedly the Thasos figure is a personification of Comedy and not a Muse. What is interesting is that on the one hand a personification of Comedy looks remarkably like a Muse, and that on the other hand a Muse of Comedy is

PLATE P. 58

PLATE 15 – Theatre at Epidauros. View of the orchestra and steps of the auditorium. 3rd century B.C. *Cf. pp. 50, 196.*

established as independent of the other Muses and looks remarkably like a personification of Comedy.

In Homer the Muses have two functions: they are invoked by the poet because they give him his song, since they have all knowledge, and they are the choir who sing with Apollo on Olympos. They were then from the beginning the givers of knowledge as well as givers of song and artists themselves: so it is perfectly natural that they should be worshipped in Plato's Academy and that Alexandrian scholarship should be pursued in their place, the Mouseion. But as patrons of poetry, dance and music, they are also concerned with the great new classical genre of poetry, drama, in spite of its close connexion with Dionysos. In Aristophanes' *Frogs* the chorus invoke the Muses to come and see the contest between the two tragic poets, Aeschylus and Euripides; and Sophokles 'collected in honour of the Muses a thiasos of the educated' (or 'of those he had trained'); it is not clear whether this was a kind of literary society or an association of actors. Much later, at Syracuse, the Guild of Artists of Dionysos (actors, musicians and poets) were associated with the Muses: the grotto with a fountain above the theatre was surely sacred to the Nymphs, who, as we shall see, had a close relation to Dionysos; but in the grotto were found inscriptions which mention the Council of Artists and the Mouseion, as well as very elegant statues of Muses in the Praxitelean tradition but dating from the second century B.C. FIG. 9

But in all this there is no sign of individual Muses specialising. The possibility is given by their names, which go back to Hesiod. If they specialise, Kleio (Fame) naturally deals with the past, Thaleia (Good Cheer) with comedy, Terpsichore (Delighting with or in the chorus) with dancing, Ouranie (Heavenly) with astronomy. In the Early Hellenistic period Kallimachos uses the fiction that Kleio and Kalliope answer his questions about the origins of cults and other ancient usages, so that they seem already to be becoming the Muses of History and Epic, and Apollonios Rhodios chooses Erato (whose name chimes with Eros) when he starts to tell of the love of Medeia in the third book of the *Argonautika*.

The Roman coin, which has a Muse of Comedy very like the Thasos Comedy statue, has a curious ancestry, which leads back to the Early PLATE P. 58

PLATE 16 – Roman silver coins from the Republican era. *Above left*: Herakles; *right*: Comedy with mask; *below*: Tragedy with mask. *British Museum. Cf. pp. 55, 57ff., 60, 123f.*

M. Fulvius Nobilior

Hellenistic period. The coin is one of a set minted in 67 B.C. by Pomponius Musa with the nine Muses and with Hercules playing the lyre. It is a reasonable conjecture, based on the unusual association of Hercules with the Muses, that both the Hercules and the Muses are reproductions of the statues set up by M. Fulvius Nobilior in the temple of Hercules Musarum, which he built on his return to Rome in 187 B.C. after his Ambracian campaign. The Roman epic poet Ennius accompanied him on his campaign, and Ennius was the first Roman poet to demand implicitly that his audience must know Greek poetry in order to enjoy him to the full: he called his work *poema* instead of *carmen;* he used Greek metre instead of Roman Saturnians; and he addressed the Greek Muses instead of the Roman Camenae. Fulvius Nobilior's dedication of a temple to the Muses was in complete accord with this.

Fulvius Nobilior brought the statues of the Muses from Ambracia, probably from the palace of Pyrrhos, king of Epeiros, who died in 272 B.C.; but no authority suggests that he imported the Herakles from there. There is in fact positive evidence that instead of the abnormal association with Herakles Pyrrhos made the normal association of a lyre-playing Apollo with the Muses: Pyrrhos had a ring with an agate on which were engraved Apollo holding a lyre and the nine Muses, each with her own attribute. Perhaps the artist of the ring reproduced the statues of the nine Muses which Fulvius Nobilior removed a century later. At any rate the style of the Muses on the coins fits perfectly with a date in the early third century: in addition, the slave mask held by the Muse of Comedy is of early third-century type and the Muse of Tragedy, who is in tragic costume, does not wear the thick-soled shoes of second-century tragic actors.

Pyrrhos of Epeiros

APPX. PL. 6

FIG. 33

The Muse of Tragedy on the coin wears Herakles' lion's skin, and holds his club in one hand and his mask in the other. Herakles was a character in the *Mad Herakles*, the *Auge*, the *Alkestis* and several satyr plays of Euripides. From now on the Muse of Tragedy very often holds the mask and club of Herakles, and we know that the *Mad Herakles* was popular in the Hellenistic period. What an actor playing Herakles in this period looked like, can be seen from a terracotta statuette found in the Athenian Agora. He wears a mask with the hair piled high over the forehead, like the Achilles mask in the painting from Herculaneum. But here the hair is partly covered by Herakles' lion's skin, which he wears so that the muzzle comes over the top of his head (like the Muse of Tragedy on the Roman coin): the inside edges of the lion's jaws can be seen on both sides just below the break. The break shows that a considerable extension upwards has been lost, and the mask was originally very like that carried by the later tragic actor from Amisos. This artist, unlike the artist of the Thasos tragic

PLATE P. 61

PLATE P. 42

FIG. 33

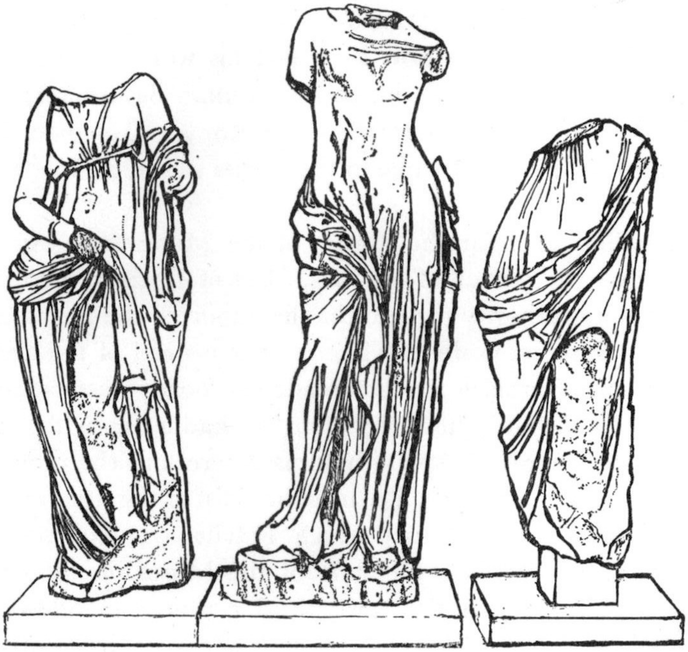

FIG. 9 – *The Muses. Marble statues from a grotto above the theatre at Syracuse. Circa 225–150 B.C. Cf. p. 57.*

FIG. 8 mask, is representing the mask itself rather than the character. Swinging brows, hooked nose, wrinkled nose, flaring nostrils would allow students of the contemporary pseudo-science of physiognomy to read off energy, self-confidence, disgust and high spirit. This is Herakles in Euripides' play when he returns from Hades and storms into the house to kill the tyrant Lykos, who has been threatening his father, wife and children. He wears the same high-girded chiton as the actor in the

PLATE P. 42 picture from Herculaneum and over it a cloak which covers his left hand; his right arm was raised and probably held his club.

PLATE P. 58 The slave mask held by the Muse of Comedy on the Roman coin is extremely like the slave mask on a plaque from Amphipolis, which is

Comic masks Early Hellenistic in date. It is a gay and engaging little piece and

APPX. PL. 4 was probably one side of a decorated box. Amphipolis is on the mainland across from Thasos; no theatre has been discovered there, but they may well have had performances. In any case the masks of comedy

PLATE 17 – Mad Herakles represented by an actor. Terracotta statuette from the Athenian Agora. *Circa* 250 B.C. *Height 8 cm. Agora Museum, Athens. Cf. p. 59.*

were by now standardised over the Greek world. These masks are: 1) an old man with neat hair; 2) a girl – this is the same as the mask held by the Tanagra figure in the British Museum; 3) a slave with triangular beard – as on the mask held by the Muse of Comedy on the Roman coin (the slave had an important, sometimes the most important role in New Comedy; more illustrations of slave masks are preserved than of any other type, and the different shapes of beard give a safe indication of date); 4) a youth with neat hair; 5) a girl with short parted hair; 6) an old woman with untidy hair. It is certainly the cast of a comedy in which true love is aided by an intriguing slave, but it is useless to guess more nearly at the plot.

PLATE P. 52

PLATE P. 58

The more successive discoveries reveal of the comedies of Menander, the more we wonder at the number of variations that he could play on the theme of love triumphing over obstacles, at the vividness of his characterisation, and at the supple elegance of his verse; the more, too, we understand the popularity of his comedy, attested by Early Hellenistic archaeology in Amphipolis, Thasos, Ambracia, Tanagra, Tarentum and many other places over the Greek-speaking world, and in 240 B.C. transferred to Rome to have a further life in Latin translation and adaptation.

PLATE P. 63

Praxitelean Women

The third of the Tanagra figures in the British Museum is the most attractive, partly because the blue of her chiton and the pink of her himation are so well preserved (the colour of terracottas is applied on a thin white slip over the clay body, and this slip flakes off extremely easily). The lines of the drapery are simple and clear, and set up a system of echoing triangles and curves with the left foot, the fan, the right hand and the head as focal points. The difference between this system of triangles and the system of triangles used for the Tyche of Antioch is that there the triangles lead into the depth and stress the volume of the figure, whereas here the figure is composed for a single view; it is relief rather than three-dimensional sculpture. The girl has an ivy-wreath on her head, and so certainly is connected with Dionysos; this need not mean, as has been suggested, that she is a maenad; nothing else suggests that she is a maenad; she is a girl who is going to a drinking-party, perhaps to entertain the guests as a musician. The ivy-wreath could be worn by the individual drinker

APPX. PL. I

PLATE 18 – Woman with fan. Terracotta statuette from Tanagra, late 4th or early 3rd century B.C. *British Museum. Cf. pp. 20, 62, 76.*

PLATE P. 21 or be put round the neck of the mixing-bowl (as on the Dherveni krater) or be suspended on the walls of the dining-room.

Essentially the same clear lines and the same frontal composition APPX. PL. 2 appear in a contemporary marble statue; but here on the large scale PLATE P. 54 in marble, as on the Comedy in Thasos, much more detail is possible for the folds, particularly for the tiny folds of the chiton. But this woman is more solid than either the Comedy or the terracotta, and PLATE P. 40 recalls a little the great seated women of the Boscoreale frescoes. She is the work of an otherwise unknown sculptor called Chairestratos. She was dedicated to Themis at Rhamnous in the north-west of Attica by a local citizen who had been successful with a team of boys and men, while he was in charge of the Gymnasium; later he also successfully produced a comedy in the local theatre and had a note of this added on the base of the statue. She is not a statue of Themis but a kore, like the archaic korai of the Athenian Acropolis, given to the goddess to serve her.

These figures give some idea of what a portrait of a woman by the sons of Praxiteles would look like. One of them, Kephisodotos, combined with Euthykrates of Sikyon, a pupil of Lysippos, – an interesting combination of two different traditions – to make a portrait statue of the poetess, Anyte of Tegea. Her lyric poetry is lost, but a number of very pleasing epigrams survive, some of which can be described as pastoral: one such is an inscription for a cup dedicated to Pan and the Nymphs by a shepherd, who in summer had drunk from a spring in a cave sacred to Pan and the Nymphs; another is an inscription for a Hermes standing at a cross-roads by a spring which gives cool water to weary travellers. Anyte was known in Alexandria, and her pastoral epigrams are rather earlier than the bucolics of Theokritos. For us she is the beginning of pastoral poetry.

Anyte and pastoral poetry

The flowering of pastoral poetry in Alexandria raises the question whether there was an analogous Early Hellenistic pastoral art. Anyte's poetry summons up a country scene which is connected with country deities. Theokritos' landscape also tends to centre round rustic deities – in the *First Idyll* an elm, a statue of Priapos, fountains, a shepherd's seat and oak – trees, or in the *Seventh Idyll* poplars, elms, water from the cave of the Nymphs, thorn-bushes, pears, apples and sloes. The land-

PLATE 19 – Deer hunt. Mosaic from Pella, signed by Gnosis. 320–300 B.C. *Cf. pp. 23, 66, 189.*

scape is ideal, and the characters are mostly mythical herdsmen, who are sometimes satyrs, and nymphs. The *Tenth Idyll* is the only complete poem which gives a consistent picture of contemporary country life, but one other contemporary figure may be added, the lean old fisherman in the description of the wooden cup in the *First Idyll;* he clearly belongs to what we have called the Old Derelicts (see p. 43).

Pastoral art

Occasional representations of rustics can be found all through the history of Greek art, but it would be fair to say that representation of nature tends to be associated particularly with the Nymphs, whether the spring Nymphs in their cave with sometimes Pan and sheep outside, or the Hesperides with their garden of fruited trees (from which the healthy Breezes blow), or the Nymphs of Nysa, who received the infant Dionysos in their sweet-smelling grotto. In all these scenes the natural elements are more emphasised in the fourth century than before. A moulded lekythos from the Athenian Agora, which dates from just before the beginning of our period, shows the child Dionysos standing in the cave of the Nymphs. He holds an oinochoe in his right hand and an enormous phiale in his left hand, to pour a libation in honour of his father Zeus. Round the mouth of the cave runs a vine from which clusters of grapes hang.

PLATE P. 22

PLATE P. 78

The vine-clad grotto of the Nymphs and Dionysos is the origin not only of the pastoral scenery of Theokritos but also of the artificial bower in which drinking-parties are held; the water of the Nymphs is as essential to a drinking-party as the wine of Dionysos. The simplest form of bower is the trailing stems either of vine with leaves and grapes or of fruited ivy or of both, pinned up or painted on the wall of the men's dining-room. But sometimes special bowers were made.

Ptolemy's symposion tent

The most splendid example is the symposion tent of Ptolemy II, which shows us also something of the magnificence of Ptolemaic Alexandria. The account by Kallixeinos of Rhodes is sufficiently detailed to permit of a reconstruction. It could take 200 banqueters. The columns were 26 metres high: the corner columns were shaped like palm-trees and the inner columns like the Dionysiac thyrsos (which was a fennel-stalk with a head of ivy-leaves). The akroteria were golden eagles, the bird of Zeus, the king of the gods, to whom Theokritos compared Ptolemy II. Thus the central hall had the air of a great bower on which birds had alighted. It was surrounded by a portico where the servants stood. Outside this was a garden, partly roofed with branches of myrtles and laurels and other suitable plants, and the ground was covered with every sort of flower. This was to provide wreaths for the banqueters, and flowers were scattered on the floor of the banqueting-hall 'so that it looked like a divine meadow'. Eagles of Zeus, thyrsoi of Dionysos, roses and violets in the depth of winter – the guests felt themselves in heaven or in the garden of the Hesperides: this is the sort of illusion that Gnosis had tried to create on a more modest scale with the mixed floral border of his mosaic in Pella.

FIG. 10

PLATE P. 65

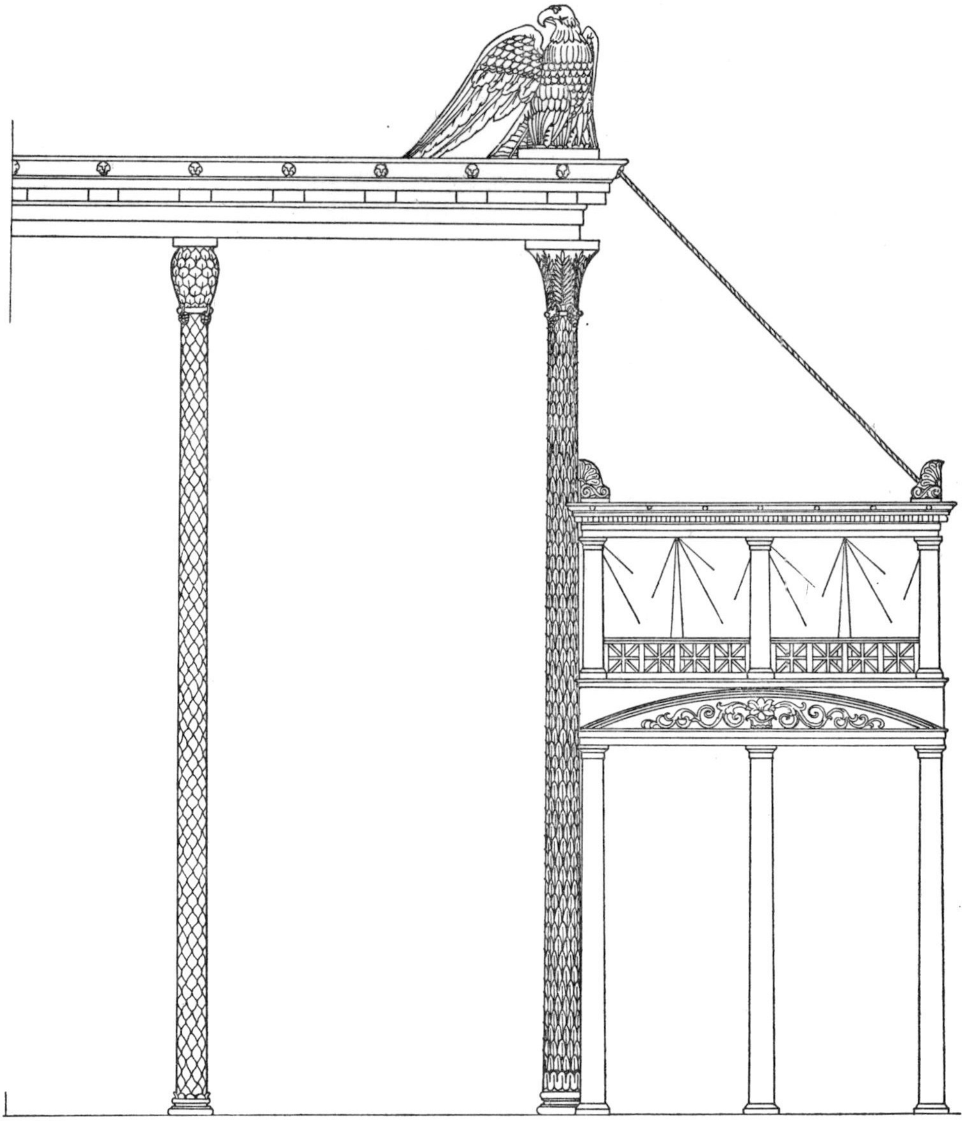

FIG. 10 – *Symposion tent of Ptolemy II at Alexandria: reconstruction. The corner columns are shaped like palm-trees, following the Egyptian tradition. The eagle of Zeus is of gold and serves as akroterion. The central hall was surrounded by a portico. Circa 275–270 B.C. Height of columns 26 m. Cf. p. 66.*

The general magnificence is shown by the hundred marble statues by the best artists standing against the columns of the portico; between the columns were hung paintings by Sikyonian artists (see p. 16; they were, therefore, already known in Alexandria before Aratos started collecting for Ptolemy III); they alternated with tapestries, some with portraits of the royal family, some with mythical scenes. Theokritos describes two women visiting the palace of Ptolemy II and exclaiming at a life-like tapestry of Adonis on a couch. That is a mythical scene; but he is thinking of a representation of the royal family (whether a tapestry or a painting or a sculptured group) when he describes Herakles, drunk with nectar, led home by Alexander and Ptolemy I.

PLATE 20 – Clay drinking-cup with Artemis hunting a feline, found in the Athenian Agora. *Circa* 300–275 B.C. *Agora Museum, Athens. Cf. p. 69.*

The couches in the symposion tent were golden with sphinx feet. Each guest had a golden table; each pair of guests had a silver wash-basin and jug. The drinking-cups were gold and gold studded with gems.

The grotto theme returns in the upper register of the surrounding portico. Here there were grottoes, 4.5 metres high; in them 'were symposia of tragic, comic and satyric figures with real garments and golden cups'. That these were characters from plays is difficult to believe. But they may have been poets and actors and perhaps also personifications of the three forms of drama. And masks suspended from vine-trailers (as often in symposion decoration) round the caves may have made the significance of each group clear.

The occasion for erecting the tent seems to have been a winter festival of Dionysos corresponding to the Athenian Anthesteria. It was therefore natural that Dionysiac imagery should predominate in it and in the great procession, which is described in the following passage of Athenaeus. Ptolemy's tent is a royal magnification of the artificial bower which the ordinary man might have for a symposion, and the grottoes with which the upper storey is decorated are related to the cave of the Nymphs where the young Dionysos grew up: his devotees, poets and actors, drink his wine in his cave, after mixing it with the water of the Nymphs.

Attic and Alexandrian pastoral scenes

PLATE P. 68

We come nearer to the mythical pastorals of Theokritos with a very large cup found in the Athenian Agora. It was dedicated to Dionysos and Artemis. The decoration is in added colour on the black glaze – the Attic equivalent of South Italian Gnathia ware. The picture shows Artemis moving from a high column on the left to spear a panther, at which a hound leaps; then a rustic shrine; then a large stag, which has perhaps been saved from the panther by Artemis' intervention. Was Menokles a successful hunter, who had this kantharos specially painted for a symposion after the hunt and then dedicated to the goddess of the hunt and to the god of the symposion? It is so large that it must have been a kind of loving cup, in which wine and water were mixed so that a krater was not needed: the use of such a cup at a symposion in the cave of the Nymphs at Phyle in Attica is described in Menander's *Dyskolos*.

PLATES PP. 3, 29

It is the amount of open space between the high column on the left and the deer on the right which makes this picture so remarkable. This reduction of the size of the figures in relation to the surrounding space marks the beginning of a tendency which leads ultimately to the

PLATES PP. 138–9 Esquiline landscapes.

One Early Hellenistic poet foreshadows this later love of wide prospects, which may, of course, have been depicted in art earlier than we know. In his *Argonautika* (I, 1112) Apollonios Rhodios sends Jason and his crew up Mount Dindymon on the southern coast of the Sea of Marmara: 'The Makrian heights and all the Thracian coast came out before their eyes as if they could touch it. They could see the misty mouth of the Bosporos and the Mysian hills, and on the other side the flowing river Aisepos and the town and Nepeian plain of Adrasteia.' They can see across the Sea of Marmara to the European coast, eastwards to the Bosporos, and westwards nearly to the mouth of the Dardanelles – a grand view described for its own sake, which is something new in Greek poetry.

FIG. 11 A bronze relief in Delos is an abbreviated representation of a sacrifice. It has the same wide spacing and a high pillar with an archaistic statue on the top. Artemis is using a torch to light a fire on the altar, while the satyr to the right is blowing the flame; the satyr on the left is carrying a winnowing-fan (containing various objects) on his head and an oinochoe in his left hand for pouring a libation. This mythical pastoral is difficult to interpret. Why is Artemis attended by satyrs?

FIG. 11 – *Artemis served by satyrs. Bronze relief from Delos. Circa 270 B.C. Height 50 cm. Delos Museum. Cf. above and p. 77.*

FIG. 12 – *A queen beside an altar with goat. Relief on fragment of fayence oinochoe. Circa 270 B.C. Istanbul Museum. Cf. p. 72.*

And why are the offerings brought in a winnowing-fan, which again belongs particularly to the Mysteries of Dionysos? Is it perhaps a joint country shrine of Artemis and Dionysos? Having got so far, we then see that Artemis looks very like Arsinoe II, the queen of Ptolemy II, and that the satyrs are not satyrs but men dressed up as satyrs. In the Roman period one grade of initiates in the Dionysiac mysteries at Pergamon were called *seilenoi* (elderly satyrs), and this usage may be old and widespread; it ties up with the use of satyrs to depict bliss in the after-life. Readers of Theokritos know only too well this kind of glide from the contemporary into the mythical world, and the same has been suspected in Kallimachos.

Arsinoe II and other early Ptolemaic queens appear on a group of fayence oinochoai, which were made in Alexandria but have been found in various places in the Greek world; presumably they were used at a royal festival by visitors and taken home afterwards. As the shape derives from the shape of jug used at the Anthesteria in Athens, these jugs may have been used at the festival for which on one occasion Ptolemy II built his tent. The queen stands beautifully draped (in some examples the word 'archaistic' can justifiably be applied to the folds) with a double cornucopia in her left hand and a libation saucer in her right. She is probably personifying Good Fortune. Beyond her is a high pillar with a long trailer wound round it, which may perhaps PLATE P. 73

have some analogy with the 'maypole' of the Athenian Anthesteria. FIG. 12 She is pouring a libation on an altar, which is set off to the left. On some examples a shaggy goat comes out from behind the altar, ready for the sacrifice. The connexion with Dionysos is further shown by the Papposeilenos and Satyr masks at the top and bottom of the handles on these jugs, which reproduce contemporary Alexandrian satyr-play masks. The high pillar and the wide spacing connect these mythical pastorals with the Delos relief and the Athenian cup; and, as in the Delos relief, the goddess has the features of the Queen of Egypt. In learned Alexandria pastoral is mythical but the figures in the myth may also be contemporary mortals.

FIG. 13 There is, however, no reason to give a mythical interpretation to a charming marble relief from Tralles in Asia Minor, which has been dated on stylistic grounds in the third century. A man wearing the short chiton of a rustic fastens a rope to a ring under a plane-tree: leaves, stem and fruit of the tree are beautifully represented. The rope was attached to an animal, which was being tied up before sacrifice at a country shrine. The wide spacing connects this with the Alexandrian and Attic pastorals, but here at last we seem to have a simple country scene with no complicated overtones.

Temple of Asklepios at Kos

Ptolemy II, who developed brilliantly the new Alexandrian civilisation started by his father, was born in Kos, and during his lifetime Kos was a sort of appendage of Alexandrian civilisation. Kos was the birthplace of the great fifth-century doctor Hippokrates and already in his time had a temple of Asklepios, of which nothing now remains. The precinct of Asklepios was greatly developed in Hellenistic times with a fourth-century altar, a third-century temple, two second-century temples, FIG. 14 as well as numerous other buildings. The early third-century temple was a simple Ionic building divided inside into an outer hall and an inner sanctuary, which included a sunken treasury. The altar, which stood some 12 metres from the front of the temple, was dedicated to a number of gods more or less nearly connected with Asklepios. On the top of the altar was the platform on which offerings were made; below, it was surrounded by a colonnade in which dedications could be placed. The altar and the Early Hellenistic temple are the setting for Herondas' *Fourth Mimiambos*, which gives a valuable picture of the reactions of a

PLATE 21 – Fayence oinochoe (wine-jug) showing a Ptolemaic queen with a double cornucopia and libation saucer. From Alexandria. *Circa* 280–270 B.C. *British Museum*. *Cf. p. 71.*

couple of ordinary Hellenistic women visiting a temple. Herondas' poems go with some of the poems of Theokritos and the last two *Hymns* of Kallimachos as a group of short poems which give a realistic and slightly tart dramatic representation of a scene of everyday life but use archaic metres and highly sophisticated dialect. The two women have come to make a sacrifice to Asklepios after one of them, Kokkale, has been ill; the other, Kynno, claims to be an expert in temple procedure. Kynno makes the prayer to all possible relevant gods and heroes, standing by the altar. She tells Kokkale to hang her tablet on the right of the statue of Hygieia (Health). The tablet is a clay or wooden tablet with either an account of the cure or a representation of the sick part or a representation of something or someone connected with Asklepios.

The statue of Hygieia makes a group with Asklepios and presumably stood against the altar wall, on which Kokkale is to hang her tablet. The women admire the statues and read the inscription, which says that they were made by the sons of Praxiteles and dedicated by Euthias,

FIG. 13 – *Man and animal. Marble relief from Tralles in Asia Minor. 3rd century B.C. Cf. pp. 72, 76f.*

son of Praxon. Fragmentary statues of post-Praxitelean style have been found near the altar and have been identified as a daughter of Asklepios, Hygieia and Aphrodite, who is elsewhere also associated with Asklepios. They then look at four other dedications before they enter the temple itself. It is not clear whether these also stood against the altar, whether they were between the altar and the temple, or whether they stood on the bases along the south wall of the temple. Kokkale exclaims: 'Look at the girl gazing up at the apple. Wouldn't you say, "She'll die if she does not get it"? And that old man. By the fates, the boy strangling the goose. If it was not obviously stone, you would say, "he'll talk". Soon men will be able to put life into the stone. Do you see that statue of Batale, the daughter of Myttes, the pose? Someone who had not seen Batale would know her completely by looking at her portrait.'

Kokkale's standard is realism, and the old man, presumably a portrait, must have been one of the Old Derelicts (see p. 43). The girl looking at the apple has been variously explained. Probably it is a relief with

FIG. 14 – *Ground-plan and façade of temple B at Kos. 300–270 B.C. Cf. pp. 72, 77.*

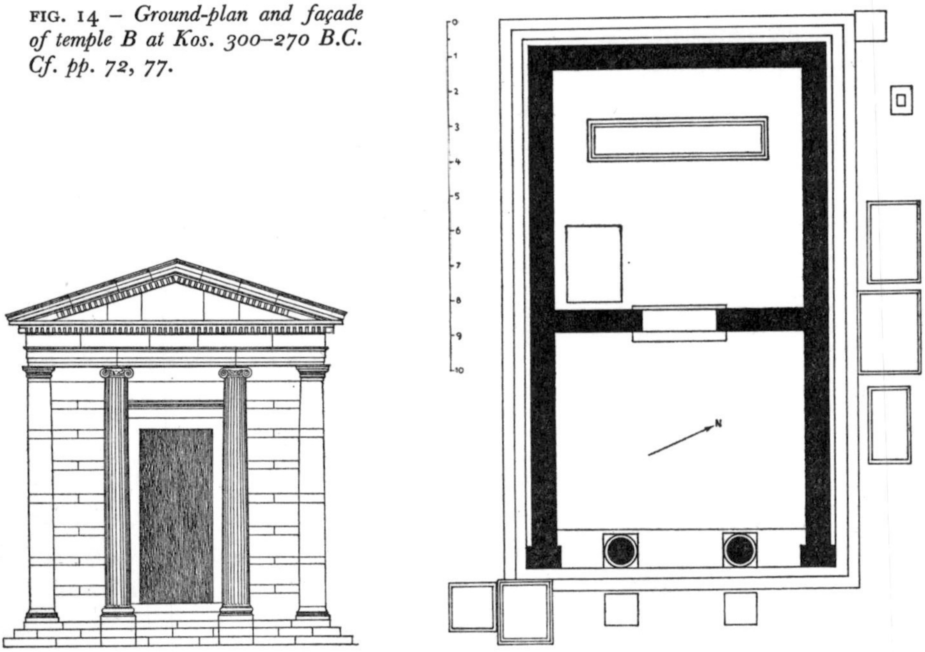

a girl reaching up to pick an apple from a tree; the theme occurs on a later grave relief from Ephesos; this is country art in the same sense
FIG. 13 as the relief from Tralles. The boy with the goose may be the group
FIG. 15 which is known from a Roman copy found in Ephesos; the sculptor was Boethos of Carthage. These two dedications do not need any complicated explanation; they are simply dedications by parents in gratitude for the recovery of two children from illness. One side of Hellenistic realism is the realistic representation of children: the chubby
PLATE P. 78 Dionysos in the cave of the Nymphs is a special instance, and there are many enchanting child Erotes in terracotta from different sites.

The portrait of Batale has been explained on the evidence of the name as a portrait of a prostitute, and Kallimachos wrote an epigram on an elderly prostitute who dedicated her picture to Aphrodite. But the masculine form, Batalos, is the name of the flute-player of the Nykterinos on the Thasos monument (see p. 49); and, as names often run in professions, Batale may have been an entertainer. Certainly her life-
APPX. PL. 13 like pose would be admirably illustrated by the bronze statuette of a dancer in the Baker Collection. She dates from the late third century and probably performed in a cult of Dionysos or Demeter, but the boundary between cult and entertainment was not very clear; after all, one might regard the symposion as a cult of Dionysos. She wears a long chiton, a himation with fringe, and slippers; in addition, a thin gauze veil hangs over her face. The statuette was probably made in Alexandria, but one tradition behind it is the tradition of the Tanagra
PLATE P. 63 statuettes leading to Praxiteles; the complication of the folds and the transparency of the himation which shows the folds of the chiton through it places it at an advanced stage of this tradition. On the other hand the very accomplished composition of triangles set in different planes belongs to the tradition of the Tyche of Antioch and
APPX. PL. 1 Lysippos. But the possibility of the blending of these two traditions was already realised in the late fourth century, if a son of Praxiteles and a pupil of Lysippos combined to make a portrait of Anyte (see p. 64). The Baker dancer is a small masterpiece. She really belongs to the Middle rather than to the Early Hellenistic period, but the links back to Praxiteles and Lysippos are so clear that it seemed right to place her here.

After exclaiming at Batale, Herondas' two women enter the temple: 'It is daylight and the crush is growing: the door is open and we can get into the sanctuary.' They cast an approving glance at the sculpture, but Kokkale is fascinated by a picture: a naked boy with tender warm flesh; a silver fire-box which would excite the greed of a burglar; an ox, a man leading it, a woman with him, a hook-nosed man, a snub-nosed man – all alive and the ox with a terrifying roving eye. Kynno tells her that this is the work of Apelles who 'hastened to touch the gods' and that anyone who does not appreciate him should be hanged. At this point a temple attendant announces the success of their sacrifice, and Kynno tells Kokkale to put the cake into the snake's hole without speaking. The snake's hole is the underground treasury which can be seen on the plan of the temple in the inner sanctuary. At this time the FIG. 14
cake was no longer a cake but an offering of money. At Ptolemais the temple of Asklepios had a similar treasury, and the lid was in the form of a snake rearing up with its mouth open to receive the coins. In Kos, however, the lid had a simple hole; the snake would surely have frightened Kokkale, and Kynno merely says 'the snake's hole'. The snake was not only sacred to Asklepios; the god himself might appear in the form of a snake.

The picture of Apelles which Kokkale admires belongs to a long tradition of pictures of sacrifice, which can be traced back to the beginning of Greek art; the bronze relief in Delos is a special instance, FIG. 11
and the Tralles relief is a fragment of a similar scene; the surviving FIG. 13
figure corresponds to the man leading the ox in Apelles' picture. The boy with tender warm flesh is lighting the fire on the altar like one of the satyrs on the Delos relief; he uses the silver fire-box; the woman probably carries on her head the basket which holds the sacrificial knife, sacrificial grain and incense; her place is taken on the Delos relief by the satyr with a winnowing-fan on his head. The hook-nosed man is probably the father of the household, who made the sacrifice and dedicated the picture. The snub-nosed man is probably a slave.

One contemporary work survives which helps to explain Kokkale's PLATE P. 81
excitement over the silver fire-box. A group of hydriai, known as Hadra ware from the cemetery in which many were found, were made in Alexandria in the third century; the sparing decoration on the body

PLATE 22 – Dionysos in the cave of the Nymphs. Plastic vase from the Athenian Agora. *Circa* 300–275 B.C. *Height 9.5 cm. Agora Museum, Athens. Cf. pp. 66, 76, 189.*

is often interesting. One has a picture of a silver bowl; it is difficult to see, but the painter was clearly interested in the effects of light on the shining metal, and 'there seems even to be a glow of reflected light on the edge of the shadowed side'. An Alexandrian painter, Antiphilos, painted a boy blowing up the fire so that the light was reflected on the walls of the room and on the boy's own face. The occasion need not necessarily have been a sacrifice, although it may have been a sacrifice inside a temple. It is our first evidence for light effects in an interior scene. Of the Alexandrian poets Apollonios Rhodios is the most obviously interested in light effects. This is seen in his descriptions and in his similes: Medeia's agitated heart is compared to a gleam of sun which 'darts about the roof, rising from water which has been newly poured in a cauldron or pail. It leaps this way and that, shaken by the swift whirlpool'; and Jason, holding the Golden Fleece in his hands, is like a girl in an upper room holding a piece of fine linen under the light of the full moon. Here, as in his love of prospects, he is at least abreast with painting.

Kynno in Herondas says that Apelles 'touched the gods', and in this practically quotes Apelles' own statement that works which have charm 'touch heaven'. It is reasonable therefore to suppose that Herondas omitted two much more famous pictures in Kos, the Aphrodite rising from the sea and the portrait of Antigonos, because the everyday scene of sacrifice contained more elements to arouse the ejaculations of the women. These women were representatives of the ordinary people

FIG. 15 – *Boy with goose. Marble. Roman copy from Ephesos. Height 55 cm. Kunsthistorisches Museum, Vienna. Cf. p. 76.*

whom Apelles said he regarded as more careful critics than himself; Herondas must surely have known this saying.

When Kynno calls down a curse on Apelles' critics, she is thinking of Antiphilos, the rival Alexandrian painter, who tried to get Apelles banished by accusing him of treachery; Ptolemy was told the truth; Apelles was saved, and embodied his experience in an allegorical picture. How much of this is true we do not know; at least we can accept as fact the rivalry between the two painters and the existence of Apelles' allegorical picture. In it appeared Ignorance, False Assumption, Slander (equipped like a Fury), Jealousy (a pale, ugly man with sharp eyes, wasted away by disease), Plotting, Deception, Repentance (a weeping woman with black tattered clothes) and Truth. Here again Apelles is working in an old tradition of representing mental states by personifications: we have noticed another Early Hellenistic example in the Mad Jealousy (*Oistros* as distinct from Apelles' *Phthonos*) on the Taren-
PLATE P. 27
tine vase with Medeia, and in the late fifth century the maenads attending Dionysos were given the names of mental states resulting from Dionysiac inspiration, such as Brightness, Good Cheer and Happiness (see p. 55). But the tradition is alive because it is a convenient method of representing in art the nice distinctions between mental states established by Aristotle and his successors. Apelles showed the psychological factors present in the mind of a man who believed a slander and then discovered it to be untrue. In the same way Menander could put on the stage, as prologue figures, personifications of psychological factors affecting his characters, when he felt that the audience needed to be told how to approach his plot: the prologue figure of the *Perikeiromene* is Ignorance, because ignorance of an essential fact set the story in motion – the hero flamed into a range and cut off his girl's hair because he did not know that the young man who had embraced her was her brother.

Conclusion

Tradition is strong in the Early Hellenistic period. The old cities clung to it because the Hellenistic kings, however Greek they were, were a recurrent threat to their inherited ideals and institutions. The new cities like Alexandria wanted to emphasise their connexion with the ancient glories of Greece: of this feeling the exedra of the Sarapieion

PLATE 23 – Clay hydria from the Hadra cemetery near Alexandria, known as 'Hadra ware'. *Circa* 270 B.C. *Height 8.2 cm. Metropolitan Museum, New York, Cf. p. 77.*

gives a very strong indication – a new god and round him the statues of Greek poets and thinkers from Orpheus to the present day: this is the right atmosphere for learned Alexandrian poetry in archaic metre and dialect. Archaism is less obvious in art, but the elegance of post-Praxitelean poses and drapery could easily become archaistic. The content of much Alexandrian poetry is nevertheless realistic in spite of the archaism of form and has a parallel in the realism of Early Hellenistic portraiture. Pastoral poetry and pastoral art develop in a new way and partake both of the mythical and the contemporary; pastoral art shows the possibility of developing into a new landscape art, which will correspond to the new vision of the poets.

Dionysos is a central figure. Some of the new kings identified themselves with Dionysos. Dionysos gave old Greeks and new Greeks alike their hopes of immortality. Dionysos was the god of the symposion, at which much Hellenistic poetry was performed, at which the beautiful women represented by the Tanagra statuettes entertained the men, for which Hellenistic artists made furniture, drinking-vessels, mosaics, tapestries, paintings and statues. Dionysos was the god of Tragedy and Comedy, which now claimed their own two Muses from Apollo; for Dionysos theatres were built or remodelled, dramatic poets wrote and producers produced with new costumes and masks; in honour of Dionysos choral lyrics were written and performed, so that the theatre has become, beside the symposion and the court, a great patron and inspirer of art. The association of Dionysos with the Nymphs and of Pan and Priapos with Dionysos brings him also into pastoral poetry and art; the satyr, herdsman or not, is an obvious link between the pastoral, the drama, and hopes of immortality.

Some of the art is court art. The mosaics of Pella and the monument of Thasos were made for a rich or even very rich patron. The Medeia krater and the Menokles cup were probably commissioned specially but would not have been very expensive; a rich man would have ordered either in bronze. The terracottas, once the original was made, were turned out in quantity and were the house ornaments, temple dedications, and tomb offerings of the poor. The difference between the rich man's art and the poor man's art is a difference of scale and material rather than a difference of style.

The styles of Early Hellenistic art continue along lines laid down by the middle of the fourth century. It has been convenient to treat these lines separately. Our documentation varies considerably for the different lines. Lysippos' pupils are known and the influence of Sikyonian painting is reasonably clear. Praxiteles' sons carry his art into the third century, and further developments are very clear in the Tanagra statuettes. The style associated with Nikias, Euphranor and Bryaxis has no documentation after its inception: yet there seems to be a recognisable common element in these large serious figures, which often communicate directly with the spectator – whether they are found in Pella, Centuripe or Alexandria. Artists and works of art travel so easily that the stylistic lines become intertwined and the new centres such as Alexandria do not develop a style of their own. It would be wrong to think of Early Hellenistic art as only traditional. It is traditional, but most noticeably in realistic portraiture and in pastoral art new developments can be seen.

PLATE 24 – The Acropolis at Lindos on Rhodes. *Cf. p. 85.*

II. MIDDLE HELLENISTIC PERIOD

In the Middle Hellenistic period sculpture seems to have a dramatic quality which was lacking earlier. This is partly because our conception of Middle Hellenistic sculpture is dominated by the Pergamon altar; but it is a quality which appears in architecture as well as in sculpture; it is not confined to Pergamon or to areas under the influence of Pergamon, and in fact the beginning lies before the Middle Hellenistic period – in sculpture with Leochares and in town planning, for example with the town of Priene, built in 350 B.C. on the grid plan and dominated by the temple of Athena in the centre. The latter was dedicated in 334 B.C., but apparently was not finished until the second century. A pure and beautifully proportioned Ionic temple, it was designed by Pythios, who had previously built the Mausoleum at Halikarnassos; he wrote a book about it which was known to Vitruvius. Vitruvius' numerous references to him show that he had a considerable influence throughout the Hellenistic period.

Architecture

But drama in architectural planning demands wide flights of steps and long colonnades. In Kos the layout of the Asklepios sanctuary (see p. 72) was remodelled in the second century, so that the Early Hellenistic temple and altar visited by Herondas' women became merely the introduction to a tremendous staircase, which led through a gateway half-way up to a large Doric temple on the top level; the new temple stood in the middle of an enormous court surrounded on three sides by a colonnade. This three-sided court echoed in reverse a corresponding three-sided court, which formed the entry to the whole precinct on the level below the Early Hellenistic temple and altar. Two Rhodian towns, Lindos and Kameiros, were also architecturally dramatised in the second century, and the effect can still be observed. PLATE P. 84
Lindos has an extraordinarily beautiful Acropolis with a sheer drop on the seaward side. The old temple at the top on the south-western edge was replaced by a new Doric one about 330 B.C. A second temple was built about 300 B.C. at the lower north-eastern edge.

About the same time the approach to the higher temple was given a noble columned Propylaia on the model of the Propylaia leading on to the Acropolis in Athens. In the second century the wide flight of steps leading up to this Propylaia was flanked on either side by a colonnade. Thus if one were visiting the Acropolis, one would first visit the lower temple; then one would turn round and face steps leading up to the court formed by the lower colonnade. Through the lower colonnade one would approach the broad steps leading up to the court formed by the Propylaia. Through the Propylaia one found oneself in another columned court with the upper temple in the far left corner. The rebuildings had the effect of veiling the upper temple by successive curtains of columns.

Kameiros was an attractive Hellenistic town, which ran up a valley from an Agora with temples at the bottom. Across the top a magnificent colonnade was built in the second century, and this again veiled the temples which were behind and above it, so that they would only burst on the eyes of the visitor when he had passed through the colonnade.

Before considering Pergamon, the most dramatic and from the point of view of the history of art the most important Middle Hellenistic Acropolis, some other buildings of this period may be briefly considered.

FIG. 16 Priene has a well-preserved meeting-house, which seated over 600 persons; presumably it was designed for the Council rather than for the Assembly. What remains today is chiefly the seating. A door leads on to a street at the back and another on to a side street on the left-hand side. The site is steep, and the passage at the bottom of the Council House also connects with the side street there. The square altar in the middle is decorated with ox-skulls supporting garlands. This kind of decoration became common from the middle of the fourth century; it is suitable either for a dining-room or for an altar; in origin the skulls were the skulls of the victims killed to honour the god and to feed his worshippers, and the garlands might equally well adorn victim and worshippers. Sacrifice was made on the altar before the Council met. The most curious feature of the building is the arrangement of a bench in the back wall so that the officials occupying it had their feet in the room and their heads and bodies in the open air:

the bench projects through an archway behind the back wall. They would not be in the sun as the wall would shelter them. They could receive or send messages along the passage behind them without disturbing the main body of the Council.

It is also interesting to find the arch as an architectural feature. The Greeks were so enslaved to the normal temple architecture, with flat elements joining columns and bridging doorways, that until the third century they only used arches and barrel-vaults when they could be put out of sight. Perhaps as a result of contact with the East, arches were now occasionally put on view; in Priene another arch was erected in the second century to form an entrance into the Agora.

One of Vitruvius' favourite sources is the second-century architect, Hermogenes of Alabanda, who firmly rejected the Doric for the Ionic order because of the difficulties of arranging the triglyphs in relation to the columns. He built the temple of Artemis Leukophryene at Magnesia on the Maeander. This was probably an old Asiatic mother-goddess, who had been Hellenised and was now renowned for her Epiphanies. The temple stood on a platform approached by steps. In front of it was a large altar surrounded by columns with statues between them, not unlike the altar at Kos, which was rebuilt more magnificently at this time (see p. 72). The actual temple building was divided into antechamber, sanctuary and back chamber, and was surrounded by columns; but instead of placing the surrounding columns FIGS. 17, 18

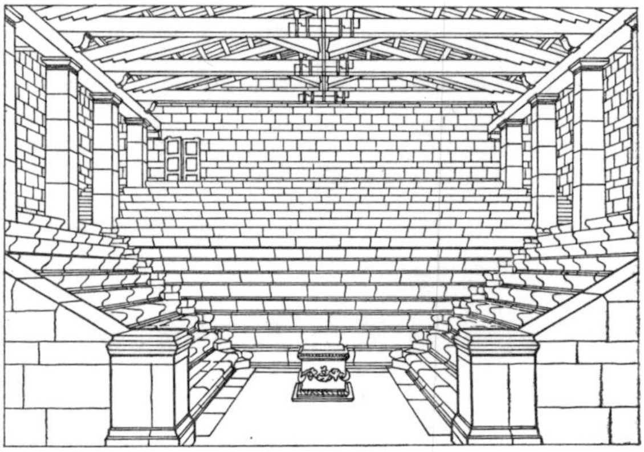

FIG. 16 – *Meeting-house (ekklesiasterion) at Priene: reconstruction. Circa 200 B.C. Cf. p. 86.*

close to the temple walls Hermogenes moved them further out, so that the width of the passage surrounding the temple was doubled. 'If,' says Vitruvius, 'an unexpected storm confined a large body of people to the temple, they had plenty of room to stay there in comfort.' The pediments had no sculpture but large floral akroteria. The columns had elaborate Ionic capitals and bases. The frieze was sculpted with battles of Greeks and Amazons. The Greek temple of Artemis at Ephesos, according to Kallimachos, was the successor to an open-air shrine of Artemis established by the Amazons; the Greeks defeated the Amazons there but took over their goddess, and this may be the allusion in this frieze. It repeats themes from earlier Amazonomachies, particularly from the frieze of the temple of Apollo at Bassai; even the angular style is repeated, but the relief is much higher. It is difficult to see here the kind of pointed reminiscence which is found in the

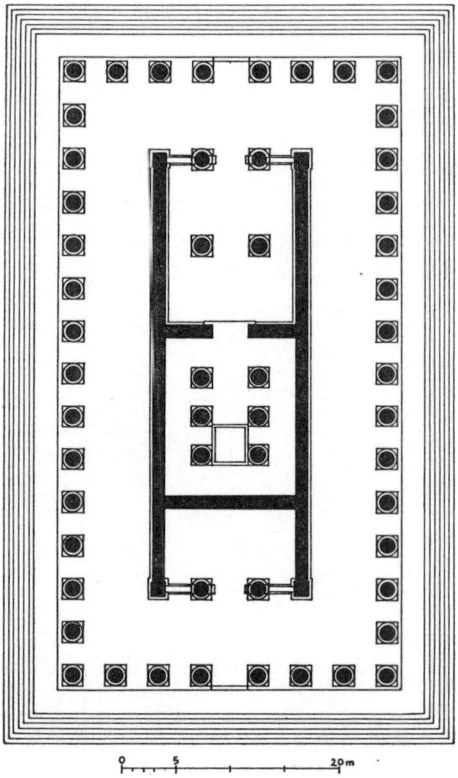

FIG. 17 – *Ground-plan of temple of Artemis at Magnesia. 200 B.C. Cf. above.*

FIG. 18 – *Order, frieze and entablature of temple of Artemis at Magnesia. Circa 200 B.C. Cf. p. 88.*

FIG. 19 – *Capitals and entablature from the temple of Olympian Zeus in Athens. Circa 170 B.C. Cf. below.*

Pergamon Gigantomachy; it seems rather that the designer of the frieze, perhaps Hermogenes himself, knew the Bassai sculpture and repeated the design.

APPX. PL. 24 In Athens the temple of Olympian Zeus, which had been begun by
FIG. 19 Peisistratos in the sixth century B.C., was carried a stage further in the second, when Antiochos Epiphanes of Syria contributed to the cost. This was a magnificent gesture to the cultural centre of the Greek world; similar gestures, as we shall see, were made by the kings of Pergamon and Egypt. This donation apparently carried the temple up to the roof, and it was finished in the second century A.D. by Hadrian. The temple was on an enormous scale and had a double row of columns round it. The columns were Corinthian – an early example of the use of the Corinthian order for a large temple. The capitals are interesting because the akanthos-leaves surrounding the lower part are surmounted by tendril-like volutes with a lily-like flower growing above them. This is the same kind of never-never plant found
PLATE P. 65 long before on the mosaic at Pella; if the symbolism is still alive here,

FIG. 20 – *Plan of the Acropolis in Pergamon, showing the library, theatre, temple of Athena, altar of Zeus and temple of Dionysos. 200–150 B.C. Cf. p. 92.*

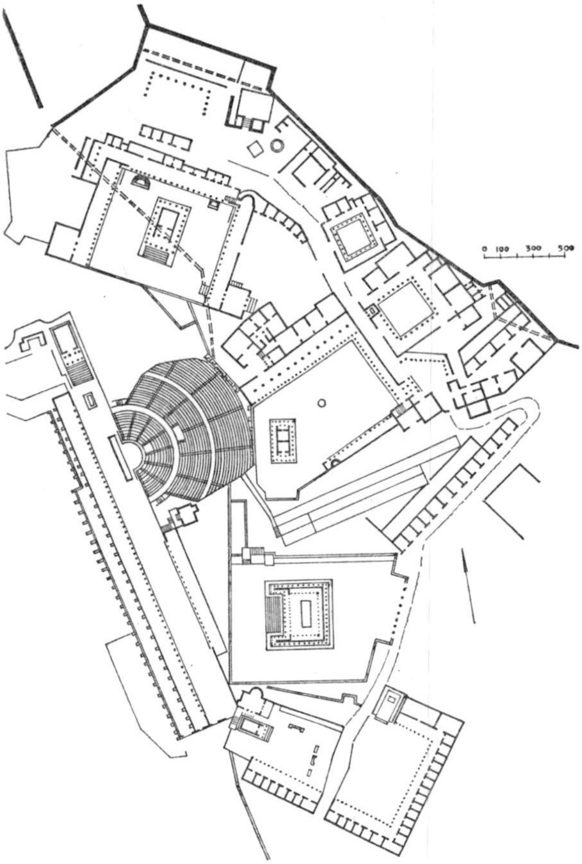

the plant indicates the heavenly flora of Olympos, where the Olympian Zeus lives. The architect of this temple is called by Vitruvius *civis Romanus Cossutius*, the Roman citizen Cossutius. This does not mean that he was a Roman any more than St. Paul was; Vitruvius would not have added *civis Romanus* to the name of anyone who was a Roman in the ordinary sense of the word. It is interesting to find that a very distinguished Greek architect was given Roman citizenship, however he may have obtained it. The information presumably came from the inscription on a statue-base found by the temple. The name occurs again in the signatures of several artists in the late first century B.C., and it is possible that these are descendants.

FIG. 21 – *Monument on a round base commemorating Attalos I's victory over the Gauls. View from above, showing arrangement of figures, Cf. p. 94.*

PERGAMON
History

The most splendid and influential Middle Hellenistic city was Pergamon. The last king of Pergamon, Attalos III, left his kingdom to Rome in 133 B.C.; thus very large numbers of works of art came to Italy when his property was auctioned. The site is on a hill which rises steeply 300 metres above the coastal plain opposite the island of Lesbos. One of Alexander's companions, Lysimachos, who set himself up as king of Thrace and northern Asia Minor, deposited a large amount of treasure in the natural stronghold of Pergamon and placed an officer, Philetairos, in command. Philetairos deserted Lysimachos in 282 B.C. and from that time Pergamon was under the suzerainty of Seleukos; Philetairos won a victory over raiding Galatians or Gauls in 278 B.C. Philetairos' nephew, Eumenes I, made himself independent in 263 B.C.; he was succeeded by his nephew Attalos I, who ruled until 197 B.C. He again defeated the Gauls in 230 B.C. and made an alliance with the Romans. This Western policy was carried on by his elder son Eumenes II and by his younger son Attalos II. Finally Attalos III, son of Eumenes II, who succeeded in 138 B.C., bequeathed his kingdom to Rome.

FIG. 20 Attalos I conceived of his capital as a centre of culture and started the building which was carried on by his successors. Like the Alexandrians, he set up a library and was sufficiently successful for Ptolemy V to try and stop its development by putting an embargo on the export

FIG. 22 – *Frontal view of monument commemorating Attalos I's victory over the Gauls. Cf. p. 94.*

of papyrus from Egypt; Eumenes II replied by introducing parchment. The library and the theatre (which was, however, later remodelled to some extent) were early additions to the extremely steep Acropolis, of which the dominant feature was the temple of Athena, a Doric building with columns round it, apparently erected in the time of Lysimachos. Eumenes II balanced the temple of Athena by building the great altar of Zeus to the south, and made a new Propylaia or gateway to give a slanting view of the temple of Athena from the landward side. Attalos II completed the layout by building porticoes to form a three-sided court round the temple of Athena.

Pergamon was to be an Athens in the East. Attalos' victory over the Gauls was to be regarded as a triumph of Greeks over barbarians like the Athenian triumph over the Persians. So the altar of Zeus was the Parthenon of the Pergamenes; and the temple of Athena, which could not carry this symbolism, was yet given a resemblance to the Parthenon when the gateway was built, because a similar slanting view faced the spectator when he emerged from the Parthenon gateway on the Athenian Acropolis.

Attalos I and the Gauls

Attalos I sowed the seeds of this grandiose development, which will occupy us later. He was the founder of the library, he set up on the Acropolis at Athens a monument commemorating his victory over the Gauls, and he may have sent his younger son to study in Athens.

The monument which he erected in Pergamon to commemorate his victory over the Gauls is known from Roman copies and can be re-
FIGS. 21–23 constructed. It stood in the sanctuary of Athena. On a large round base with an inscription the centre was taken by the towering figure of the Gaul plunging his sword into his neck after having killed his wife; round this pair were grouped four dying Gauls, of which the best known is the so-called Dying Gladiator of the Capitoline Museum. The slanting bodies of the dying Gauls led the eye upwards to the twisting flame of the central group.

What makes this monument so arresting is partly the characterisation of the figures and partly the composition. Here, brilliantly, the victors were omitted, and the might of the victory was to be appreciated from the splendour and agony of the vanquished. The agony is shown in their utter defeat, but they die proudly and defiantly in the glory of splendid physique, with their wild, thick hair, and with their golden

FIG. 23 – *The Gaul plunging his sword into his neck after killing his wife. From the monument commemorating Attalos I's victory over the Gauls. Roman copy. Marble. Terme, Rome. Cf. above and p. 95.*

FIG. 24 – *Artemis and Iphigeneia. Marble group from Rome. 220–200 B.C. Height 1.22 m. Ny Carlsberg Glyptotek, Copenhagen. Cf. pp. 96, 120.*

torques round their necks. Here the realism of the Old Derelicts in the Early Hellenistic age (see p. 43) is transferred to these magnificent non-Greeks. To call them barbarians is to miss the spirit of the dedication; the artists may have remembered that Alexander so respected those other non-Greeks, the Persians, that he caused noble Greeks to marry noble Persians: Gauls may have been uncivilised and unlearned but they stood for something which a Greek could respect.

The monument set up on the Acropolis of Athens did not have this restraint. Pausanias says that Attalos dedicated the war of the Giants, the battle of the Athenians against the Amazons, the action at Marathon against the Persians, and the rout of the Gauls in Mysia. As we know from Plutarch that the war of the Giants included Dionysos, it seems likely that all the groups contained victors as well as vanquished. In Athens Attalos I (like his son later in Pergamon when he built the altar of Zeus) wanted to point out that his victory over the Gauls ranked with Marathon and the legendary victories to which Greeks of the fifth century had compared Marathon.

The central pair of the monument in Pergamon has, of course, the tradition of Greek sculpture behind it. The deep savage eyes recall FIG. 23

Skopas, the dramatic striding pose recalls Leochares, the composition with its insistence on the third dimension and its absence of a single viewpoint recalls Lysippos; but these elements have been combined into a new superb unity. This three-dimensional composition can be illustrated elsewhere by the Tyche of Antioch at the beginning of the third century B.C. and by the Baker Dancer, which is contemporary with the Pergamene group (see p. 76).

APPX. PLATES I, 13

Other groups

Some other groups and figures reflect the style of the central group of Gauls. The composition is repeated most obviously in groups representing Menelaos carrying the dead body of Patroklos and Achilles carrying the dead body of Penthesileia, the Amazon queen. The originals of these must have been works of an artist very close to the artist of the pair of Gauls. It is, of course, possible that these groups also had dying figures round them. Menelaos only saved the body of Patroklos after a major battle, and the great classical picture of Achilles killing Penthesileia showed another Amazon at her feet. It is, of course, even possible that these groups also belonged to Attalos' monument in Pergamon. If they did (and the common composition is the only evidence), they were set on separate round bases and the Gauls lost nothing essential from the comparison with earlier Greek victories. Less close but still sharing the essential idea of a falling figure supporting a drooping figure is the original group of Artemis, Iphigeneia, and deer in the Ny Carlsberg Glyptotek, Copenhagen, which is said to be made of marble from Asia Minor with restorations in Italian marble; it was found in the Horti Sallustiani in Rome. The dates given to it have varied from 340 to the first century B.C. The composition suggests the late third century; but the formalism of the hanging folds may bring it down into the early second century, as they find a close parallel on dated terracottas from Myrina. The group goes right back into depth with Artemis behind Iphigeneia and the deer behind Artemis; at the same time a strong diagonal movement is set up, which runs from the altar in the front right corner to the head of the deer. But in spite of the composition into depth the group is meant to be seen from the front, and it cannot have stood on a circular base like the Gauls. Iphigeneia is sinking to the ground as the priest is about to strike her; at that instant Artemis arrives, pulls her away and

FIG. 24

substitutes the deer, so that the priest kills the deer instead of Iphigeneia. Another deep composition with very strong diagonal movement is the Laokoon group. The treatment of the torso and particularly of Laokoon's head brings it near to the Pergamene Gauls and still closer to the rather later giants on the altar of Zeus, so that the style can be dated to the early second century B.C. The new reconstruction makes the group much more compact, and emphasises the certainty that Laokoon and the son on the left will be destroyed, whereas the son on the right has a chance of escape. Laokoon was a Trojan priest, who protested against the Trojans' willingness to accept the Wooden Horse as an offering to Athena; the gods sent two snakes across the sea to kill him; according to Arktinos, who wrote a *Sack of Troy* in the late eighth century B.C., one son escaped, and the artist alludes to this version. Pliny describes the group, which he saw in the palace of

Laokoon
FIG. 25

FIG. 25 – *Laokoon group by the sculptors Agesander, Polydoros and Athenodoros of Rhodes. Presumably a Roman copy. Marble. Height 2.42 m. Vatican Museum, Rome. Cf. above.*

the Roman emperor Titus, as 'preferable to all other works of painting and statuary' and names as the artists Agesander, Polydoros, and Athenodoros of Rhodes. Signatures of artists with these names are known from the first century B.C. and later and the Vatican group may therefore be a copy, but it is more likely that it is an original by artists who were the ancestors of a long succession of Rhodian sculptors.

PLATE P. 99 Another famous original, which has long been associated with the Pergamene sculptures because of its style and dramatic composition, is

Nike of Samothrace

the Nike or winged Victory from Samothrace in the Louvre. Excavations on the island have confirmed the date in the early second century B.C. and have illuminated the original setting of the statue. In a swirl of draperies she lands on a ship's prow, which was erected in a basin fed from an aqueduct with water that reflected the Nike. The colouring of such a statue, which is inadequately given by the rare traces left on PLATE P. 100 ancient marbles, can be imagined from a rather later terracotta Nike from Myrina, on which the colours are well preserved even down to the tiny white sea-monsters which decorated the borders of her chiton. This Nike has lost her wings, but the slots in which they were inserted can be seen on the back and between them are the hang-holes, which show that she was meant to be suspended. Another example from the same mould has the mask of a slave of comedy in one hand and a papyros roll in the other, so that it was presumably a present to a victorious comic poet. Such Victories were sometimes used in pageants: in 87 B.C. Mithradates of Pontus, who (like several other Hellenistic kings) called himself the New Dionysos, was celebrating his power in the theatre at Pergamon and a Victory holding a crown was lowered on a crane towards his head; the Victory broke in pieces and the crown fell into the theatre. This Nike was presumably a life-size figure. The essential idea is the same also in the Myrina terracotta and the marble figure from Samothrace, which celebrates a naval victory.

Art and scholarship

The subjects of the Laokoon, Iphigeneia, Achilles and Penthesileia, Menelaos and Patroklos show interest in mythology. Two other well-

PLATE 25 – Nike from Samothrace. Marble. Early 2nd century B.C. *Height 2 m. Louvre, Paris. Cf. above and p. 120.*

PLATE 26 – Winged Nike from Myrina. Terracotta statuette. *Circa* 150–130 B.C. *Leland Stanford Jr. Museum, Stanford University, California. Cf. pp. 98, 124.*

known groups which have the same general style and also the cruelty of so much Pergamene sculpture are the Apollo and Marsyas and the punishment of Dirke. Apollo sits nonchalantly at ease, while a Scythian slave whets his knife to flay the satyr Marsyas, who is hanging from a tree in agonised apprehension. The other group was based on the messenger speech of Euripides' *Antiope* and showed Zethos and Amphion tying Dirke to the bull to be torn to pieces instead of their mother Antiope; the late copy has many additions and restorations but still gives an idea of the tremendous power of the original pyramidal composition; according to Pliny the original in Rhodes was by Apollonios and Tauriskos of Tralles, who were adopted sons of Menekrates of Rhodes, a sculptor and perhaps the architect of the altar of Zeus at Pergamon.

The Laokoon alludes to a single version of the story in which one son escaped. The helmet of Menelaos is decorated with a leopard and with an eagle which has a tail ending in snakes. These have been interpreted as symbolic of Menelaos' wanderings to Libya and Aithiopia. These details go beyond popular interest in mythology; they show an interest in scholarship. They do not necessarily imply that the artists themselves were scholars, and there is no reason to attribute the works to Antigonos of Karystos, although he did make sculpture at Pergamon and according to Pliny wrote books on his art: any artist could go to a scholar for details.

Library

At Pergamon, as at Alexandria, scholarship was at home in the library, which was started by Attalos I. The library consisted of four large rooms above the theatre and to the north of the temple of Athena. The rolls were kept on wooden shelves which surrounded the walls. Eumenes II, who introduced parchment to counter the embargo on papyrus from Egypt, also adorned the library with statues, and Attalos II connected the library with the temple of Athena by building the two-storeyed portico which ran round the courtyard of the temple. The library gave on to the upper floor of the northern portico.

Eumenes II emphasised the connexion of Pergamene scholarship with Athens by installing a marble copy of the Athena Parthenos of Pheidias to preside over the library. It was impossible to make a mechanical copy of the colossal statue in gold and ivory; the marble statue is less

FIG. I

than half the size of the original; the copyist has simplified the helmet, made the eyes pathetic, and complicated the folds. As the statue is of Pentelic marble, he presumably went to Athens to make it, like the painters who were sent by Attalos II to copy Polygnotos' paintings in Delphi (see p. 17).

The Athena was not only a symbol of Pergamon's connexion with Athens but also an example, even if slightly modernised, of Athenian classical art for sculptors to consider. Like the copies of classical frescoes from Delphi (see p. 16f.), she joined the originals in the royal collections, which included the Graces of the archaic sculptor Boupalos and the Apollo of the early classical sculptor Onatas, as an inspiration to Pergamene artists. It is much to their credit that Pergamene art did not become classicistic. Earlier art was a source of inspiration and of allusions which the spectator would understand.

Eumenes II also put statues of poets in the same room as the Athena. They included Homer, Sappho, Alkaios and Timotheos (the choral lyric poet of the late fifth and early fourth centuries). This room was probably a committee- and lecture-room, so that the scholars of Pergamon, like the scholars of Alexandria, met in the presence of the great poets of the past and literally under the aegis of Athena. The epigram on the base of the statue of Sappho was written by one of the best contemporary poets, Antipater of Sidon: 'My name is Sappho. I surpassed all women in song as much as Homer surpassed all men.' The reference to Homer implies that the statue of Sappho was placed near the statue of Homer. The Homer may be the original of the well-known blind head which survives in Roman copies; in style it is close to the Laokoon and to the frieze of the altar of Zeus.

Scholarship shows itself in much Middle Hellenistic art. Eumenes II and Attalos II built a sanctuary at Kyzikos in honour of their mother, Apollonis, who came from there. They set up nineteen reliefs on pillars which showed dutiful sons and their mothers. Two were historical; one was Roman (Romulus, Remus and Servilia) – an interesting compliment to their great Western ally. The rest were taken from Greek mythology, and ten of these (including Antiope and her sons, as in the Dirke group) were taken from tragedy: we only know these reliefs from the epigrams inscribed beneath them, which have been

PLATE 27 – Dove mosaic from Hadrian's Villa at Tivoli. Copy of an original, *circa* 170 B.C. *Height 85 cm. Capitoline Museum, Rome. Cf. below.*

preserved with a brief prose description in the Palatine Anthology. A more striking example of Pergamene scholarship showing itself in art is given by a recent interpretation of the well-known Dove mosaic. Two copies with minor variations survive and they agree closely enough with a description in Pliny to be attributed to Sosos of Pergamon.

Dove mosaic

PLATE ABOVE

They are highly competent, particularly in their rendering of the light and shade of the metal vessel on which the doves sit. A very strange feature of this bowl is the shadowy figure of a naked man rising from the foot with his arms raised to support the handles. The new suggestion is that the mosaic is a light-hearted interpretation of Nestor's cup in the eleventh book of the *Iliad*. This passage was a crux for ancient as for modern scholarship. Was a *depas* a cup or something much larger? Where were the 'ears' and the doves? What were the two *pythmenes?* Sosos interpreted the doves as real doves instead of modelled or cast doves; it looks as if he interpreted the 'ears' as feet. The enigmatical *pythmenes* (which may, in fact, have been a double bottom so that the liquid could be kept hot) are for him the two supporting figures under the handles. This interpretation is, at least, seductive.

Hiero's ship

The enthusiasm for Homer was immense. Hiero II of Syracuse, who reigned from 265 to 215 B.C., built an enormous ship; one of its dining-rooms had a mosaic floor on which the whole story of the *Iliad* was represented. When the ship was loaded, Hiero decided to send it as a present to Ptolemy IV. Ptolemy IV was another Homer-lover. He founded a shrine in honour of Homer in which was a seated statue of the poet (echoing, as we have seen, the scheme of Bryaxis' Sarapis; see p. 35) surrounded by statues of the cities which claimed to be his birthplace. The painter Galaton painted a picture for the shrine, in which he showed Homer as a river-god pouring water from his mouth for other poets to collect in jugs, a not very happy conceit which naturally led to satire.

FIG. 3

Homeric bowls

The Homereion, like the Sarapieion (see p. 35), may well have been used for banquets of scholars and poets. The so-called Homeric bowls may possibly be connected with these and may even have been inspired by the Homeric mosaics of Hiero's ship. Vast quantities of gold and silver cups are mentioned in the description of Ptolemy II's symposion tent (see p. 69) and procession; Ptolemy IV could easily have ordered a special set of cups for a symposion in the Homereion. The so-called Homeric bowls are hemispherical clay cups which have been found chiefly in Boeotia but also in Athens and date from 170 to 130 B.C., but it is agreed that they derive from Alexandrian silver cups of about 200 B.C. (Some of them were cast from moulds taken directly from

PLATE 28 – Herakles with Telephos as a child. Detail from the Telephos frieze on the Pergamon altar. *Circa* 160 B.C. *Height 1.58 m. Department of Antiquities, Staatliche Museen, Berlin.* *Cf. p. 121.*

FIG. 26 – *Scenes from Euripides' 'Iphigeneia in Aulis'. Relief on a clay cup. Circa 200 B.C. Metropolitan Museum, New York. Cf. below.*

the originals, but others were cast from moulds into which stamps of individual figures taken from the earlier originals were pressed.) Stylistically they go closely with Alexandrian painting of the late third century. Somehow a selection of moulds taken from rather more than forty Alexandrian cups must have reached Boeotia and appealed to the literary tastes of the Boeotians, who reproduced them in clay (we have evidence for dramatic and other poetic competitions at various places in Boeotia throughout the Hellenistic age).

The subjects of the preserved bowls are taken from twelve books of the *Iliad*, five books of the *Odyssey*, six post-Homeric epics, one play of Aeschylus, one play of Sophokles, and five plays of Euripides. Two of the Odyssey bowls have the relevant lines of Homer inscribed by their pictures, and these have given rise to the theory that the pictures on the bowls are derived ultimately from illustrated texts of epic and drama, but we have no evidence for book illustration before the Christian period and the bowls imply an illustration every thirty lines, which would make a very long book. Moreover, the other fourteen inscribed bowls have prose captions, which occasionally give information not contained in the text. The artists therefore had access to scholarship and the drinkers were expected to know their texts.

FIG. 26 A bowl in New York illustrates the earlier part of Euripides' *Iphigeneia in Aulis*. The scenes are: 1) Agamemnon handing over to the old man the letter which was to delay the arrival of Iphigeneia; 2) Menelaos seizing the letter from the old man; 3) Agamemnon receiving 'the

FIG. 27 – *Clay cup illustrating part of Euripides' 'Phoinissai'. Circa 200 B.C. British Museum. Cf. below.*

messenger about the presence of Iphigeneia', as the inscription says; 4) Menelaos trying to comfort Agamemnon; 5) the arrival of Iphigeneia. There are two strange points here. The artist has not given the scenes in the Euripidean order; the order round the cup is 1, 4, 5, 3, 2. It is of course possible to read leftwards 1, 2, 3, and then go back to 1 and read rightwards 4, 5. But other cups (including the cup which illustrates the rest of the *Iphigeneia in Aulis*) show a similar confusion. The confusion must go back to the originals. It looks as if the master artist planned the scenes and captions and then distributed them to the craftsmen to put on the bowls, and they sometimes dislocated the order. The other strange point is that the names written over the figures in the scene of Iphigeneia's arrival are Orestes, Iphigeneia and Elektra. Elektra is not mentioned in the text of Euripides. The artist has shown Orestes and Iphigeneia in the chariot but not Klytaimnestra, possibly because of lack of space. Elektra stands behind the chariot and is ready to help Iphigeneia down. Perhaps some learned commentator in Alexandria pointed out that Elektra could not be left at home when her mother and family went to Aulis and that she could act as nurse to the young Orestes.

One of the bowls illustrating the *Phoinissai* also introduces a name which is not in the text: the girl accompanying Teiresias is labelled Manto; in Euripides Teiresias says 'lead me, my daughter', and the ancient commentator on the line notes that her name was Manto. The scenes on this bowl, which starts half-way through the play, are: 1) Kreon FIG. 27

appealing to Teiresias for his help; 2) Polyneikes fighting Eteokles, who comes out from a seated Thebe; the city-goddess sits on her rock with APPX. PL. I her hand to her chin, like the Tyche of Antioch (see p. 19); 3) a messenger summons Iokaste, who in turn summons Antigone. In the play the first messenger only reports that Polyneikes and Eteokles are going to fight, but perhaps the preceding picture does not mean much more than this. More surprising is the omission of the scene between Kreon and his son Menoikeus and the self-sacrifice of Menoikeus; 4) Antigone appeals to Kreon. In the play the second messenger reports the death of the sons, the suicide of Iokaste, and the rout of the invaders (which are illustrated on a second bowl); Antigone returns and summons Oidipous out of the house. Antigone only appeals to Kreon when he proposes to expel Oidipous and refuse burial to Polyneikes. Therefore the whole of the second bowl belongs between scenes 3 and 4 of this bowl. A fragment of a third bowl illustrates a later part of this scene: its inscription reads 'Oidipous gives orders that he shall be led to the dead body of his mother and wife and of his sons'. This is the end of the play and one wonders whether the artist went on to another play or went back to the beginning of the *Phoinissai*. The whole set may well have been a special order to celebrate some festival in the Homereion. We have positive evidence for a poetic competition in the Homereion from a marble relief in the British APPX. PL. 6 Museum, which dates from the third quarter of the second century. Vitruvius has an amusing story about an Alexandrian poetic competition in the late third century. Ptolemy (probably Ptolemy IV) found six judges and needed a seventh; the library authorities put up Aristophanes of Byzantion. The six judges put the poets in an order which reflected the amount of applause they had received. Aristophanes put first the poet who had received least applause. He justified this unpopular verdict by saying that this poet was the only one who had not recited stolen poetry, and he confirmed this by bringing the relevant books from the library and compelling the poets to admit their thefts.

PLATE 29 – Herakles and Telephos. Large fresco from the basilica at Herculaneum. The allegorical female figure seated majestically upon the rock personifies Arkadia. Copy of an original, *circa* 200–150 B.C. *Height 2.02 m. Museo Nazionale, Naples. Cf. p. 122.*

Apotheosis of Homer

The relief in the British Museum was found at Bovillae in Italy. Its connexion with the Homereion is given by the bottom register. Behind the seated Homer are Time and the World, but Time has the face of Ptolemy IV and the World has the face of his queen, Arsinoe. The artist means that by founding the Homereion they gave Homer Immortality over the World. The identifications are in the same spirit as the identification of the earlier Arsinoe with Artemis (see p. 71). The artist signs himself (under the seated Zeus at the top) Archelaos of Priene, and comparison of the inscriptions with dated inscriptions from Priene makes a dating 150–125 B.C. probable. The figure on the extreme right of the second register from the bottom is a poet; he stands on a base with a roll in his right hand, and a tripod is represented behind him. This would naturally mean that he won a competition at the Homereion, was awarded the tripod as a prize, and that his fellow-citizens set up a statue in his honour; the fact that he has a roll and not a lyre probably means that he wrote in hexameters rather than lyric metre. It is impossible to say whether the relief was set up in his own city or in Alexandria; he may himself have been an Alexandrian and have employed an artist who came from Priene; the Muses in the upper registers copy a group of Muses which was probably made in Asia Minor, but the artist may have seen them before he came to Alexandria; on the other hand the hump-backed bull in the lowest register is said to be Carian. It does not much matter to us where the relief was originally set up, since we know the artist and what it celebrates.

It is tempting to suppose that the relief gives us the content of the successful poem. The beginning naturally invoked the Muses. At the top Zeus reclines on Olympos with eagle and sceptre; he speaks to Mnemosyne, the mother of his daughters, the Muses. Terpsichore, the Muse of Dancing, runs down to the assembled Muses, who are differentiated by their attributes: concert lyre, small lyre, double flutes, globe, scrolls. The poem may have told of the different arts that they patronised. If the top of the relief is Olympos because of Zeus, the two last Muses are at Delphi because of Apollo. The artist (or the poet) has thought back beyond the temple and placed Apollo and the omphalos, the centre of the world, in a cave of Parnassos. The last Muse is giving

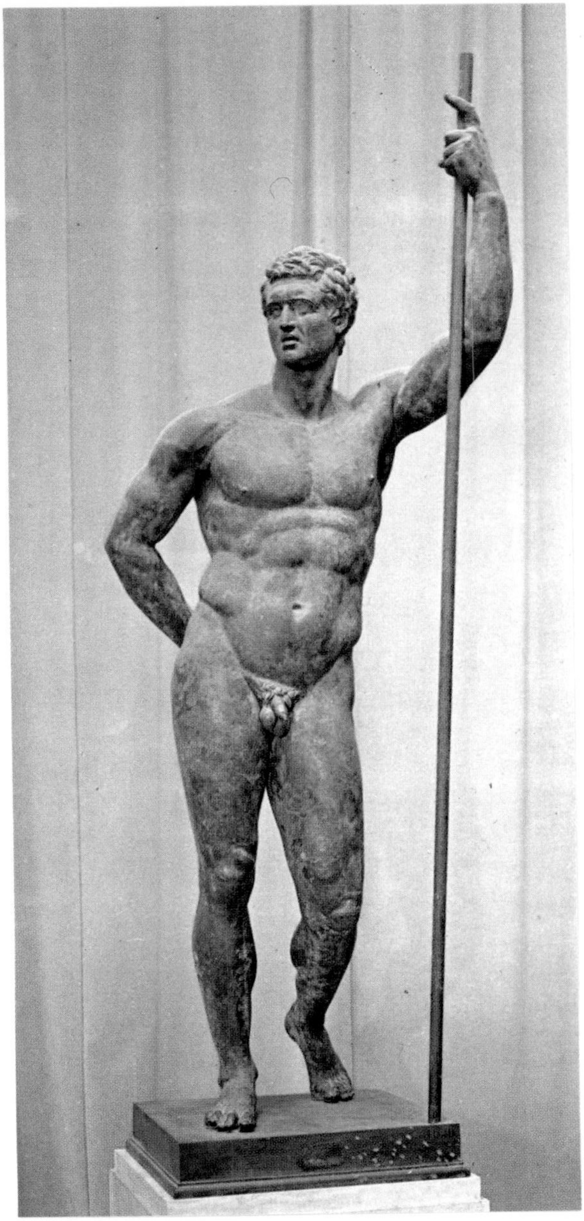

PLATE 30 – Bronze statue of a Hellenistic ruler (Demetrios I?). *Circa* 150 B.C. *Height 2.33 m. Terme, Rome. Cf. pp. 123, 181.*

Apollo a scroll, possibly the poem. We are perhaps meant to remember that Kallimachos claimed that the received his great poem, the *Aitia*, in a dream from the Muses on Helikon.

This was the prelude. The bottom register is an assessment of Homer in the Middle Hellenistic period, and this may have been the burden of the poem. Homer is crowned by Time and the World in the guise of Ptolemy IV and his queen. The *Iliad* crouches on one side of his throne and the *Odyssey* on the other. A frog and a mouse by the footstool allude to the *Batrachomyomachia.* Mythos pours a libation; Historia sprinkles incense on the altar on which the bull will be sacrificed. At this time they probably have their modern connotations of Myth and History, of which the Homeric epic is a blend. A long string of figures come to do Homer honour: Poiesis holding two torches is in this context non-dramatic poetry; Tragedy wears mask, tragic costume and thick-soled shoes; Comedy, behind her, wears the mask of a young hetaira of Comedy.

So far the theme is the same as the theme of Galaton's picture, which showed the poets collecting the stream of Homer in their jugs. Homer is the inspiration of all poetry, dramatic and non-dramatic. But the relief (and the poem?) take Homer's influence a stage further. In the corner a child labelled Physis is evidently in the keeping of four women who raise their hands in reverence for Homer: they are Arete, Mneme, Pistis, Sophia. Physis is Nature, both Nature in general and the Nature of an individual. At first sight one thinks that Homer's nature or genius is compounded of these qualities and Pistis has its natural interpretation as Credibility, power of persuasion. But surely these figures cannot be qualities of Homer; their position shows that they belong to an outer circle, outside the poets, who feel Homer's influence. Physis then is the nature of the ordinary man, and the women are the qualities which he gets by reading Homer: excellence (perhaps particularly courage), memory of the heroic Greek past, loyalty (a quality much prized by the Ptolemies whether it came from reading Homer or not) and wisdom.

The relief gives a fascinating glimpse of Middle Hellenistic literary and educational theory. Many of the individual figures are reminiscences of figures that we know. The Muses go back to a set probably made in

PLATE 31 – Aphrodite standing beside a herm. Terracotta statuette from Myrina. 2nd century B.C. *Height 22.5 cm. British Museum. Cf. p. 124.*

PLATE 32 – Theatre at Pergamon, looking toward the stage across the auditorium. 2nd century B.C. *Cf. p. 127.*

Asia Minor in the third century. The Apollo recalls the fourth-century Apollo Patroos of Euphranor. The Homer is the Homer of the Homereion. The group of the child and the women is a reminiscence of the reliefs with three Nymphs and a child. The artist has contributed his knowledge of art history to make the poet's meaning plain. The meaning is all the clearer because the spectator immediately recognises the figures. It is the same sort of allusion that Eumenes II made by putting a copy of the Athena Parthenos rather than a new Athena in the library (see p. 101).

It is tempting to call this classicism, but perhaps that name should be reserved for works which use traditional figures and schemes of composition without achieving any such overtones by the allusions that they make to their original. A pretty mosaic in Alexandria can be dated near the Archelaos relief. The scheme of Erotes hunting a deer demonstrably goes back to earlier originals. One is in fact known on a third-century Hadra hydria. At that date the scheme was taken over from works like the Pella mosaic (see p. 23), and carried the meaning: look at these funny little winged boys doing the things that young heroes do. By now it is simply a pleasant reminiscent picture, and that may justly be called classicism. *Classicism* PLATE P. 65

This long digression on scholarship as shown in art started from the library at Pergamon. Scholarship in the library also had its influence on the altar of Zeus, in which reminiscences of earlier works are used extremely effectively. But here no one would consider using the term classicism: the tremendous vigour of the gods and the violence of the giants excludes it. *Altar of Zeus*

The altar is a magnification of the altar at Kos (see p. 72). Here the scheme is a raised inner court surrounded by colonnades with the Telephos story in relief on the walls and in the centre the altar proper on which offerings could be made. The inner court was approached by a wide flight of steps flanked by projecting wings, which on the level of the inner court carried the continuation of the colonnade: below that level ran the Gigantomachy frieze, which surrounded the whole of the outside of the building and came back up the steps. The akroteria on the projecting wings were Tritons, and along the roof of the inner courtyard on the side above the steps were set dramatic figures of gods and goddesses. FIG. 28

This was the great conception of Eumenes II, although in fact the colonnade surrounding the altar proper was never completed, and work was apparently terminated at his death. The sculptors came from Athens, Rhodes and Tralles, according to the surviving signatures; probably they came from elsewhere too, but the style was uniformly Pergamene and continued the splendour and cruelty of the monuments of Attalos I.

Athena presided over the library; the Gigantomachy is also an Attic *Gigantomachy*

FIG. 28 – *Altar of Zeus at Pergamon: reconstruction. 200–150 B.C. Cf. p. 115.*

theme: it was woven in the robe which was presented to Athena at her Athenian festival, and a Gigantomachy was carved on the eastern metopes of the Parthenon and on the inner side of the shield of the Athena Parthenos herself; for the Athenians in the fifth century it symbolised the triumph of discipline over violence, which was also exemplified by the Greek victory in the Persian wars. Here again Eumenes was stating that his capital was the Athens of Asia Minor.

By changing the majority of the Giants into monsters ending in snakes, the designers achieved wonderful twisted forms to writhe between the limbs of the gods, strong brutal bodies on which to exercise their realism, and an immediate and obvious contrast with the victorious gods. Classical Giants were represented as men, sometimes very large, sometimes bearded and uncouth, but still men; the snaky ending was kept for the most part for Typhoeus and Triton. By this means the Pergamene Giants were attributed to another race from the Greek gods, as sharply distinguished as the Gauls of Attalos I and equally tremendous as adversaries.

PLATE 33 – Scene from a comedy. Mosaic from a villa at Pompeii, signed by Dioskourides. *Circa* 100 B.C. *Height 44 cm. Museo Nazionale, Naples. Cf. pp. 18, 129, 172.*

PLATE 34 – Women at Breakfast: from the first scene of Menander's comedy of the same name *(Synaristosai)*. Mosaic from a villa at Pompeii, signed by Dioskourides. *Circa* 100 B.C. *Height 42 cm. Museo Nazionale, Naples. Cf. pp. 18, 129.*

Much scholarship must have been needed to establish their names and to decide which Giants should have lion's heads, which should have wings made of leaves, and which should have a watery transition to their snaky limbs. Originally the names were all inscribed, and no doubt the differences had some justification. We can at least see that the opponents of Artemis and Apollo, the giants Otos and Ephialtes, are beautiful young men such as they are described by Homer in the *Odyssey*, 'far the most beautiful after famous Orion'. Their divine victors recall two great Early Hellenistic statues, known to us as the Diana of Versailles and the Apollo Belvedere; we do not know where the originals stood – they have been plausibly ascribed to Leochares. In the group of Zeus, Porphyrion, Alkyoneus, Athena, Ge, Nike, the gods recall the east pediment of the Parthenon. The Parthenon Zeus has left his throne here and is plunging to the left. The Pergamon Athena is in the same position as the one in the Parthenon pediment, but she moves faster. Here a winged Victory flies down to crown her from the right; there she came from the left. Thus the designer reminded the spectator again that the gods of Pergamon were the gods of Periclean Athens, the Athens of Pheidias and Sophokles. APPX. PLATES 7–8

The young Giant to the left of Zeus has fallen pierced by a flaming thunderbolt. On Zeus' right a fallen Giant has been struck by the aigis hanging from Zeus' left arm. But Zeus' chief adversary is the tremendous Porphyrion, who raises his left arm, wrapped in an animal's skin, against Zeus' eagle, which descends on him. Probably his right hand had a boulder in it, a weapon which will not avail against the thunderbolt in Zeus' right hand. Athena is pulling a giant (Alkyoneus or Antaios) off the ground by his hair; his right hand stretches towards his mother Ge (Earth), who rises from the ground with tortured eyes to supplicate Athena; if the Giant is torn from the earth, he loses his strength. Victory flies down to crown Athena.

The spectator who entered the main gateway would see the east frieze first: Ares, Athena, Zeus, Apollo, Artemis, Hekate. Then he would walk down the south side and there find an older generation of gods fighting, such as the Moon, the Sun and the Dawn; round the south-west corner and up the steps he would find Dionysos and his following in the battle. On the other side of the steps he would see the FIG. 31

old sea-gods doing their part, and finally on the north side Poseidon and Aphrodite.

Telephos frieze After the splendour and the cruelty of the Gigantomachy it must have been a relief to climb the steps and contemplate the Telephos frieze in the inner court. This story meant much to the Pergamene kings: Telephos was the son of Herakles, from whom they claimed descent on the Macedonian side; his mother Auge took refuge with Teuthras of Mysia (the area of Pergamon), from whom they also claimed descent, presumably on the maternal side. The story also included the transfer of two cults from Arcadia to Pergamon: the cult of Dionysos and the cult of Athena. It had therefore some of the feeling of the Parthenon frieze, which showed the Panathenaic procession, the most splendid festival of the city's goddess, Athena.

The story is told in successive separate scenes like the scenes on the 'Homeric bowls' (see p. 106); this was an old method of pictorial story-telling, which can be traced back to the sixth century B.C. About a third of the frieze is lost, and the interpretation and position of some of the slabs are doubtful. Violence only appears here in the battle scenes, but some figures storming forward in long chitons recall the Nike of Samothrace (see p. 98). The drapery of the women in a cult scene has formal folds like the Iphigeneia (see p. 96). Landscape is indicated by a sphinx on a high pillar, rocky ground and plane-trees – elements of the pastoral style, which continues from the Early Hellenistic period (see p. 70 ff). Couches, pillows and a bed are shown in interior scenes. This does not mean that the sculptors had not also worked on the Gigantomachy frieze, but that the subject matter was different; and the low relief also set a different artistic problem. The sculptors occasionally introduced small-scale figures rather perhaps to dissociate them from the main scene than to show distance; the clearest instances are the veiled Auge and her two attendants, who appear on a smaller scale above the workmen who are building the chest, and the small woman who runs away when Telephos seizes the infant Orestes.

PLATE P. 98
FIG. 24

The story, so far as it can be reasonably recognised on the frieze, runs as follows: 1) King Aleos of Arkadia consults the oracle and hears that the son of his daughter Auge will kill his sons; 2) he receives

PLATE 35 – Six Comedy masks on a golden necklace from Palaiokastron in Thessaly. *Circa* 100 B.C *Museum für Kunst und Gewerbe, Hamburg. Cf. p. 131.*

Herakles in his palace; 3) Herakles enters the grove to rape Auge; 4) (Auge bears a child, Telephos, which is exposed), and a chest is built in which she will be set adrift; 5) (the chest drifts to Mysia), and King Teuthras hurries to the shore to receive it; 6) a maenad heats water to bathe the infant Telephos under the eyes of Arkadia seated on her rock (a personification very like Thebes on the 'Homeric bowl'; see p. 108); 7) Herakles discovers the infant Telephos being suckled by a lioness; 8) the young Telephos arrives in Mysia looking for his mother, and Aleos finds him a successful warrior; 9) Aleos presents him Auge as a bride; 10) Auge tries to kill Telephos, but a snake rises from the ground and prevents her, (recognition of mother and son follows); 11) Telephos, now king of Mysia, battles with the invading Greeks; 12) Dionysos entangles Telephos with a vine so that Achilles can wound him; 13) (Telephos goes to Greece to get his

PLATE P. 105

wound healed), is in danger of being put to death as a spy, but snatches up the infant Orestes and takes refuge on an altar; 14) Telephos shows his wound to the Greek chiefs (and Achilles heals him in return for Telephos' service in guiding the Greeks to Troy); 15) the cults of Athena and Dionysos are transferred from Arkadia to Mysia in the presence of seated satyrs.

The long series, which can be thus partially reconstructed, is rich in literary allusion: Euripides' *Auge* dramatised the rape of Auge; Sophokles' *Mysoi* dealt with Telephos' arrival in Mysia and Auge's attempt to kill him; Euripides' *Telephos* showed him in Greece and carried the story to his healing. The frieze therefore satisfied Pergamene scholarship, besides illustrating the ancestry of the kings and the origin of the two very important Pergamene cults of Athena and Dionysos.

PLATE P. 109

The subject of the slab with Herakles watching the infant Telephos is repeated in a fresco from Pompeii, which must go back to a contemporary Pergamene original. In both the Telephos is an enchanting example of Hellenistic child art (see p. 76). The freer medium of painting allows the artist more easily to place the little satyr and the winged woman behind the main figures without the drastic reduction of scale used to express dissociation in the sculpted frieze. Here he uses scale to emphasise the importance of the personification of Arkadia. He achieves considerable depth, because the diagonals, which run from the satyr's face to the lion and from the wings to the infant Telephos, lead out of the depth as well as across the picture. The shallow stage and backdrop of Early Hellenistic painting have been completely abandoned (see pp. 23, 32).

Here, as in the literary versions, Telephos is suckled by a deer, not by a lioness; and the royal future of Pergamon is symbolised by the eagle of Zeus and the lion. Perhaps the sculptor of the frieze substituted the lioness because he wanted at that moment to point to Telephos' royal successors. The winged figure is Parthenos, both the Arkadian mountain on which Telephos was born and the constellation Virgo,

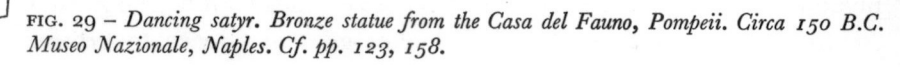

FIG. 29 – *Dancing satyr. Bronze statue from the Casa del Fauno, Pompeii. Circa 150 B.C. Museo Nazionale, Naples. Cf. pp. 123, 158.*

who has led Herakles to his child. The solid figure of Arkadia is like the Arkadia of the frieze. On that slab a Dionysiac maenad heated water for the baby; here bunches of Dionysos' grapes are in the basket by Arkadia's side, and a young satyr leans over her. The young satyr is a herdsman; he holds Pan pipes in one hand and a crook in the other and has a rough skin over his shoulder. We remember that the initiates of Dionysos in Pergamon were called *Boukoloi* or herdsmen, so that this cult too is foreshadowed in the picture.

The muscled back of Herakles and his heavy bearded face have some kinship with the Giants on the altar of Zeus. The stolid figure and the placing of the hand on the back recall the over-life-size bronze of a Hellenistic ruler in the Terme Museum, Rome. An identification has been suggested with Demetrios I, who became king of Syria in the mid-second century B.C. The head has lost the inset eyes which would have made it come alive. The heavy brows and the thick hair bring it near the Herakles of the picture. PLATE P. 111

Another bronze can be placed here, the statuette of a dancing satyr which gave the Casa del Fauno in Pompeii its name. The wild hair and heavy brows recall the Giants; the heavy torso and the wide stride of the thin legs recall the Hellenistic ruler. The twisted pose with limbs going in different directions is a late development of Lysippan three-dimensionalism. The statuette may well be a Pergamene original which was brought to Pompeii after the death of the last king of Pergamon. The mosaic with tragic masks hung on a garland of realistic fruit and flowers, which comes from the same house, has also been regarded as a copy of a Pergamene original, and if the original of the Alexander mosaic (see p. 38), which covered the floor of an exedra in the same house, was really by Apelles, it too may have been painted in the East and have been copied there. FIG. 29

Hercules Musarum

The Satyr leads us to Dionysos and his various manifestations in Pergamon. But first let us notice that these twisted figures, and here we may include the Gallic chief and the other figures like him (see pp. 76, 96), belong to the late third and early second century B.C., and they are the natural parallels for the lyre-playing Herakles on the coin of Pomponius Musa. The artist has had to accommodate the statue to the low relief of the coin, but it seems clear that the original was a FIG. 23 PLATE P. 58

striding figure with twisted torso which fits well with these twisted Pergamene figures, whereas the Muses with which it is associated belong in the early third century. Thus style too suggests that the Herakles was a new or at least modern statue which was added by Fulvius Nobilior in Rome to the Early Hellenistic Muses brought from Ambracia.

Dionysos cult

PLATE P. 160

Dionysos was the god of mysteries and the god of drama in Pergamon. The paintings of the Villa dei Misteri in Pompeii may be copies of the decoration of the shrine of Dionysos Kathegemon in the palace. The quality of the paintings has been destroyed by the Roman copyist, and they were probably multiplied up from an original on a smaller scale; but they tell us something of the terror and elation of initiation. The young Dionysos reclining against the seated Ariadne is both the symbol and the guarantee of the bliss to be attained in the after-life by participation in the Mysteries.

FIG. 30

Myrina terracottas

PLATE P. 100

FIGS. 34–36

The strongest evidence for the connexion of these paintings with Pergamon is the likeness of the Dionysos and Ariadne to a terracotta group from Myrina. Myrina is some 25 miles from Pergamon and had a flourishing terracotta industry, which continued and developed types known earlier at Tanagra but also introduced many new types, such as the Nike mentioned on p. 98: the very interesting actor terracottas, which will be considered later (see p. 130f.), probably reflect Pergamene theatre practice.

PLATE P. 113

Two of the actor terracottas, like the Dionysos and Ariadne, seem to have been copied from a contemporary painting. Other terracottas are reduced copies of sculptures. This, it has been suspected, is the case in regard to a group in the British Museum with a naked woman beside a herm. Essentially the theme of a pliant body beside a rigid support is Praxitelean: the Apollo Sauroktonos is the best-known example. The use of a herm in this kind of context recurs in the bronze group from a shipwreck off the coast of Tunisia: there a winged boy stands by the herm as he puts a wreath on his head. He has been interpreted as Agon, the personification of Competition; the herm bears the signature Boethos of Kalchedon. The herm in the bronze group presumably belongs to the place where the competition is held, perhaps the palaistra or wrestling school. In Athens the Stoa of Herms was used by competing choirs.

The god's head both on the bronze herm and on the British Museum terracotta is archaistic with its rows of curls over the forehead and with formalised moustache and beard. But the fashion for archaising herms was set in the late fifth century, when Alkamenes made the herm for the Propylaia leading on to the Acropolis in Athens; this herm was famous and has survived in many copies, one from Pergamon. But it is probably right to recognise not Hermes but Dionysos in the head of the terracotta herm. The woman, who may be Aphrodite, is crowning it with a wreath of ivy and the basin for offerings contains a bunch of grapes as well as the pomegranates of Aphrodite. The offerings are suitable for Aphrodite and for Dionysos. If the woman is Aphrodite, as her nudity suggests, she is making an offering to Dionysos as well as to herself. This is a collocation of divinities rather like the collocation FIG. 11 of Artemis-Arsinoe and satyrs on the bronze relief in Delos (see p. 70). The collocation is very natural: not only are the god of the symposion and the goddess of love naturally connected, but the maenads of Dionysos in Euripides' *Bakchai* pray to Dionysos to take them to 'Cyprus, the island of Aphrodite, where the Erotes live and charm the soul'; in late fifth-century Athens the circles of Aphrodite and Dionysos overlap. This pretty conception with its accomplished contrasts of male and female, archaic and modern, stiff rigidity and pliant, twisting,

FIG. 30 – *Dionysos and Ariadne. Terracottas from Myrina. 1st century B.C. Height 24 cm. Louvre, Paris. Cf. p. 124.*

naked flesh, is probably the conception of a major sculptor, and the terracotta is a cheap copy which anyone could possess.

Dionysos with his devoted thiasos of satyrs and maenads often appears, FIG. 30 as he does with Ariadne in the Myrina group (see p. 124), young and beardless, quite unlike the stately head of the herm. In his youthful FIG. 31 form he leads his satyrs to battle with the Giants on the altar of Zeus at Pergamon, and in the same form he entangles Telephos with the vine on the Telephos frieze (see p. 121). One of the most attractive rep- APPX. PL. 17 resentations of a maenad is the relief from a round marble base which was found in Pergamon. The drapery is elaborately carved with many gradations of folds; even the hem on the inside bottom edge of the chiton is rendered. This treatment connects it with the goddesses of the Gigantomachy frieze. Compared with the maenads of the Lysippan PLATE P. 21 krater from Dherveni (see p. 20), this maenad has much more elaborate drapery but much less violent movement. Her elegant advance on tiptoe, with two fingers lifting up the skirt of her chiton, reminds us rather of the neo-Attic maenads (see p. 169), which were themselves copied from Attic reliefs of the late fifth century. Once again in Pergamon this is a reminiscence of classical Athens, and a claim that the god of mysteries and drama in Athens is also the god of mysteries and drama in Pergamon.

Drama in Pergamon

Dionysos Kathegemon was the name of the god both of the mysteries and of drama in Pergamon. Kathegemon means 'guide': it is a natural title for a god of mysteries, but perhaps a Pergamene would hear in it also that the god first guided Telephos to Mysia and later guided the Attalids to Pergamon. The guild of actors, poets and musicians was called 'the guild of artists of Dionysos, those from Ionia and the Hellespont and those of Dionysos Kathegemon'; the Ionian-Hellespontine guild went back well into the third century and had its headquarters in the old Ionian city of Teos, on the coast about forty kilometres beyond Myrina. The artists of Dionysos Kathegemon were a branch of the guild concerned with performers at Pergamon.

But there was yet another association in Pergamon, called the Attalistai, founded by a famous flute-player, Kraton of Chalkedon, who had held high office in the Ionian Hellespontine guild and received many honours from them. He left the Attalistai a house near the palace and a building near the theatre adequately endowed for their sacrifices and meetings. The building near the theatre, the Attaleion, has been identified with a site just south of the lower part of the auditorium; this has been compared with the Early Hellenistic exedra and rectangular room in Thasos (see p. 49); here its function as a meeting-place is known. The duty of the Attalistai was to look after the cult of the kings, but they were closely linked with the guild both through their founder, Kraton, and through the kings' reverence for Dionysos Kathegemon, who was the god of the guild.

Theatre

PLATE P. 114

The theatre was built into the hill below the library and the temple of Athena. The auditorium was very steep, and the level of the orchestra was 56 metres below the top row of seats. The eighty rows were divided into three blocks by two horizontal passages, and the blocks were subdivided by vertical stairways – eight in the lowest block and four in the two blocks above it.

FIG. 32

The stage-building had to be erected for each performance, because it blocked the broad road running along the bottom. This led from the Agora and the temple of Dionysos Kathegemon in the south to the predecessor of the temple of Caracalla in the north; the god of this northern temple is unknown, but it may have been another temple of Dionysos. This broad road looks like a processional way, and one reason for making the stage-building temporary may have been to allow the seats of the theatre to be used for viewing processions. The sockets in the road permit of the erection of a normal Hellenistic stage-building with projecting stage and three doorways in the background.

FIG. 31 – *Dionysos relief from the frieze of the Pergamon altar. Marble. Circa 200–150 B.C. Height 2.30 m. Pergamon Museum, Berlin. Cf. p. 119.*

Tragedy The theatre is so steep that anything that would give elevation and definition to the actors would be helpful. Nothing could be done about actors of comedy because they had to be mobile, but tragic actors, who did not move about so much, could be given thickened soles to increase their height and mark off their feet. It may not therefore be chance that the earliest representations of tragic actors with thick-soled shoes and the only representations going back to the second century B.C. have an actual or possible connection with Pergamon.

APPX. PL. 10 The earliest is the large marble figure from the neighbourhood of the Altar of Zeus: where exactly it stood is unknown, nor is it certain whether it is a personification of Tragedy or the Muse of Tragedy, but one of the two a woman in tragic costume with a sword at her side must be: the sole of her right shoe is clearly visible and is thick. In APPX. PL. 6 proportion the Tragedy of the Archelaos relief has still thicker soles (see p. 112); the drapery is very like the figure from Pergamon, but the sword is omitted; Archelaos came from Priene, which is in the territory of the Ionian-Hellespontine guild, and we have seen that for his Muses also he drew on models in Greek Asia Minor. A round base from Halikarnassos, also in the territory of the guild, has a seated tragic Muse, who wears thick-soled shoes and holds a bearded male mask in her hand. The earliest surviving actor with these thick-soled shoes FIG. 33 is a very fine terracotta statuette from Amisos on the Black Sea, which would also come under the Hellespontine-Ionian guild. The actor has played Herakles (see p. 59); he wears a long, sleeved chiton with high girding, and a small cloak over his left shoulder; he holds his club by his side and his mask in his left hand. This is the actor when he takes PLATE P. 61 his applause; the earlier statuette from the Athenian Agora (see p. 59)

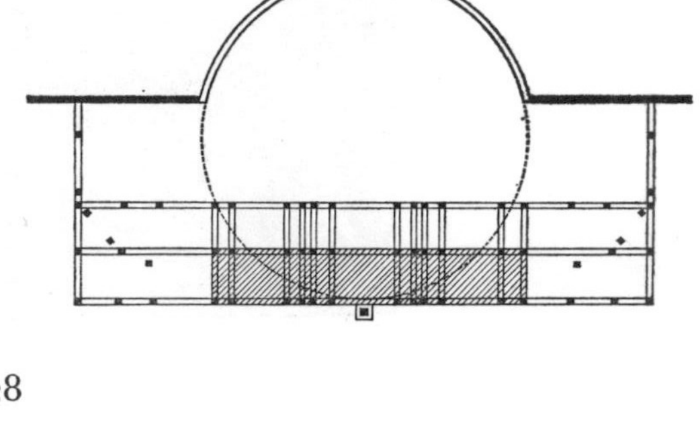

FIG. 32 – *Ground-plan of the theatre at Pergamon. Cf. p. 127.*

shows Herakles on the stage. Probably a century separates the two, but the traditional costume and mask continue; the Agora statuette has lost its legs and feet, but there is no reason to suppose that it had shoes with thick soles. Once the new shoe was introduced it became standard practice, and we shall find evidence for it in Rome by the middle of the first century B.C. (see p. 193). FIG. 53

Comedy

Myrina produced a large number of very fine terracotta statuettes of comic actors. A good example is the old slave (his hair and beard are white) hurrying along, neatly wrapped in his short himation. He reminds us of many running slaves of comedy, who bring news to their young masters, and in general the ebullience of the slaves from Myrina suggests that slave parts had become more important in the plays of Menander's successors. FIG. 34

Dioskourides mosaics

Two of the statuettes from Myrina, a young man playing the tympanon and a young man playing the kymbala, are so similar to two figures in a mosaic found in Pompeii that a common original must be supposed. This raises a fascinating problem of translation and transmission. The terracottas come from Myrina. The mosaics were found in a house at Pompeii, and one of them is copied in a wall-painting in a house in Stabiae of the first century A.D. Thus we have one certain instance of a Campanian painting copied from an original in mosaic. The mosaics themselves are small and miraculously fine in technique. The lettering of the signatures, Dioskourides of Samos, dates them about 100 B.C.; Samos points eastwards but the artist could have migrated, and safer pointers are other known imports to Pompeii from the East and the identity of the two young men with the terracottas from Myrina. We have seen that Myrina terracottas sometimes reflect paintings and a painting seems the likely ancestor for both the terracottas and the mosaic. The date of the painting behind the other mosaic is FIGS. 35–36 PLATES PP. 117–118

FIG. 33 – *Actor playing Herakles. Terracotta statuette from Samsun. 2nd century B.C. Louvre, Paris, Cf. above.*

FIGS. 34–36 – *Terracotta statuettes from Myrina. Fig. on p. 130 above: Slave from a comedy. Height 21 cm. National Museum, Athens. Fig. on p. 130 below: Comedian playing kymbala. Height 19 cm. National Museum, Athens. Fig. on p. 131 above: Comedian playing drum. Antikensammlung, Berlin. All statuettes circa 125 B.C. Cf. below.*

fixed in the third century by the shape of the cup held by the old woman, and both mosaics have the Early Hellenistic convention of a narrow stage with a backdrop, although, of course, they are both theatre pictures. But the very elaborate drapery of the young men, both in terracotta and on the mosaic, would put them right at the end of the third century. It is natural to think of Pergamon as the place where these paintings could be seen, because the terracottas of Dionysos and Ariadne led to Pergamon, but the headquarters of the Ionian-Hellespontine guild at Teos might equally well have such paintings of theatre scenes.

In either case the two mosaics give us very delicately executed copies of two theatre pictures painted in Greek Asia Minor in the late third century. In one two young men dance with tympanon and clappers outside a door; they are accompanied by a flute-girl. A scene of revelry not unlike this survives in a Latin adaptation, in Plautus' *Mostellaria.* These three figures are the masked actors; the unmasked boy in the corner is probably a stage-struck youth who is allowed to play a mute part. The long low group of three figures on the left balances the high narrow figure on the right, which is itself picked up by the high door, and the grey-green of the door is balanced by the narrow grey-green strip along the front of the stage: the whole is held together by strong low light from the right, which casts heavy shadows.

The other mosaic illustrates the first scene of Menander's *Synaristosai* (Women at Breakfast), which Plautus translated as the *Cistellaria.* The old procuress (right) and her daughter (left) have visited the young woman in the centre, who gives them breakfast. The old woman has complained of the strength and amount of the wine. The little slave (unmasked again because it is a mute part) is going to remove the table. Here the light comes from the left and makes high-lights on the masks and on the face of the slave, and causes a heavy shadow where

the cushion overhangs the seat on the left. Again the light is strong and low, and we remember that at the beginning of the century the painter Antiphilos in Alexandria had illuminated an interior scene by fire-light (see p. 79).

In the Revellers the artist has shown the masks, costumes and stage of the theatre performance; the wall and the door are an ordinary house-wall and door and not a theatre background, and the darker strip along the top of the wall is a pure painting effect with no counterpart in reality. In the Breakfast scene the three steps come from the stage, and the text of the play mentions the table, but the seats belong to real life rather than the stage. The artist wants to show that three people are seated round a table in a room, although the room could not be shown in the theatre. He has therefore used coloured strips much more elaborately than in the other mosaic, to show recession both at the left side and at the top of the picture; the coloured strip on the right acts as a frame and cuts off the servant. This is purely a device to represent depth; it is, of course, possible that in the original painting the individual strips were neither so uniform in colour nor so sharply divided from each other as they are in the mosaics.

The masks are standard New Comedy masks and the types represented have not changed from the Early Hellenistic period. A good set, which can be dated in the second century, can be seen on a necklace which was found in Thessaly. PLATE P. 121 The masks are of the following: one old man, two types of young men which correspond to the young Revellers on the mosaic, three types of hetairai, one of which is the mask worn by the flute-player in the Revellers mosaic and by the girl seated in profile on the Breakfast mosaic, and three types of slave. The slaves' beards are shorter and more rounded so that their mouths appear wider than APPX. PL. 4 those of the Myrina slaves or those on the Amphipolis plaque (see p. 60): Middle Hellenistic slaves in comedy were evidently more talkative and greedier than their predecessors.

Scenery

The theatre set was not represented by the painter whom Dioskourides copied in mosaic. He was only interested in the actors. Sets for the theatre were painted by first-rate artists; they were costly and they lasted a long time. In the Early Hellenistic theatre the artist was restricted to comparatively narrow panels set between columns in the spaces between and outside the doors. About the middle of the second century some theatres, at any rate, were rebuilt so as to have much larger panels in which the doors themselves were set. These large panels gave much more room for the wide prospects in which the painter was interested. For tragedy and satyr play only the central door was used so that the wide side panels were entirely free for scenery; in some comedies the central door was not used and that panel could be pure scenery. But even the panels which contained a practicable door had more room than the narrow panels of the earlier period.

FIG. 37 The theatre at Oropos in Boeotia was rebuilt about 150 B.C., and inscriptions record the dedication by one man of the *proskenion* and the *pinakes* and by another man of the *skene* and the *thyromata*. A glance at the reconstruction of the theatre explains the distinction. The *proskenion* is the lower range of columns which supports the stage, and the *pinakes* are the narrow panels between the columns. The *skene* is the stage-building where it rises above the stage and the *thyromata* are the wide panels that surround the doors on to the stage.

We can also form an idea of the scenery. Vitruvius, tracing the history of decoration in houses, places well before his own day a time when it was the fashion to paint walls with tragic, satyric or comic scenery. When he is speaking of the theatre, he says that tragic scenery has columns, pediments, statues and other royal things; comic scenery has private houses, balconies and windows; satyric scenery is decorated with trees, caves, mountains and other rustic things in landscape-painting. These themes can be recognised in a bedroom of the Villa at Boscoreale (which has in another room the copy of the Early Hellenistic paintings of Aratos, Macedonia, and Syria; see p. 32). The Boscoreale paintings date from soon after the middle of the first century B.C., but realistic scenery of this kind was already used in Rome in 99 B.C., when the backgrounds of plays given at the games of Appius Claudius Pulcher were so realistic that the crows tried to settle on the painted tiles. But the word which Vitruvius uses for landscape,

Boscoreale cubiculum

PLATE 36 – Comic scenery. Fresco at Boscoreale. Detail from the wall-painting in the room reproduced on p. 137. *Cf. p. 134.*

topoeidis, takes us back to the middle of the second century, when *topographos* was the word used to describe the landscape-painter Demetrios and to distinguish him from a colleague who was *anthropographos*, a figure-painter. Demetrios lived in Rome but came from Alexandria, and we have seen that the Homeric bowls are a contemporary link between intellectual and artistic Alexandria and intellectual and artistic Boeotia (see p. 104). It is quite possible that the idea of large realistic panels for scenery came to Oropos ultimately from Alexandria. But however the lines of influence ran, the cubiculum of Boscoreale can give us an idea of Middle Hellenistic scenery and landscape-painting.

PLATE P. 135 The tragic panel (to the right of the corner) is an architectural prospect, a small round building between colonnades and viewed through a colonnade; this colonnade has a central opening crowned by a pediment and blocked by a wall with an altar carrying fruit offerings at each side and a round table for offerings in the middle. Such an arrangement is decorative rather than practical, but it is not the structurally impossible architecture to which Vitruvius objects when he sees it in contemporary paintings. Architectural prospects have a long history going back to the scenery which Agatharchos painted for a revival of Aeschylus in the late fifth century. What is new here is the use of the wide panel, the nature of the architecture, and the extreme competence of the perspective.

PLATE P. 135 Similarly, simple rocks with vines growing across them were represented on the panels for satyr plays in the fifth century, but in Boscoreale the wide panel (to the left of the corner) accommodates a considerable cave with vines growing across it and a bird sitting on the vine. The water of the Nymphs has been channelled into a marble fountain, in which it flows from three spouts into a basin. Above, an arbour is roofed with greenery and recalls the arbours of Ptolemy's symposion tent (see p. 66).

PLATES PP. 133, 137 For comedy the bedroom at Boscoreale gives all three panels of the normal stage front. The doors and windows of the outside panels represent practicable doors and windows. The central panel is a shrine of Hekate without a practicable door. This comedy evidently only used the two houses. The young satyr masks at the top of the house panels and the old satyr mask on the shrine of Hekate should probably

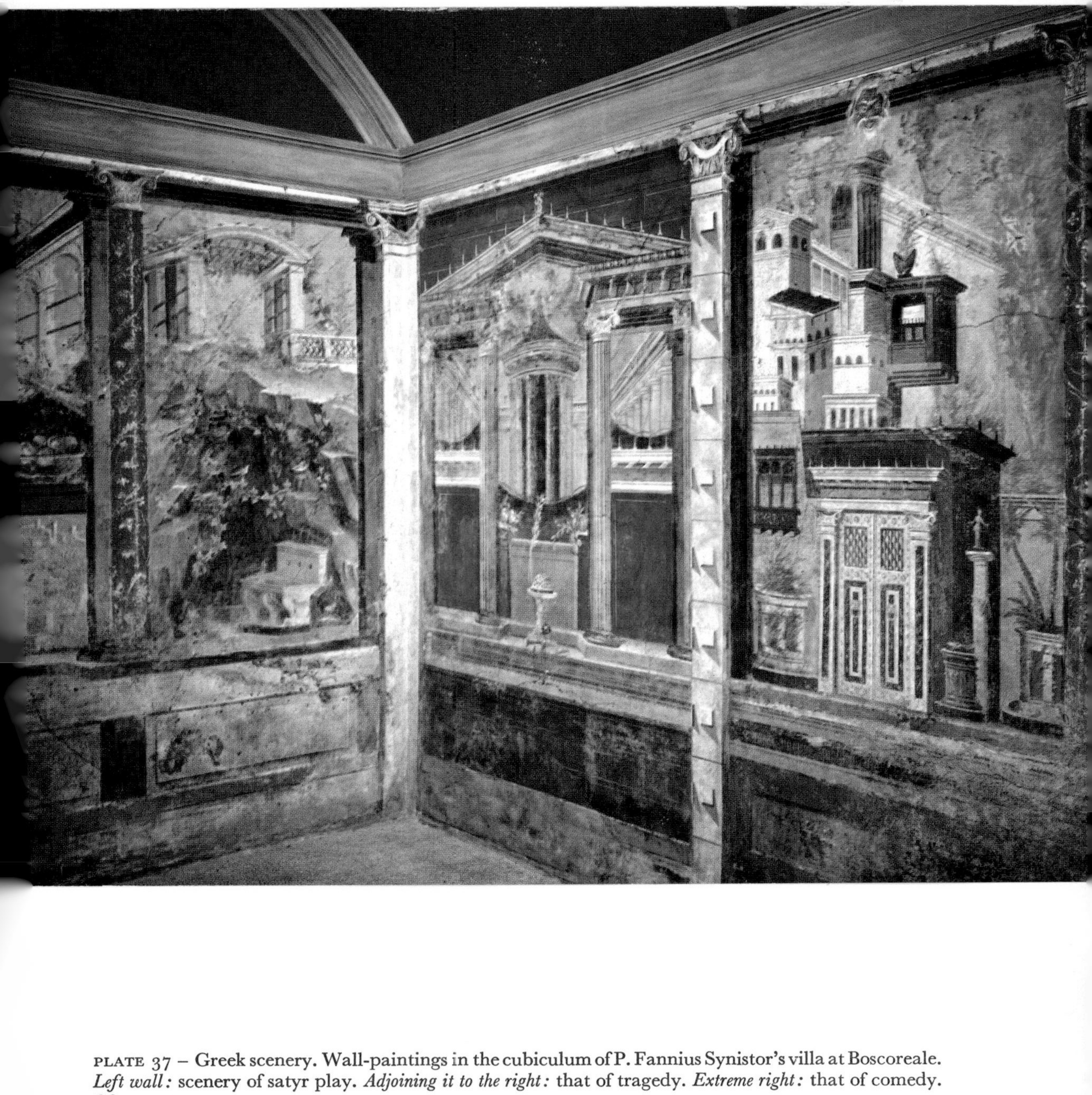

PLATE 37 – Greek scenery. Wall-paintings in the cubiculum of P. Fannius Synistor's villa at Boscoreale. *Left wall:* scenery of satyr play. *Adjoining it to the right:* that of tragedy. *Extreme right:* that of comedy. *Cf. p. 134.*

FIG. 37 – *Stage-building of the theatre at Oropos in Boeotia: reconstruction. Circa 150 B.C. Cf. p. 132.*

be thought of as additions by the painter of the bedroom and not part of the comic scenery.

The house architecture, like the prospects in the tragic scene, is decorative rather than real; it might even be called fantastic but it is not impossible. Such houses probably never existed, but they could have. It is interesting to see that in this very elaborate and imaginative representation of two houses on either side of a shrine, elements are preserved which were found in their simplest form at the beginning of pastoral painting (see pp. 69 ff.): round altars, and columns bearing statues on either side of the doors; moreover, the shrine of Hekate has the same essential shape – uprights and cross-piece sheltering an image – as the rustic shrine on the Attic kantharos of Menokles (see p. 69).

PLATE P. 68

One allusion in the comic scene is doubtful: on the roof of the balconies, which project above the inner side of the doors, is a broken flower-pot with a plant growing in it. These are certainly the so-called gardens of Adonis: plants which grew and died quickly like Adonis, whom the women lamented. Some have supposed the comedy was called 'Women at the Adonis Festival', a title borne by more than one comedy. But

PLATE 38 – Cubiculum decorated with frescoes, from P. Fannius Synistor's villa at Boscoreale. 3rd quarter of 1st century B.C. from originals, *circa* 150 B.C. *Height 2.44 m. Metropolitan Museum, New York. Cf. pp. 132ff., 159, 195.*

PLATE 39 – Mythological landscape from the *Odyssey*, showing Antilochos and Anchialos. Fresco from a house on the Esquiline in Rome. Copies from original, *circa* 150 B.C. *Vatican Library, Rome. Cf. pp. 20, 70, 139, 181.*

special scenery for a single comedy is unlikely, and it may rather be that comedy was sometimes produced at an Adonis festival.

Mythological landscape

In the same passage in which he mentions the dramatic scenes as good old decoration, Vitruvius also mentions the Wanderings of Odysseus, which he puts in the same category. Such a sequence of pictures was found in a house on the Esquiline and is now in the Vatican. Four pictures tell the story of Odysseus among the Laistrygones; another shows the palace of Kirke; another two show Odysseus in Hades.

PLATE 40 – Mythological landscape from the *Odyssey*, showing Nomai and Laistrygones. Fresco from a house on the Esquiline in Rome. Copies from original, *circa* 150 B.C. *Height 1.16 m. Vatican Library, Rome. Cf. pp. 20, 70, 140.*

Again these seem to be first-century copies of second-century originals. They are primarily landscape paintings, but the painter knew his Homeric text. Odysseus sails into a land-locked harbour, which is clearly shown on the third and fourth of the Laistrygones pictures. He sends three men to inquire of the inhabitants, and they meet the daughter of Antiphates, king of the Laistrygones, when she is coming down to fetch water. This is shown in the first picture. The artist has added the names of the men, Antilochos and Anchialos; they are not PLATE P. 138

named by Homer, and this is a piece of gratuitous scholarship akin to the names Elektra and Manto on the 'Homeric bowls' (the artist of the 'Homeric bowl' which illustrates the Kirke story knows the names of the men whom she turned into animals). To the left the spring Nymph reclines with a jug beside her; high to the left the wind-god is nearly hidden in his wind; to the right the mountain-god reclines on his mountain. These personifications, in contrast to Early Hellenistic personifications (see p. 20), are quite small in relation to their elements.

FIGS. 26–27

PLATE P. 139

Antiphates' daughter took the Greeks to the town, of which the fortified walls can be seen high on the second picture. Antiphates is summoned; he kills one of the Greeks for dinner, but the other two escape. He then summons the gigantic Laistrygones to attack the Greek ships with enormous boulders. This is the action of the right-hand side of the second picture. The attack, which destroyed all Odysseus' ships except his own, continues into the third picture; in the fourth Odysseus' ship is seen making good its escape to the shores of Kirke's island: the shores again have their nymphs with AKTAI (shores) written above them.

Between the opening scene with Antilochos and Anchialos meeting the king's daughter and the giant Laistrygonian who is pulling down a tree to use as a missile, the landscape on the right of the first picture and on the left of the second picture is filled with pastoral themes, for which the *Odyssey* provides no text. Sheep occupy the foreground, cattle and a herdsman the middle distance, and goats are on the hill at the back. The theme is made clear by the two figures to the left of the tree which the Laistrygonian is attacking: a reclining nymph and a satyr herdsman with the label NOMAI (pastures) above them.

This is an echo of the pastoral art which began in the Early Hellenistic period (see p. 69). There the spacing was already wide and the figures small. On the Telephos frieze (see p. 120) some figures above or below the base-line were on a reduced scale to dissociate them from the main scene. Here the figures are disposed over great spaces, and their scale is reduced according to their distance from the front of the picture. This is landscape-painting in the sense that the landscape and the seascape dominate the figures, but the landscape is also very skilfully arranged to show off the figures: the lighting, which comes from the left, provides light surfaces to set off dark figures and dark surfaces to set off light figures.

This is clear in the first two pictures, but it is particularly effective in the last two pictures which show Odysseus' arrival in Hades and what he sees there. Odysseus sails in over a sunny sea. Then the light pours down through a rocky arch to illuminate the ghosts so that they appear insubstantial: this is a special light effect for a special situation. In the last picture the landscape is arranged to provide a light surface for Sisyphos and Krataiis and another light surface for the sprawling figure of Tityos. In this picture scholarship has suggested including the group of Danaides drawing water; they are taken from a later account of Hades and do not occur in Homer.

It is perhaps an oversimplification to speak of domination by the landscape. In these pictures, where the artist has a much freer field even than in the wide panels of the new theatres, he has re-thought the *Odyssey* narrative in Hellenistic terms. Apollonios Rhodios loved wide prospects and would have described the coast much more fully than Homer, who is only concerned with its convenience for shipping; he might easily have interested himself in the effect of light on insubstantial ghosts, and he might have inserted a pastoral interlude. The artist's vision is Hellenistic rather than Homeric.

Pergamon and mainland Greece

The consideration of these developments in painting has led us far from Pergamon, where only the Telephos frieze with its variations of scale, with its rocks and trees, its satyrs and maenads, gives a hint of contemporary landscape. The Telephos painting (see p. 122) is dominated to such an extent by the mighty Arkadia that it leaves little room for landscape. We have now to consider how much influence Pergamene art had on Greece itself and what Greece itself was doing in the Middle Hellenistic period. Attalos I set up a memorial to his victories on the Acropolis at Athens (see p. 93). Eumenes II gave the Athenians the colonnade or Stoa which ran under the Acropolis west of the theatre. In the precinct of Dionysos under the theatre is a round base with masks and garlands, which is so similar to the mask relief from the theatre at Pergamon that it must be Pergamene even if it is somewhat later than the Stoa.

PLATE P. 109

PLATE P. 148

FIG. 38

The base in Athens is decorated with satyr masks, over which runs

FIG. 38 – *Satyr masks and garlands on a marble relief from Pergamon. Circa 150 B.C. Istanbul Museum. Cf. below.*

a heavy wreath of fruits and leaves tied on to the masks by broad ribbons with hanging ends. The leaves certainly include ivy, akanthos and laurel; the fruits include grapes, pomegranates and ivy-fruit. The tradition of these heavy garlands goes back a long way, and an
PLATE P. 29 early example was noted round the belly of the Gnathia oinochoe in Cleveland (see p. 30). An example of comparable richness is the mosaic garland with tragic masks from the Casa del Fauno (see p. 123), which
FIG. 38 is also thought to be Pergamene in origin. The marble mask relief which comes from the theatre at Pergamon has the same wild-haired Satyr masks alternating with Papposeilenos masks (the old bald father of the satyrs); instead of the thick garland of mixed fruits this has a simpler garland of ivy-leaves and ivy-fruit. The reliefs with tragic and comic masks which were found in the Pergamene Agora have still thinner ivy trailers. It is clear that all these derive from symposion decoration (see p. 24). The reliefs from the theatre belong to a gateway linking the auditorium with the stage-building; it was the gift of one Apollodoros, but is probably part of the rebuilding plan of Eumenes II.
Athenian Agora Attalos II gave Athens the Stoa, which has now been reconstructed
FIG. 39 on the east side of the Agora. This great two-storeyed portico was part of a general remodelling of the Agora. It filled the whole of the east side. The so-called Middle Stoa ran at right angles to its southern corner, and separated the southern part of the Agora from the rest: this whole area was probably the Gymnasion given by Ptolemy VI. The west side under the Hephaisteion already had the fifth-century Stoa of Zeus, and now a new portico in front of the Metroon was added south of that. On the north side the Stoa of Herms had been

built early in the fifth century and the painted Stoa was built about the middle of the fifth century. Only the Stoa of Attalos had two storeys, and its enormous length and height gave a new unity to the Agora. Then as now, it must have looked tremendously impressive from the eminence of the Hephaisteion. The top storey gives a superb view across the Agora, and in those days must have been a wonderful position from which to view the Panathenaic procession. On both levels the whole length was open to walkers; arbitrations and trials could be held there; philosophers could talk to their pupils. Along the back at each level were twenty-one separate rooms for shops. The stairs went up outside at each end, and under them was an exedra (see p. 35) covered by that rarity in Greek architecture, a round arch. Outside, the extension holding the staircase had its own upper gable roof, a triple window on the top floor with the arch over the exedra under it, and a sloping roof over the lower flight: thus the north end, as reconstructed, gives the kind of collocation of shapes that appear in the house architecture of the Boscoreale comedy scenery. The outside row of columns are Doric below and Ionic above; the columns down the centre of the lower storey are Ionic, those of the upper storey have Egyptian palm-leaf capitals. The two-storeyed Stoa is used to frame an important public area, as in Pergamon itself round the temple of Athena.

PLATE P. 147

PLATE P. 144

PLATE P. 133

L. Aemilius Paulus

The violent style of the Pergamene gigantomachies is rarely found in Greece. It can perhaps be seen in the reliefs on the monument of L. Aemilius Paulus at Delphi; the cavalry engagements here bear some relation to the battles between Greeks and Mysians on the Telephos frieze, and they have also been compared with contemporary reliefs in South Italy, which illustrate equally violent subjects in violent style. L. Aemilius Paulus defeated Perseus of Macedon at Pydna in 168 B.C.; the reliefs are a representation of this battle; the high base had already been prepared by Perseus to receive his own statue. Plutarch, who tells us this, also says that after the victory Aemilius went on a sightseeing tour of Greece and in Olympia made the famous remark that Pheidias had sculpted the Zeus of Homer. His visit had a considerable effect on art and literature in Rome. Not only did he bring home a large number of statues, paintings, and golden and silver cups; he also

FIG. 40

PLATE 41 – General view of the Stoa of Attalos II, built on the east side of the Agora. *Cf. p. 142.*

allowed his sons to bring back Perseus' library with them, and he appointed an Athenian philosopher and painter, Metrodorus, as their tutor. More important still, one of the Achaeans sent to Italy after the battle of Pydna was the soldier, philosopher and historian Polybios, who had an immense influence on the young Scipio Aemilianus and his circle in Rome.

Neo-classical style

When Aemilius Paulus saw the Zeus of Pheidias in the temple of Zeus at Olympia, it had recently been restored by a sculptor called Damophon, who made a number of cult statues in Achaia and Messenia. The classical style of Pheidias influenced his work in the great group of Demeter and Despoina, which he made for Lykosoura in Arkadia. In this sanctuary the cult legend made Artemis as well as Despoina

APPX. PLATES 9, 18–20

(who was identified with Persephone) the daughter of Demeter, and told that Despoina was brought up by Anytos, one of the Titans. The father of Despoina here was Poseidon, but he did not appear in the great group of four statues: Demeter and Despoina were seated and Artemis stood beside Demeter and Anytos beside Despoina. The representation of Demeter and Persephone as a pair of seated goddesses with a single cloak draping them is an old idea found in several different places in the archaic period and later. The cloak here has elaborate patterns including a remarkable border with a dance of women wearing animal masks, which presumably represents some very ancient cult dance. APPX. PL. 9

The influence of Pheidias can be seen in the great size of the figures,

FIG. 39 – *Plan of the Athenian Agora. 2nd century B.C. Cf. p. 142.*

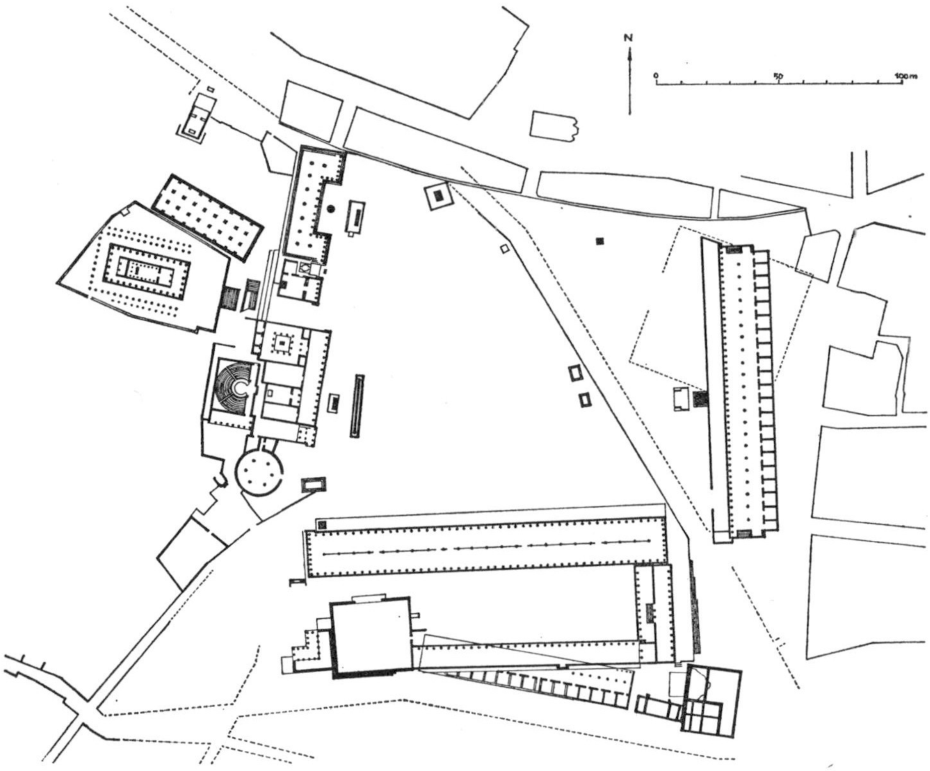

their frontality and their calm expressions. But the heads, like the figures in the Pergamene Gigantomachy (see p. 115), were enlivened by

APPX. PL. 20 inset eyes, and the Anytos has the wild hair and beard of Hellenistic satyr masks.

FIG. 41 The same mixed style appears in the head of Zeus from Aigeira in Achaia. The sculptor was an Athenian called Eukleides. The calm frontal, classical face had inserted eyes and has Hellenistic brows, beard and hair. Perhaps neo-classical is a reasonable name for this style; certainly its classical reminiscences are meaningful; rightly or wrongly, one feels that here the meaning is different from the meaning in Pergamon. In Pergamon the Parthenon is recalled because the Attalid kings are claiming Pergamon as a new Athens. In Greece the sculptors, living in a dangerous world at the mercy of the Hellenistic kings to the East and of Rome to the West, are bravely asserting their belief in the values of classical Greece, to which they are the heirs.

FIG. 42 The same style can be seen in the fragments of a colossal marble statue found in Rome; it may have been made by a Greek artist imported by Aemilius Paulus or by some other Philhellene with his taste for classical sculpture.

Euboulides, the grandson of the Euboulides who made the realistic portrait of Chrysippos (see p. 44), was a favourite sculptor of portraits in the mid-second century. The statue of Karneades, set up by an Attalos and an Ariarathes in the Agora at Athens, perhaps actually in the Stoa of Attalos, although it cannot be certainly ascribed to Euboulides, may give an idea of his style: the lined elderly face has orderly hair and beard, the himation is neatly draped over a fine chiton. This breaks with the tradition of representing philosophers as Old Derelicts and looks back to statues like the Lateran Sophokles. The dedicators only give their names and an Athenian deme-name, but they were presumably the kings of Pergamon and Cappadocia, using their honorary Athenian citizenship to honour a great contemporary philosopher.

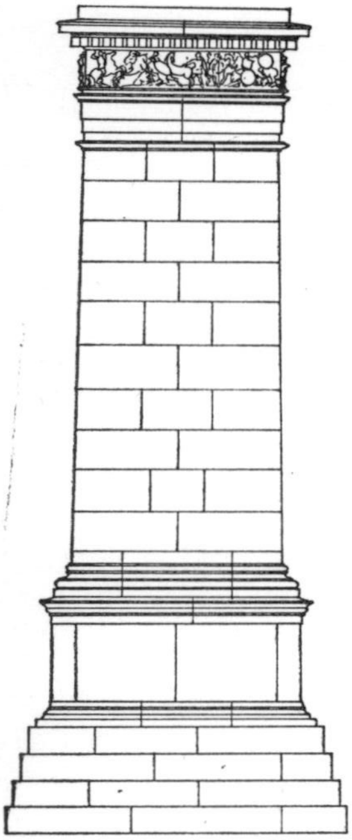

FIG. 40 – *Base for the statue of Aemilius Paulus at Delphi. 167 B.C. Delphi Museum. Cf. p. 143.*

PLATE 42 – The Stoa of Attalos II. View through the two-aisled portico. *Cf. p. 142 and plate on p. 144.*

Neo-classical is the kindest name also for the Aphrodite of Melos in the Louvre. The head is a hard and insensitive adaptation from Praxiteles' Aphrodite of Knidos. The fourth-century original of the Aphrodite of Capua, which held a shield between raised left hand and lowered right hand, was also in the mind of the artist. But the body has been given a more complicated twist with breasts turned to the left, hips turned towards the right, and right leg drawn behind the left leg; the drapery, too, is much more fussy and realistic. The reconstruction remains uncertain, and it is not known whether the lost base, which had both the signature of a sculptor from Antioch on the Maeander and a square-socket to receive a pillar, belonged. The left PLATE P. 151

PLATE 43 – Round base with masks and garlands, from the Dionysos theatre in Athens. *Cf. pp. 141, 199.*

arm was raised above the level of the shoulder; the right arm was lowered across the body. The mass of naked body must have been balanced by something of different texture on the right; the general scheme must have been not unlike that of the Apollo of Kyrene, which may derive from a contemporary original. There an elaborate structure is built up from the base ending in the lyre which Apollo is playing. What corresponding structure was designed for this Aphrodite we do not know. Another large neo-classical statue from the island of Melos is the Poseidon, which is also a dramatic recreation of an earlier type.

Delos

The nearby island of Delos had flourished during the Early Hellenistic period and received many gifts from the kings; it also became the central corn-market of the Aegean. But the Delians sided with Perseus of Macedon against the Romans, and the Romans handed the island over to the Athenians after they had defeated Perseus at Pydna in 168. The Athenian period lasted until the destruction and evacuation of Delos in the early first century. This again was a period of great prosperity, and the large Italian settlement must have been one of the channels through which Greek artistic ideas passed to Rome. 'An Agora rich in food and an enormous crowd of worshippers' is how an Athenian comic poet described Delos, probably in the early second century. Theatre records in Delos go back to the fourth century B.C., and a long series describes improvements made in the theatre and gives lists of performers through the third and down into the second century. The performances at the festivals of Dionysos included choral dithyrambs, tragedies and comedies; there was also a performance in honour of Apollo in which apparently poets, actors, musicians, jugglers and marionettists might give a turn. The actors were international stars who came from all over the Greek world, some of whom are known to have played also in Athens, Delphi and Thasos. As early as 259 B.C. one of the jugglers describes himself as a Roman citizen and has a slave-girl to help him; in 170 B.C. one of the marionettists is

FIG. 41 – *Head of Zeus from Aigeira. Marble. 150 B.C. Height 87 cm. National Museum, Athens. Cf. p. 146.*

FIG. 42 – *Marble head from Rome. Circa 150 B.C. Cf. p. 146.*

described as *Romaïstes,* which presumably means that he gave a Latin recitation while operating the puppets.

This lively theatrical life is sometimes reflected in the decoration of the rich houses which have been excavated on the island. Numerous terracottas with comic subjects (and a few with tragic) have been found in the houses and elsewhere: many of them are statuettes, others masks – some of them large enough to affix to the wall of the dining-room; some small ones were the lids of terracotta lamps. Terracotta braziers with masks from comedy, tragedy and satyr play helped to warm the houses. One house (called the House of the Comedian) had frescoes with one tragic scene (possibly Antigone and Oidipous in the prologue of the *Oidipous Koloneus* of Sophokles) and several comic scenes.

House of the Masks

FIG. 43

Another house has been called the House of the Masks, because it contained three mosaics with dramatic subjects. They were in three adjoining rooms. The largest is the Mask mosaic. The main pattern consists of perspective cubes painted in black, white, dark red and light red. On two sides this 'carpet' has a border of comic masks hanging from a trailer of fruited ivy (see p. 142). These borders are very like the contemporary frieze of the Agora at Pergamon, and belong to the long tradition of symposion decoration which goes back at least to the fourth century B.C. The masks in one border include a Pan mask and in the other border a Satyr mask; the artist may therefore have been thinking of two different comedies in which Pan (as in Menander's *Dyskolos*) and a Satyr spoke the prologues.

FIG. 44

The mask mosaic is in the room labelled *andron* on the plan, the main dining-room. The antechamber of the small room next it has a mosaic with a flute-player seated on a rock. The nudity of the flute-player and the rock are imaginary; the artist has transposed the theatre flute-player into the country because he is thinking of a comedy set in the country like the *Dyskolos*. The dancer wears the same costume as the walking slave from Myrina (see p. 130), but he has a bald mask with a wreath round it. This type of mask is especially associated with

PLATE P. 155

FIG. 34

PLATE 44 – Aphrodite of Melos. Marble. 2nd century B.C. *Height 2.04 m. Louvre, Paris.* *Cf. p. 147.*

the cook: the cook kills the animal which he intends to cook, and this is a sacrifice to a god; therefore he wears a wreath. In the *Dyskolos* Menander provides a beautiful example of a cook in comedy: Sikon, who sacrifices a sheep to Pan.

PLATE P. 156 The third mosaic comes from the larger room on the right of the *andron*. A beardless figure rides a leopard. The face with its hard features seems to me to allude to the mask of the young Dionysos, a type which can be traced from the early fifth century. He rides a leopard because his travels have taken him as far as India. He is the god of maenads and satyrs, of initiation and hopes of immortality, and so he carries a thyrsos in his right hand and a tympanon in his left hand. He is the god of tragedy, and therefore wears the clothes of a tragic actor, chiton with long sleeves, long himation and red shoes; the fashion of thick soles had evidently not reached Delos yet. He is the god of the symposion; he himself wears a wreath with ivy-leaves and fruit, a tainia is tied round the thyrsos, and the leopard has a wreath of vine-leaves and fruit round his neck. Thus Dionysos displays the various aspects of his divinity, in which the Hellenistic age was particularly interested. Here again the label neo-classical may be applied. The conception of Dionysos riding a leopard goes back to the

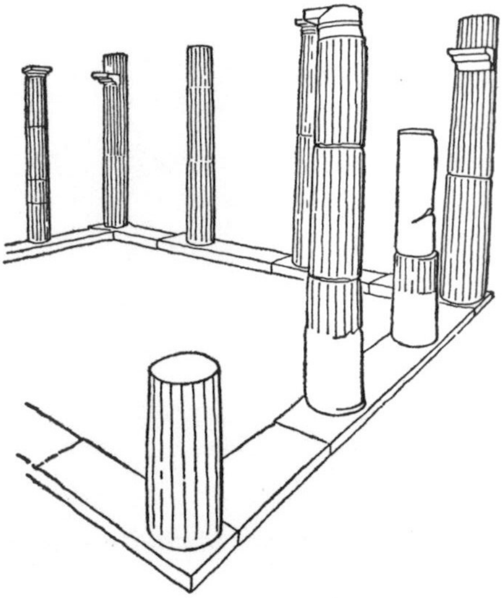

FIG. 43 – *Court in the House of the Masks at Delos: reconstruction. 2nd century B.C. Cf. pp. 150, 154.*

fifth century, and the artist intentionally recalls this tradition by the mask-like face and the very formal folds along the bottom of the chiton; as in Early Hellenistic paintings and mosaics (see p. 23), the background is a plain drop and the panther prowls along a narrow stage.

Opposite the room with the Dionysos mosaic is another large room labelled *bibliotheca* on the plan, and this had a mosaic with a Panathenaic FIG. 44 amphora on the floor. This was a special form of wine-jar which was given as a prize to victors in the Panathenaic games in Athens; it was filled with olive-oil from the sacred olive-trees on the Acropolis. This combination of subjects, coupled with the discovery in the house of statues of an elderly man and a young man, led the excavators to suggest that the house, which was only a hundred yards from the theatre, was put at the disposal of the theatre, for storing properties and perhaps entertaining visiting actors, by a patron of drama or a poet, who was the father of a victorious athlete.

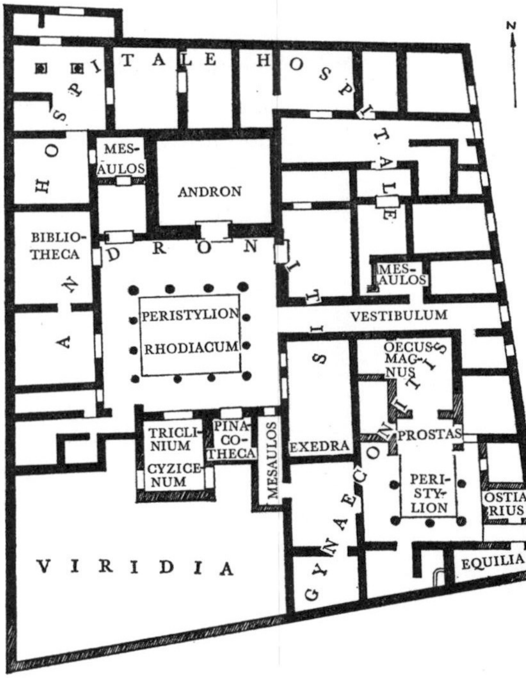

FIG. 44 – *Ground-plan of the House of the Masks at Delos. 2nd century B.C. Cf. pp. 150ff.*

This suggestion is perhaps more precise than is justifiable. Certainly the Panathenaic amphora alludes to Athens and to Athenian culture, but it need not imply a victory, musical or athletic, in the Panathenaic games. And Dionysos is the god of the symposion, so that anything connected with Dionysos is a suitable subject for the part of the house connected with drinking.

The layout of the house has been shown to agree well with Vitruvius' description of a Greek house, and Vitruvius' names are entered on the plan. It has also been noticed that Vitruvius' account of the Greek theatre has a close correspondence with the theatre at Delos. He may, therefore, have been following here some Athenian handbook which drew on examples from Delos. If we follow Vitruvius, we enter the house by a passage in the south-east corner with a porter's lodge on the left and stables on the right. The passage leads into the main court of the women's part of the house, *gynaeconitis*. The *oecus magnus* is the large room in which the family weaving is done. One passage from the women's quarters and another from the street leads into the men's quarters, *andronitis*. Their main court can be reconstructed. It is called a Rhodian peristyle, because the colonnade has higher columns on the north side than on the others. Round this court the main rooms are grouped. Vitruvius recommends a main dining-room, *andron*, on the north, a lecture-room, *exedra*, on the east; a picture gallery, *pinacotheca*, and a garden dining-room, *triclinium Cyzicenum*, on the south; a library, *bibliotheca*, on the west; the rest of the house is used for guest-rooms, and was arranged so that the guests could live independently of their hosts if they wished. It is impossible to tell whether the rooms in the House of the Masks in fact had these uses, but the names from Vitruvius fit easily into the plan, and the writer on whom Vitruvius drew must have had a house like this in mind.

FIG. 43

The main decoration of the walls in the more elaborate rooms was stucco-modelled and painted to represent marble slabs, but paintings were also used. The House of the Comedian had frescoes of dramatic

PLATE 45 – Flute-player and dancing slaves. Floor mosaic in the House of the Masks on Delos. *Circa* 150 B.C. *Height 88 cm. Cf. p. 150.*

PLATE 46 – Dionysos riding a panther. Floor mosaic in the House of the Masks on Delos. *Circa* 150 B.C. *Height 1.08 m. Cf. p. 152.*

subjects round the upper part of the walls, and some houses had pictures in painted frames set in the stucco background; Vitruvius speaks of the possibility of cutting out such pictures and removing them elsewhere, and that is presumably how some of the very fine small pictures, such as that of the tragic actor, came to Herculaneum and Pompeii (see p. 37). In his account of decoration Vitruvius makes it clear that larger pictures were reserved for exedrae and porticoes.

Conclusion

The houses at Delos give some idea of how wealthy Greeks lived in the second century, and we can think of them using the 'Homeric bowls' to drink from, made in silver, bronze or clay according to the wealth of the owners. They too, like the Boeotians and the Alexandrians, liked learned allusions to the great literature of the past. Reverence for the past is the most obvious common factor in the Middle Hellenistic period. It was not only the inspiration of scholarship and of art and literature which derives directly from scholarship; for the old Greek cities to remember the past was to assert their heritage and their right to kindly treatment in a dangerous world; the new kingdoms felt the need to claim a connection with the great Greek past whose glories they believed they were renewing. The Romans, who had always been open to Greek influence, indirectly through the Etruscans and directly through imports, and increasingly through contact with the Greek cities of South Italy, were now in ever closer contact with the old Greek cities and the Hellenistic kingdoms; Romans were visiting the Hellenistic Greek world, Greek artists were visiting Italy, and works of art were pouring into Italy. Reverence for the past not only inspired traditional works like the Zeus of Aigeira and the Aphrodite of Melos, but also provided at least subject matter for such startlingly new experiments as the Telephos frieze and the Odyssey frescoes.

ADDITIONAL NOTE ON POMPEIAN HOUSES AND DECORATION

In the foregoing chapters Roman paintings from Herculaneum, Pompeii, Boscoreale and the Esquiline have been illustrated for the information that they give about the Greek originals from which they were copied, and something has been said about the evidence for copying. It will be convenient to consider here briefly their place in the sequence of Roman wall decoration.

The earliest houses at Pompeii date from the third century B.C. The House of the

PLATE 47 – Street in Pompeii.

Surgeon is the best-known example. The plan seems very like a contemporary Greek house with rooms opening off a courtyard, but the courtyard was roofed; this room was the *atrium*, and the roof drained into a tank in the centre. The upper storey ran round the *atrium* and the room immediately behind it. From the second century B.C. onwards much larger and more complicated houses were built. The essential change was the addition of an open court with columns round it, like that in the house at Delos (Fig. 43), to the original complex; thus in the House of the Tragic Poet this peristyle court was added behind the *tablinum*. Very large houses, like the House of the Faun, from which comes the bronze dancing satyr (Fig. 29), might have two *atria* and two peristyle courts.

The early history of wall decoration is given by Vitruvius (VII, 5). He speaks of an early style in which the decorators imitated marble slabs. This is the incrustation style known at Pompeii from 150 to 80 B.C., and in Delos in the second century B.C. (Earlier still at Olynthos in the fourth century B.C. the walls were decorated in

PLATE 48 – Court in the House of the Deer at Herculaneum, looking toward the apse decorated with mosaics. 1st century B.C.

blocks of plain colour separated by narrow bands, flat, sunk or raised.) This decoration did not exclude friezes with figure decorations and small pictures in panels.
The Second Style, which runs roughly from 80 B.C. to A.D. 14, has large pictures set in simple architecture which appears functional. It is to this stage that the pictures from the House on the Esquiline (see above p. 138) and the pictures from the Villa at Boscoreale belong (see above pp. 32, 132). Another good example is the Villa dei Misteri. In all these the pictures are large and the figures in them are large in scale. The pictures are seen through and beyond a fairly simple architectural framework which appears to project into the room. Toward the end of this period, as Vitruvius says, the architecture becomes fantastic with decorative candelabra, scrolls etc. instead of functional members. PLATE P. 160
The Third and Fourth Styles go beyond the chronological limits of this book but may be briefly described. In the Third Style, which lasts till about A.D. 63, the painted architecture does not pretend to be functional; it is a light, fantastic and

PLATE 49 – Wall-painting in the large hall of the Villa dei Misteri near Pompeii, extending around a room measuring 5 by 7 metres and containing 29 figures. Detail shown: Initiation of a woman into the mysteries of Dionysos. *Height circa 1.85 m. Cf. pp. 124, 159.*

very delicate system, which decorates the wall and surrounds the pictures; the figured scenes themselves are now much smaller in relation to the wall and are correspondingly lacking in depth: the House of M. Lucretius Fronto is a good example.

The Fourth Style, which continues until the eruption of A.D. 79, is much less restrained and has the baroque character of contemporary sculpture and architecture. The painted architecture is on a larger scale and more fantastic than before: the individual elements appear to have much greater depth than in the Third Style. Many of the pictures are larger than in the Third Style, have greater depth and figures on a larger scale in relation to their frames. The Herakles and Telephos (see above p. 109) is one of many Fourth Style pictures which seem to be good copies of Greek originals. The House of the Vettii and the House of the Dioscori are good examples of this final Pompeian style.

III. LATE HELLENISTIC PERIOD

Introduction

In the Middle Hellenistic period three rather different attitudes to classical Greek art can be seen: in the new kingdoms allusion to the great past is a claim to have revived it; in the old cities allusion to the great past is a claim to have inherited it; and thirdly we see classicism in the form of reminiscence and free copies, classicism with no further aim than the production of pleasant old-fashioned work. It is this third attitude which dominates the Late Hellenistic period. One of the reasons for this is that the Greek centres, new kingdoms and old city-states alike, all with the exception of Egypt, had come under Roman domination in the course of the second century and remained under Roman domination – except for the false flicker of freedom in the early first century when they sided against Rome with Mithradates of Pontus, a mistake for which the Athenians paid by the Sullan sack in 86 B.C.

Rome and Greek art

Roman acquaintance with Greek art goes back to the beginnings of the city's history. Besides their direct imports they knew Greek art through the medium of Etruscan art, which reflected the changes in Greek style; in the Middle Hellenistic period the mythological scenes on Etruscan ash-chests reflect the same learned strain in Greek art as the 'Homeric bowls', and the terracotta statue of Apollo from Falerii has the dramatic grandeur of early Pergamene art. Through the whole Hellenistic period Roman knowledge was also being enriched by their increasing contacts first with South Italy and Sicily, and then with Greece and Greek Asia Minor; and from the time of the victory over Pyrrhos at Beneventum in 275 B.C. Greek statues, paintings, tapestries, gold and silverware flowed into Rome in increasing quantities as booty. Mummius, who destroyed Corinth in 146 B.C., had his attention called to painting by the high price which Attalos II of Pergamon (see p. 17) paid for an Old Master; this story is always quoted as illustrating Roman insensitivity to art, and both Horace and Virgil must bear part of the blame for this. Two other stories probably illustrate the Roman attitude better. When Marcellus captured Syracuse in 212 B.C., he dedicated Syracusan statues and paintings not only in the temple of Honos and Virtus in Rome, but also in Samothrace and Lindos. This was not only a demonstration of Roman power but also an acknowledgment that there should be some sort of community between Greeks and Romans, symbolised by dedicating Greek works of art to Greek gods in Greek islands.

The other is the story already quoted of Aemilius Paulus' admiration for Pheidias' Zeus at Olympia (see p. 144). This raises a question which cannot be answered. If Aemilius thought that Pheidias sculpted the Zeus of Homer, did he also think that neo-classical gods, like the one found in fragments in the Largo Argentino (see p. 146), added to Roman religion the majesty and ethical content of the Pheidian gods which inspired their sculptors? At least we can say that the Romans of the Middle and Late Hellenistic periods regarded Pheidian and post-Pheidian forms as a suitable embodiment of their gods. FIG. 43

Art galleries

We should probably be wrong to rate too high the religious content of Late Hellenistic art, and where works of art were dedicated in temples, we should think of them perhaps rather as additions to an art gallery than as dedications to secure the favour of a god. Undoubtedly the old idea, that the god would be grateful because he loved the same kind of beautiful things as the dedicator (see p. 17), survived, but already in the early third century Herondas' women, in the interval between handing over a cock to be sacrificed and receiving news that the sacrifice was successful, treated the temple as an art gallery and admired the dedications from an aesthetic point of view: they never consider the relevance of this or that work to Asklepios. And in the first century B.C., although Cicero talks a lot about Verres despoiling the gods (see p. 199), the real charge against him for taking the paintings from the temple of Athena in Syracuse is that he denuded the Syracusan art gallery.

Cicero objects strongly that Verres should have a large private collection, when the ordinary man has to go to the temple of Felicitas, the portico of Catulus, or the portico of Metellus to see works of art. The temples and porticoes (or as the Greeks would say *stoai*) rank equally as art galleries. The dates are mid-second century for the temple of Felicitas and for the portico of Metellus and the very end of the second century for the portico of Catulus. The portico of Metellus made a court round the temples of Jupiter and Juno, which were built at the same time. This whole arrangement is obviously Hellenistic Greek, and the architect of the temples was a Greek, Hermodoros of Salamis. The works of art on display here included Lysippos' equestrian group of Alexander's friends, Aphrodite washing herself by Doidalsas (who was a follower of Lysippos), and an Artemis and Asklepios by Kephisodotos, the son of Praxiteles. The cult statues of Jupiter and Juno were made by the Athenians, Dionysios and Polykles, sons of Timarchides; at this date it seems virtually certain that Athenian sculptors would work in the neo-classical style of Damophon. (Dionysios was the younger of the two brothers and worked with his nephew, the younger Timarchides, at the end of the second century in Delos.) FIG. 51

Patrons

Late Hellenistic artists were producing for patrons who had ample opportunities of seeing masterpieces of classical and earlier Hellenistic art in public and private galleries. It is small wonder that their art was so largely classicising. This was what Roman collectors wanted, and if we may trust Virgil Romans had no doubt that artists were inferior to soldiers and administrators. The poets had some slight advantage over the artists here because those who wrote Latin had the creative task of Hellenising the Latin language. But for both artists and poets the main line is classicising until Augustus and the Empire produced a new stimulus for both.

Greek artists were working in Rome in the Middle Hellenistic period; the Athenian sculptors discussed above and the Alexandrian painter Demetrios are obvious examples. But probably the influx was greater after the sack of Athens by Sulla in 86 B.C. In studying the tendencies of Late Hellenistic art as they begin, objects originating in Greece which can be dated before 86 B.C. are of particular interest.

Athens and neo-Attic art

Technically and stylistically a curved relief found in the Agora at Athens can be dated in the late second century B.C. Here for the first time the term archaistic can and must be used. A touch of archaism (APPX. PLATES 14–16) was noted in the drapery of the queens on the fayence jugs and of the Artemis and Iphigeneia (FIG. 24) (see pp. 71, 96); but here all the drapery is archaistic, the treatment of the relief is archaistic, and the long feet and fingers are archaistic. The terminology is imperfect: ideally one should have three words to distinguish the three earlier styles, archaic, classical and Hellenistic, which Late Hellenistic artists used as models; in practice archaistic and classicistic are used both as general terms to describe any style which uses earlier models merely to evoke pleasure in the spectator and not for any ulterior purpose, and as particular terms to describe styles which use either archaic or classical models to evoke pleasure.

Archaism

The Agora reliefs are archaistic in the particular sense of using archaic models. The drapery is based on ripe archaic drapery of the Persian War period, but in that period the stacked folds would never kick up sideways, as they do both on the female figure and on the draped male figure. On the surviving evidence archaism seems to have been introduced in the fifth century for special purposes. The Athena on the amphorai given as prize-vases in the Panathenaic games develops in style naturally from 560 to about 480 B.C.; from then onwards the artists imitate in a more and more exaggerated form the Athenas of 480 B.C. A similar archaism appears on a group of late fifth-century jugs, which may also be connected with the Panathenaic festival. We have already noticed also that Alkamenes gave the Herm outside the Propylaia of the Acropolis an archaic hair-style (see p. 125). In these instances the artist seems to have wanted to give an added solemnity to his Athena or Hermes by showing them as they appeared in the great past period of the Persian Wars.

The other common use of archaism in the fifth century was for statues in mythological scenes such as the rape of Kassandra or Iphigeneia among the Taurians: here the artist certainly used the stiff archaic posture and clothes to differentiate the statue from the heroes and heroines of the story; sometimes the goddess herself stands or sits nearby in contemporary clothes and attitude. This last collocation was taken up by the sculptors in the fourth century when they represented, for instance, a modern Artemis with her arm resting on the head of her own archaic statue.

The sculptors of archaistic reliefs took these archaic images and animated them into archaistic figures of gods and heroes. The earliest is a four-sided base from the Acropolis at Athens with Hephaistos, Athena,

FIG. 45 – *Victories and shield on a limestone relief found in Rome. 100–50 B.C. Conservatori, Rome. Cf. below.*

Zeus and Hermes. Dating has varied between the early fourth century and the second century B.C. The simpler treatment favours the earlier century. Later many archaistic reliefs survive: the subjects include Pan and the Nymphs, processions of gods, Dionysos and the seasons. They go right on into the Roman Imperial period, and the figures may be found on flat reliefs, curved reliefs or marble vases. A relief with archaistic nymphs from Rhodes is firmly dated by the inscription about 70 B.C.

The relief from the Agora is curved and stood between the legs of
APPX. PL. 14 a great bronze tripod, which was won as a prize in some contest. The boy with the thin club can be certainly identified as Theseus. He rests
APPX. PL. 15 his club on a rock because he has just arrived in Athens. The man with the sceptre, therefore, in spite of his being a copy of the Zeus on the Acropolis base, must be Theseus' father, Aigeus. Then the woman, who
APPX. PL. 16 is running away with a phiale in her hand, must be Medeia who tried to poison Theseus to secure the succession for her own son. The three reliefs allude to a well-known Athenian story dramatised by Euripides, and the archaistic style removes these heroic figures from the unpleasant realities of the second century.

The same stacked swallow-tail folds, which on the Agora Medeia seem an elegant and formal stylisation of an archaic garment, appear rather
FIG. 45 less well suited to the robust Victories on a frieze found in Rome, which

is believed to have decorated a monument erected by Sulla to celebrate his triumph over Greece. Here the archaism is confined to the himation which the Victories wear over their long chitons. The rest of the frieze is a combination of elements known elsewhere in Hellenistic relief. The section illustrated shows the Victories between two large incense-burners decorating with a laurel-wreath a shield, on which the eagle of Jupiter is represented in relief, standing on Jupiter's thunderbolt; above the eagle two tiny Cupids hold a scroll, from which the inscription has vanished. The other preserved section has a profile bust of Roma on a shield between two trophies. The execution is extremely competent, and the decoration is relevant, if reminiscent.

Victories carrying incense-burners appeared on the robe of Despoina at Lykosoura, but then they did not have archaistic folds. The portrait in a shield is known from other first-century monuments, for instance the monument of Mithradates in Delos, and Pliny quotes them on the Basilica Aemilia, which was built in 78 B.C. Pliny curiously says that the portraits were set in shields like those used in the Trojan War. To judge from Greek heroes in Pompeian pictures, he would think of such shields as round and bronze-faced. Shield blazons go back to the eighth century B.C., and one of the earliest was a frontal Gorgon's head. In the long history between the archaic and Late Hellenistic periods shields, particularly shields used as decoration, influenced and were influenced by other forms of tondo, such as mirrors and coins, which contained profile, three-quarter and full-face heads and busts. Probably the Hellenistic rulers first put their portraits on shields, and this was the more natural because they were equated with gods; Mithradates called himself the New Dionysos. The Romans took over the custom without making the equation; nor was there any reason for them to do so since already in Athens in the first century B.C. it had become a decorative convention which could be used for private persons. APPL. PL. 9

In our frieze Rome is personified as a war-goddess, as in the Greek hymn by the poetess Melinno, who addresses her as a daughter of Ares, the Greek god of war. Trophies already appear in the later fifth century on the balustrade of the Athenian temple of Nike, the source of much neo-Attic inspiration. Later the Stoa round the temple of Athena at Pergamon had shields and other weapons in its frieze. Thus this frieze in Rome is a typical and successful eclectic work of its time.

Neo-Attic classicism

The majority of the reliefs which, like the Agora reliefs, are called neo-Attic are not archaistic in the narrow sense but are archaistic or classicistic in the wider sense. The description neo-Attic is convenient even if only some of the artists were Attic and if many of the objects were made elsewhere, particularly in Italy, where many artists migrated after the sack by Sulla. Many of the models are Attic; the Acropolis basis is a forerunner; some of the artists who signed their works were Athenians; and neo-Attic reliefs were still being made in Attica in the first and second century A.D.

Besides the Agora relief, good early examples which were certainly made in Attica were found in the wreck of a ship which foundered off the coast of Tunisia, when conveying a cargo of works of art, including the bronze Agon noted on p. 124, to Italy about 100 B.C. or soon after. Among the works were fragments of four marble kraters with neo-Attic reliefs. The four kraters were in fact two pairs of identical kraters, and together they show something of the range and complicated ancestry of these neo-Attic works.

The first pair are decorated with a thiasos showing a youthful Dionysos and Ariadne (if she is the lady playing the lyre), satyrs and maenads; it belongs to the general tradition of Dionysiac thiasoi, which goes

PLATE P. 21

back through the Dherveni krater to the fifth century and beyond (see p. 20). But this is only a tradition of subject matter; the style has been completely modernised. For instance, the wonderful group of a young satyr supporting an old satyr as he falls is unthinkable before the Pergamene Gauls. In fact the artist seems to have found his model in a Pergamene original of the early second century B.C. The same original, probably through the medium of another Late Hellenistic krater which arrived safely in Italy, was copied by an artist of the early first century A.D., who made a marble krater now in the Louvre. The second pair of kraters from the wrecked ship also have a thiasos of Dionysos, satyrs and maenads but without Ariadne. The artist (and he may indeed have been the same man as the artist of the first pair) did not follow a single model but has combined figures from several sources into a pleasing new whole. Again a much later copy is preserved,

FIG. 46

a marble krater of the second century A.D. now in Pisa. Two of the

FIG. 46 – *Thiasos of Dionysos with satyrs and maenads. Frieze from a marble krater. 50 B.C. Campo Santo, Pisa. Cf. p. 168.*

elements in this composition may be taken as examples of how these artists worked. The maenad with her right hand above her head and her left hand holding her follower's wrist is a copy with only slight remodelling of a maenad known from twenty other neo-Attic works. This maenad held a sword in her left hand and half a deer in her right hand; the Mahdia–Pisa maenads only differ in omitting the sword and animal. The style is so akin to that of some Victories from the balustrade of the temple of Nike in Athens, that a late fifth-century Attic original must be assumed for this and for the eight other types of neo-Attic maenad which go closely with it. A recent reconstruction supposes that the original was a bronze relief with three maenads moving to the right and three to the left, and that the other three types of neo-Attic maenads were later creations. At least we can accept that six of the neo-Attic types are copies of a late fifth-century Attic original.

Another element on the Mahdia krater has a later and more complicated origin. This is the group of Dionysos, the two satyrs, one untying Dionysos' shoe and the other supporting him, the two satyrs in front, the one immediately behind him, and the old satyr supporting the falling maenad. The Dionysos is based on a well-known statue which is known from several copies; the original has been ascribed to Praxiteles. The rest of the group seems from its exciting postures to be Hellenistic, and presumably the earlier Dionysos was adapted to fit in with it. APPX. PL. 12

Visit to a Comic Poet

But why should Dionysos have his shoe untied unless he is entering a house? The artist of the Mahdia krater must have transferred the group from a context where this made sense. One such context appears on the reliefs in which Dionysos visits a comic poet. Here he is having his shoe removed because he is entering the house of the poet. The group is known in many versions which have variations of detail and background, but in all of them the curtain behind the poet, the couch on which he is reclining, and the table in front of the couch show that he is at home, and therefore a visitor may reasonably take off his shoes. This scene occurs on a marble base in the Vatican which has been dated in the first century B.C. It adds on the extreme right a rustic statue of Priapos. The revellers have, therefore, come from the country to visit the poet. The British Museum example, which has been dated in the first century A.D., has a much more elaborate background with another satyr standing on the wall. The poet has been given a basket of comic masks by his side to make his identity certain. The artist has removed the girl from the couch, and has reduced the group of satyr supporting maenad to a single figure of a maenad. One wonders whether he was working from a model, such as a plaster cast, which had become obscure at this point.

But was the group of Dionysos and his thiasos invented for the 'Visit to a Comic Poet', and should we therefore postulate an original 'Visit to a Comic Poet' earlier than the Mahdia krater? There are two difficulties. The first is the awkward position of the poet; one expects him to lie the other way round so as to face Dionysos. This position is much better suited to a man who is in the middle of a party of three and turns to speak to the man on his right. A Paestan bell krater has just such a figure as the central member of three symposiasts playing kottabos. The poet of the reliefs may well derive from such a figure.

The second reason against supposing that the group on the Mahdia krater was originally devised for the 'Visit to a Comic Poet' is that a much more convincing 'Visit to a Comic Poet' is found on a relief in the Louvre, which has been dated in the second century B.C. Here a young Dionysos supported by a satyr arrives from the left so that the comic poet faces him without turning round. This is an entirely satisfactory composition, and the young Dionysos is a much more suitable visitor for a comic poet than the solemn, bearded, heavily-draped figure of the Mahdia krater.

Dionysos and Ariadne

It is tempting to speculate further on the origin of the group on the Mahdia krater. Dionysos is sometimes bearded when he comes to find Ariadne on Naxos, and one South Italian vase of the late fifth century shows Theseus departing to the left to join his ship. An original which gave all three elements – Theseus departing to the left, Ariadne asleep, and a bearded Dionysos arriving from the right with his thiasos – would provide exactly the original needed for the group on the Mahdia krater. The bearded Dionysos, from which the Mahdia Dionysos is derived, has been dated in the fourth century. The original of the marble statue of Ariadne asleep has been dated in the late fourth to early third century. It looks as if a great late fifth-century conception (possible the painting recorded by Pausanias in the temple of Dionysos by the theatre in Athens, although it has been claimed as the original of a quite different tradition, in which a young Dionysos comes on Ariadne from the left, while Theseus escapes to the right) was several times remodelled in the style of later periods. One of these remodellings, a Hellenistic original, whether a relief or painting, was the source from which the artists of the Mahdia krater and of the earliest standard 'Visit to a Comic Poet' took the group of Dionysos and his thiasos for their separate purposes.

These Late Hellenistic artists were excerptors: they took from any source they liked to make an interesting composition to fill the space available. Dionysos and his thiasos were the visible symbols of a Greek's hope of immortality, whether he lived in Athens, Pergamon, Alexandria or South Italy. The story of Dionysos finding Ariadne on Naxos was interpreted in two very different ways in the late fifth century – as a story of passionate bliss when the gay young god comes upon the sleeping beauty and as a story of mystical exaltation when the solemn bearded god moves slowly up to her. These are the opposite poles of ecstasy which Euripides, who understood the whole range of Dionysiac religion, represented in the *Bakchai*. The ecstasy is only a distant echo in neo-Attic art, produced for the most part for Roman purchasers, who wanted decorative art for their houses and gardens.

Copies All the individual figures in neo-Attic art were derived from earlier creations, but the earlier creations were translated into the medium of the new work. Even where the earlier work was itself a relief, the new work differed in scale. Here there was no question of mechanical copying, but this also had begun at least early in the first century B.C. By mechanical copying, as distinct from free copying, is meant the process by which points are transferred from a cast of the original to the block of marble which is being used for the copy. An early example is the marble copy of the Polykleitan Diadoumenos in Delos; this marble copy of a fifth-century bronze was certainly not made later than the early first century, since sculpture in Delos is unlikely to date after the destruction by Mithradates. The copyist has added the support at the side, which would have been unnecessary in the bronze original. Other copies have a simple tree-trunk, but here a quiver hangs from the tree and this is presumably an allusion to the Apollo of Delos. From this time onwards the Roman could and did own mechanical copies of Greek masterpieces.

FIG. 47

In one respect, however, the copies apparently did not follow the originals: they were not coloured. This seems a fair deduction from Vitruvius when he says that naked marble statues are covered with melted wax, which is then worked over with waxed cords and clean cloths. When statues were coloured, the colours were put on with melted wax; Vitruvius describes a process of polishing uncoloured marble *(ganosis)*. Classical bronzes would have often lost their golden colour before they were copied, and the copies of marble statues must often have been made at a distance from the original. When the Romans wanted colour, they had their statues made of coloured stone.

Less is known of the copying of painting, but all the paintings from Rome and the Campanian towns which have been used to reconstruct the history of Hellenistic painting are in fact copies or adaptations. The only evidence for the method of transmission is the Dioskourides mosaic (see p. 129) which is itself copied in painting in a Campanian house, but such very fine small mosaics must have been expensive and rare, and the ordinary painter presumably had some sort of pattern-book. In the second century copies of classical paintings were made in Delphi for the Pergamene royal collection (see p. 102); in 86 B.C.

PLATE P. 117

Sulla removed a late fifth-century painting, Zeuxis' Centaur family, from Athens and left a copy in its place; and in 84 B.C. Lucullus bought a copy of Pausias' Garland-maker when he was serving in Athens.

Adaptations

PLATE P. 175

There is plenty of evidence also for adaptations as well as mechanical copies of classical sculpture. The Idolino in Florence was long supposed to be a fifth-century bronze original by Polykleitos, but it has been shown that it belongs to a group of bronze boys, who initially all held candelabra in their hands. Their bodies are alike, but they have different heads: the Idolino has a copy of a Polykleitan head; another bronze boy is equipped with a girl's head of about the same date, which is known in several copies; another has a Hellenistic head. The one with the girl's head was originally gilded. For gilded boys holding candelabra a Roman text can be quoted. Lucretius, in a poem left unfinished when he died in 55 B.C., contrasts the simple pleasures of the Epicurean philosopher with the elaborate banquets of rich houses, where 'gold statues of youths hold flaming torches in their right hands'.

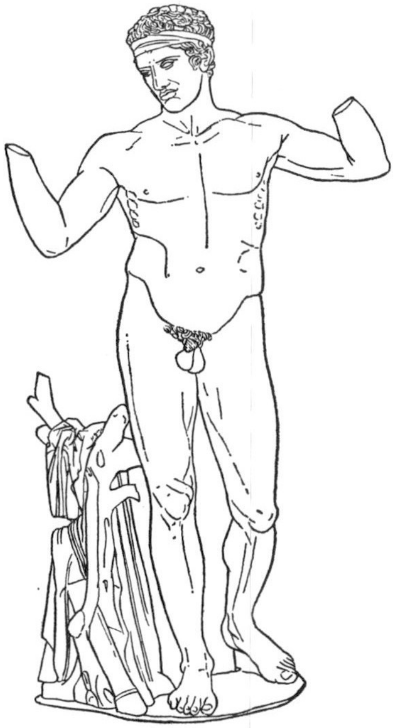

FIG. 47 – *Young man putting on victor's garland (Diadoumenos). Copy of the Polykleitan Diadoumenos. Circa 100 B.C. Height 1.86 m. National Museum, Athens. Cf. p. 172.*

The gilded bronzes show that this was a Roman fashion known to the poet. It was not only the poet but also the inventor of this fashion who remembered the description of Alkinoos' palace in Homer's *Odyssey:* 'Golden boys stood on well-built bases, holding blazing torches in their hands, making the nights in the halls bright for the banqueters'. The Romans enjoyed the allusion to Greek literature.

FIG. 48 A marble statue known in several replicas can be dated soon after 50 B.C. because one replica is signed by Stephanos, who was a pupil of Pasiteles. Two of the examples are combined with figures in a similar style to make groups; one has been called Orestes and Elektra and the other Orestes and Pylades. Even when viewed in three-quarter, which was the popular modern viewpoint for all these classicising figures, the figure has little merit. It has a softness which jars with the early fifth-century stance, and the head with its insipid smile has no placed on a naked athlete's body. For us it is an unsatisfactory combination of old elements.

Stephanos, who himself had a pupil called Menelaos, known from his signature on another classicising group, is interesting chiefly because his master Pasiteles was presumably an artist in the same genre. Another pupil, Kolotes, came from Herakleia and worked at Olympia in the neo-Attic tradition. Three of his recorded works were made of ivory, and the tradition that he worked with Pheidias on the Olympian Zeus and on the Athena in Elis may mean that he restored these statues.

Pasiteles Pasiteles himself is one of the few artists of the first century B.C. who is known from literary sources. He was a contemporary of Pompey the Great, was born in a Greek city of South Italy and given Roman citizenship in 89 B.C.; he was therefore not born after 110 B.C. He wrote five volumes about notable works of art in the world (in another passage Pliny calls them 'wonderful works'). The works were presumably masterpieces of classical art. Pliny has a short passage which gives a chronology of artists: it starts with Pheidias and runs through to the pupils of Lysippos and Praxiteles, whom he dates 296–3 B.C.; 'art then stopped and revived again in the 156th Olympiad (156–3 B.C.) with Polykles and Timokles etc.' Pliny's source was only interested in classical and neo-classical art and neatly excluded violent and realistic Pergamene art. This might well be drawn from the 'notable

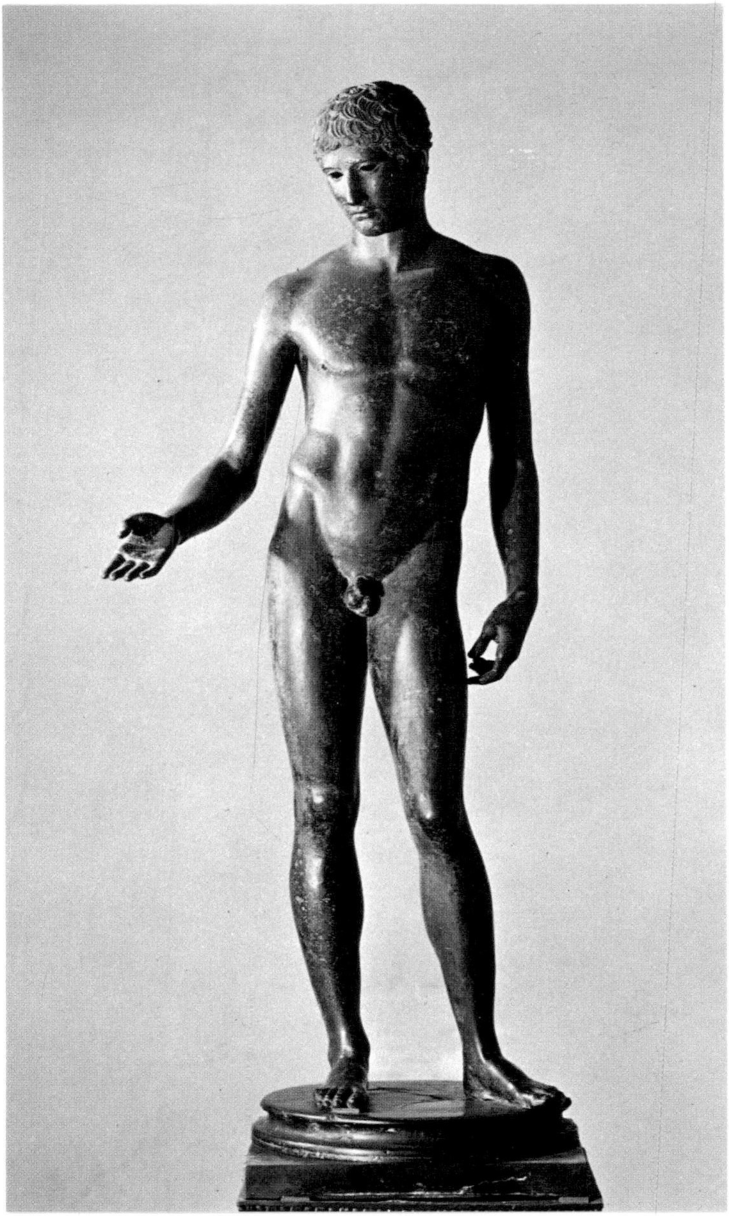

PLATE 50 – Idolino. Life-sized bronze figure of a boy. *Height 1.57 m. Museo Archaeologico, Florence. Cf. p. 173.*

works' of Pasiteles. Polykles in this list was the sculptor who made the marble statue of Jupiter for the temple of Metellus (see p. 164); Pasiteles made an ivory Jupiter for the same temple. Unfortunately we have no idea how these two statues were related; in view of Kolotes' work in Olympia it is tempting to think that Pasiteles copied the Olympian Zeus in the same material.

Pasiteles and Kolotes both worked in ivory; Stephanos worked in marble. Pasiteles also worked in silver. He himself said that 'modelling was the mother of engraving, statuary and sculpture', and Pliny adds, presumably also from Pasiteles' own writings, that though he was supreme in all these arts he never made anything before he had made a model for it. The last sentence has reasonably been taken to mean that he perhaps invented and certainly used the mechanical pointing process; that he was in fact a typical academic artist of the first century, mechanical copyist when this was possible, free copyist and adapter when it was not. The three arts by which he translated his models into new works were fine metalwork, bronze statuary and marble sculpture.

Arkesilaos

Another sculptor of the same date and approximately the same range was Arkesilaos. He was a friend of L. Lucullus and made the Venus Genetrix for the temple built by Julius Caesar in Rome; this was almost certainly a copy of a well-known fifth-century statue, which in style accords with the Nike balustrade in Athens (see p. 169) – the style of the maenads copied in neo-Attic reliefs. The material of the Venus is not stated. His marble works – Centaurs carrying Nymphs and Cupids playing with a lioness – perhaps reliefs rather than free-standing groups, must have been inspired by Hellenistic rather than classical originals; this is no more surprising than the use of Hellenistic originals by the artist of the Mahdia kraters.

This kind of Hellenistic art is sometimes called Rococo, but it is better to avoid the misleading associations of the modern term. Tiny Erotes (or as the Romans called them Cupids) are amusing when they do the things that strong men can do. An Eros drives a chariot with two

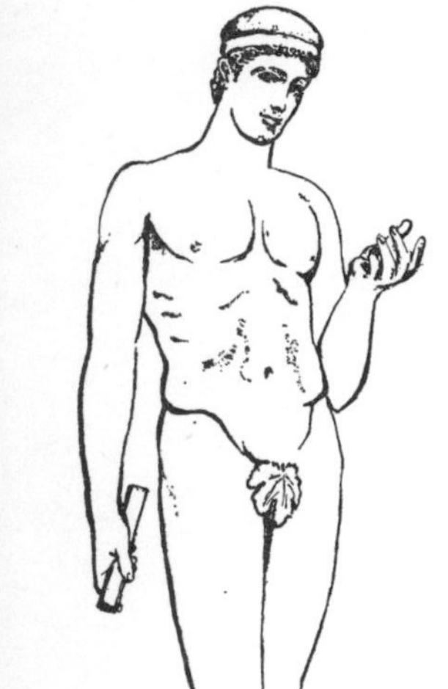

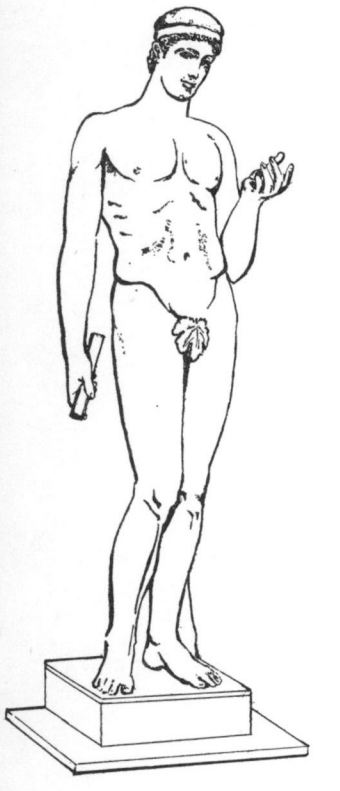

FIG. 48 – *Young athlete. Marble statue signed by Stephanos. 50 B.C. Villa Albani, Rome. Cf. p. 174.*

panthers as horses on a Gnathia krater (see p. 28). Erotes hunt deer on a Hadra vase and on a later Alexandrian mosaic (see p. 115). Cupids put up the inscription on the shield on the Capitoline frieze. FIG. 45 Similarly monsters are amusing when they do the sort of things that weak human beings do. The love-life of the monstrous Kyklops is sympathetically treated in Theokritos' Polyphemos and Galateia, which dates from about 270 B.C. The two centaurs harnessed to a chariot PLATE P. 3 driven by a tiny winged Victory on a Gnathia vase is roughly contemporary (see p. 38). Sea-centaurs carry off Nymphs on the bowl of a marble fountain of the first century B.C.; this might even be the work of Arkesilaos himself and certainly exhibits the same late stage of the same Hellenistic tradition.

Art trade

Two further notes show something of the art trade at this time. Arkesilaos' models were sold to artists at higher prices than those fetched by the finished works of other artists. The artists presumably were craftsmen, who made mechanical copies for the trade. Arkesilaos also made a plaster model for Octavius, a Roman knight who wanted to make a krater. Here one naturally thinks of the neo-Attic kraters (see p. 168); FIG. 46 we are not told whether Octavius reproduced the model in bronze or marble, but it is interesting to find a well-to-do-Roman, like Verres to whom we shall return, engaging in the art trade.

Evidence from the Augustan period shows something of this intermingling of the arts. The plasters found at Begram in Afghanistan have already been quoted for the range of models from which they are derived (see p. 36); equally interesting is the range of objects which have been adduced to illustrate them; these include free sculpture, marble relief, and paintings, as well as bronze reliefs, which are much nearer in scale to the plasters. The late fifth-century sculptor Kallimachos made Laconian dancers, girls in short tunics with basket head-dresses; they were probably on a bronze relief. The neo-Attic artists copied them in marble, but they are also found on Arretine ware – the very pretty clay bowls produced in the Augustan period with stamps, which were made in moulds taken from silver or bronze vessels. For the Laconian dancers a metal vessel must be assumed as a stage between the Augustan clay bowls and the neo-Attic reproductions in marble.

The major artists like Pasiteles and Arkesilaos were undoubtedly superb craftsmen in many media, and they had the taste and knowledge to choose the right originals to copy or adapt to suit the requirements of the particular customer. They also had more opportunities than the minor craftsmen. Pasiteles made a statue for the powerful Metelli, who in the middle of the second century had built the portico and filled it with classical works and had dedicated the temples of Jupiter and Juno with their neo-classical cult statues; Arkesilaos was a friend of Lucullus, who brought an early classical Apollo by Kalamis to Rome. These artists must have seen many originals and have been able to get casts from them with which to work.

FIG. 49 – *Propylaia erected by Appius Claudius Pulcher at Eleusis. 48 B.C. Cf. p. 180.*

PLATE 51 – Round temple at Tivoli. 1st quarter of 1st century B.C. *Cf. p. 180.*

Late Hellenistic architecture

Three examples will show the same classicistic strain in Late Hellenistic architecture. The round temple at Tivoli is a charming building in a PLATE P. 179 charming setting. The use of materials dates it in the early first century B.C., but the individual elements of decoration would be equally compatible with a date a hundred years earlier (see p. 65). The pro- FIG. 19 portions of the columns agree with those in the Olympieion at Athens, and the Corinthian capitals are in the same tradition, except that here the central flower is twisted into the horizontal, the volutes are more deeply cut and more plastic, and the akanthos-leaves are softer and more fleshy. The frieze of ox-heads and heavy garlands recalls the frieze of ox-skulls and garlands on the altar of the Council House at FIG. 16 Priene (see p. 86).

FIG. 49 In 54 B.C. Appius Claudius Pulcher vowed during his consulship to erect a new Propylaia for the precinct of Demeter at Eleusis, and this inspired Cicero to think of giving a gateway to the Academy. The Propylaia at Eleusis was completed after Appius Claudius Pulcher's death in 48 B.C. Much is modern and interesting, but the inspiration seems to come from the fifth-century Erechtheion. There one porch had Ionic columns and frieze, and another had Karyatids. Here the gateway is set back within side-walls: the outside porch has Corinthian columns, and the inside porch has Karyatids. They are in a rather florid late fifth-century style and carry elaborately decorated cylindrical boxes on their heads, the sacred boxes of Demeter. The Corinthian capitals on the outside are more elaborate than those at Tivoli. Winged griffins take the place of the corner volutes; the akanthos-leaves are surmounted by mixed floral ornament, tendrils, grapes, lilies and roses. Here in Eleusis the artist surely meant the griffins to be symbols of the resurrection and the mixed florals to belong to the land of bliss. The frieze on this side is also relevant to Demeter: the roses and ox-skulls in the metopes are traditional, but instead of triglyphs the sculptor has put wheat-sheaves and cylindrical boxes, which are peculiar to Demeter. Whether Appius Claudius commanded the details we do not know, but whoever was responsible had thought out what was relevant to this particular monument. He would fairly be termed neo-classical rather than classicistic.

FIG. 50 The attractive Tower of the Winds in Athens housed at once water-clock,

sun-dials and wind-indicator. It was built about the middle of the first century B.C. by Andronikos from Kyrrha in Syria. The octagonal tower had on its roof a bronze Triton which swung round with the wind and held a rod above the side of the tower on which the wind blowing at the moment was sculpted. The main reminiscence here was the Pharos or lighthouse at Alexandria, which is known from descriptions and representations. Originally this was an octagonal tower with a fire burning on the top, but before the time of Andronikos it had been given Tritons at the corners and a male figure holding a torch on the top. The reliefs of the winds on Andronikos' monument are not particularly competent. Their flight is somewhat unconvincing, but the painter of the Esquiline Odyssey pictures had an easier problem as he PLATE P. 138
could insert his winds in stormy clouds (see p. 140). Here the youthful West Wind holds a himation full of flowers, and the bearded North Wind lifts a shell trumpet to his mouth. The folds at the edges of the garment have a slightly archaistic look as befits the date.

Portraiture

The only link between the sculptors mentioned so far and portraiture is a very significant one. Dionysios, who worked with his brother on the cult statues for the temples of Metellus (see p. 164), signed a partially preserved statue of a Roman, C. Ofellius Ferus, in Delos; his partner here was his nephew, so that the statue may have been made late in FIG. 51
the second century B.C. On the whole Hellenistic portraiture had used certain well-defined types – variations of standing draped male and female figures and seated male figures – and when, as in the Early FIG. 5
Hellenistic period, portraiture was realistic, the realism extended to APPX. PLATES 3, 5
the clothing as well as to the face and hair (see p. 44). There was also FIG. 11
a clear distinction between ordinary men and women, however distin- PLATE P. 111
guished, and the Hellenistic kings and queens, who were often shown with the bodies of gods or goddesses but with portrait heads. Their faces were sufficiently idealised to avoid any violent clash with their bodies: Queen Arsinoe is not unfit to be an Artemis, and King Demetrios of Syria can pose as a youthful Herakles. Indeed in the eyes of their subjects they had a real affinity with these gods and heroes, and they

FIG. 50 – *Tower of the Winds. 40 B.C. Cf. above.*

would at least have a cult after their death, as their ancestors already had.

Roman generals, when they conquered Hellenistic kings, felt themselves their equals; Flamininus defeated Philip V of Macedon, and was hailed by the Greeks as the equal of Herakles and Apollo. We do not know in what guise he appeared in his bronze statue in Rome, but it had a Greek inscription. Lucius Scipio Asiagenus had a statue on the Capitol which gave him Greek chlamys and sandals. These are both works of the early second century, and may well have followed the tradition of the Hellenistic kings.

But for an ordinary Roman like C. Ofellius Ferus to appear as a
FIG. 51 neo-classical Hermes seems strange to us. The head is not preserved,
APPX. PL. 21 but another contemporary statue in Delos has a realistic, bald and most unheroic Roman head on a nude body, which is also probably a copy of a Hermes. A particular honour paid by Greeks in Delos to a Roman or the re-use of an existing body may account for these two, but the same practice is also found in Italy. A statue from Tivoli of
APPX. PL. 11 the early first century B.C. combines an elderly Roman head with a body which recalls the Poseidon of Melos. Here in Italy, a few miles from Rome, a successful Roman commander (the corselet beside him may be his own, but it is perhaps more likely that it symbolised a defeated enemy) is represented as a Greek god. The neo-classical style of the naked body and drapery contrasts oddly with the homely, lined, ordinary face. The face recalls the bronze 'Arringatore' in Florence, but there the face and the clothes correspond; the 'Arringatore' is
APPX. PL. 5 realistic in the sense that the Demosthenes of Polyeuktos is realistic, an unidealised portrait of a public figure in his normal dress. The 'Arringatore' was in fact a Roman, Aulus Metellus, whose portrait was made by an extremely competent Etruscan bronze-worker working in the Hellenistic tradition. The bronze 'Brutus' is not unlike in style, but probably represents a philosopher; it has been rightly compared with the portraits of Cicero and Poseidonios. These three were busts and not whole statues, but the busts in every case show that the statue would have been draped if it had been completed. The Tivoli statue is therefore an exception.

Probably, therefore, a special explanation is justified for the Tivoli

FIG. 51 – *C. Ofellius Ferus by Dionysios and Timarchides. Partially preserved marble portrait statue from Delos. 100 B.C. Delos Museum. Cf. p. 181.*

statue and the two portraits from Delos. The erectors wanted to pay some special honour to these men, and the sculptors could provide bodies of Greek gods on request. For ordinary men and women the sculptors had clothed or partly clothed bodies at their disposal, which they could directly copy or adapt. Where the feminine types had been used in classical or earlier Hellenistic times for goddesses, no one would raise the question whether this Roman lady was being equated with a goddess because Greek goddesses (with the exception of Aphrodite) were dressed like ordinary women. It is true that the daughter of Balbus, who dedicated the theatre at Herculaneum in the first century B.C., has the body of a late fourth-century Persephone, but the late-fourth century Persephone was herself clothed like contemporary Tanagra statuettes (see p. 62), which represented ordinary women.

Polybios

If the Tivoli commander had been given a chiton, he would not have looked very unlike the neo-classical portrait in relief of Polybios, the Greek statesman and historian, which was made after his return to Greece from Rome in 150 B.C. Again the pose and the low sweep of the himation across the legs recall the Poseidon of Melos, but Polybios is not posing as a god; his chiton, shield, helmet and spear show him as a military commander addressing his people. Pausanias notes four such reliefs set up in honour of Polybios: one of them, in Megalopolis, had an epigram which said that Polybios wandered over land and sea, became an ally of the Romans, and stopped their anger against the Greeks. These reliefs, which were over life-size, were a very remarkable tribute to a man who had deserved well of his country; he is represented not as a god or hero but as he appeared when in office, like the Roman 'Arringatore'.

Roman funerary portraits

Polybios was himself impressed by Roman funeral customs: 'They put a portrait of the dead in the most conspicuous place of the house, surrounding it with a wooden shrine. The portrait is a mask, which in modelling and outline has been finished to make a remarkable likeness'. He then goes on to say that at funerals the masks of ancestors are worn. Pliny looks back with regret to the same custom, which had vanished

in his day: 'Faces modelled in wax were displayed in cupboards' (these are the 'wooden shrines' in Polybios' account) 'so that they could be the likenesses used in family funerals.' What is known of the back history of portraiture in Italy suggests that it followed the same lines as Greek portraiture, as in fact Italian art was always strongly influenced by Greek art, and realism is unlikely before the third century B.C. But Polybios clearly found a remarkable realism in these masks, and his description has suggested that these wax portraits were actual death-masks. If this is so, the practice of moulding death-masks on the face will not have begun earlier than the beginning of the third century, when Lysistratos, the brother of Lysippos, started taking casts from the human face. This was presumably part of the realistic movement which produced the portraits of Demosthenes and Chrysippos (see
APPX. PLATES 3, 5 p. 43). It may well be that this style became popular in Rome and that it continued to be used for funerary portraits, which were unaffected either by neo-classical grandeur or by classicism. Comparatively little is known of Greek funerary monuments in the Hellenistic period; many of the surviving reliefs are attractive pictures of children in a more or less pastoral setting; the grown-ups often follow the scheme of well-known statues and their heads are seldom portraits in the true
APPX. PL. 21 sense. But the few portrait statues and heads which survive from Delos (see p. 182) and date from the late second and early first century
APPX. PL. 11 have the same realism as Roman heads like that of the Tivoli commander. Greek portraiture seems therefore to have become more realistic again in the late second century, and the Romans welcomed this tendency with open arms. To this revived realism we owe the numerous statues and reliefs of elderly and ugly Romans which have survived. The artists' signatures when preserved are Greek, and the whole class was probably made by immigrant Greek artists. Whether they took casts from living faces or from the newly dead we cannot tell, but as the practice was known it seems likely that in some cases they did.
FIG. 52 *Roman grave-relief* A grave-relief in Rome will serve to illustrate Roman funerary sculpture, although the heads have not the full complement of warts and wrinkles expected, and a reaction against excessive realism had already set in. The four busts presumably represent son, mother, father and daughter. The hair-styles are those of the first century B.C., but the

FIG. 52 – *Funerary relief with four busts set in concave circular frames surrounded by laurel-wreaths and floral ornaments. Late 1st century B.C. to 1st century A.D. Rome. Cf. below.*

relief may have been made in the early first century A.D. The faces are strongly individualised and the subjects would easily be recognised. The heads are set in concave circular frames surrounded by laurel-wreaths. These circular frames are midway between convex shields and concave mussel-shells, which appear on later reliefs. We have seen on p. 167 a good traditional Greek use for the portrait in the shield, where the bust of Roma appears on a shield between two trophies. Pliny, discussing portraits in shields, says that others will be inspired with courage by seeing the portrait of the user rendered on his shield. This is a pretty idea, but certainly in our relief the mother and daughter did not use shields, and the circular framework had long before become a decorative convention.

Floral ornament

But it is interesting that Pliny, looking back at the portraits on shields exhibited on the Basilica Aemilia, could so interpret them. This prompts the question whether the floral ornament, which fills in the spaces on our relief, is purely decorative, or whether to some observers at any rate it would carry the furthei meaning that the dead are enjoying the superior vegetation of the other world.

This mixed floral ornament is a late member of the long series which goes back into the fourth century B.C. but not much further. Its ancestors seems to be stylised floral ornaments such as palmettes and lotuses, which suggest that a symbolical interpretation is permissible. We have noticed mixed floral ornament associated with funerary vases

FIG. 2 and monuments in the Early Hellenistic age (see p. 24), where the reference must be to the Elysian fields. The personification of healthful PLATE P. 22 Breezes, Aura, is sometimes surrounded by mixed flowers; she is the Breeze that brings the souls of the dead to the Elysian fields, but when she appears carrying a formal flower on a marriage-vase, she is a Breeze bringing health and fecundity to the young wife. She is entirely in place among her flowers on a frieze in the precinct of Asklepios at Pergamon, because Asklepios is the god of healing and Breezes are healthy. She is in place also on the frieze of the temple of the deified Julius in Rome because here she alludes to the bliss of life FIG. 49 on Olympos. The floral capitals of the Propylaia at Eleusis (see p. 180) allude to Demeter as the goddess of all vegetation and as the guarantor of immortality. Finally the superb mixed floral ornament is in place on the Ara Pacis because Virgil tells us that in an era of peace the earth without cultivation will blossom with ivy, valerian, lilies, akanthos and vines. Perhaps we cannot in any particular case be sure of the artist's intention or of the intention of the man who gave him his commission, but we can be sure, particularly when we have ancient texts to support us, that some ancient spectators would give the same interpretation as we do.

Library portraits Pliny has a special short section on portraits of authors in libraries. He dates them from the time of Asinius Pollio, who opened the first public library in Rome in 39 B.C. and included many other works of art as well as portraits of writers. In fact, of course, in spite of Pliny's doubts the kings of Pergamon had already put statues of poets in their library (see p. 102), and the Sarapieion at Memphis is good evidence of Alexandrian practice. The library of the Pisones at Herculaneum had many bronze and marble busts, including those of Philetairos of Pergamon, Ptolemy III of Egypt (the patron of the great scholar Eratosthenes), Seleukos I, Sappho, Solon, Pythagoras, Demosthenes, Aristotle, Zeno the first Stoic, Epikouros and Hermarchos. Most, if not all, of these probably date from the refurbishing of the villa in the first century A.D., but they are interesting as showing the range of portraits expected in a library. This is a special branch of commemorative portraiture, to which we owe large numbers of surviving heads and busts, which were often copied from substantive statues.

PLATE 52 – Silver cup with flowers and tendrils. 1st century B.C. *Height 8.9 cm. British Museum. Cf. p. 189.*

In Alexandria and Pergamon we have supposed (see p. 36) that the reason for having statues of present and past writers in the library or lecture-room was to emphasise the continuity of Greek tradition, and Kallimachos' poem in which Hipponax rises from the grave to warn the scholar-poets to make up their feuds, suggests this interpretation. Pliny attributes the portraits in libraries to the readers' desire to know what their authors looked like. Cicero gives the same reason for the Syracusans' dislike of losing the portraits of their kings which Verres had removed (see p. 163). This is a Roman rather than a Greek feeling, a feeling natural to people who kept the portraits of their ancestors in their houses and were fascinated with the details of their physiognomy.

Book-illustration

The same desire for portraits of the great men of the past led to the invention of book-illustration. Pliny tells us that Varro inserted seven hundred portraits in his work *Imagines*. This was a work about famous men in the past, who were grouped in Sevens. We have no evidence for any book-illustration before this, and it may well be that the Roman desire to see what the great men of the past looked like suggested the idea of converting the library busts into illustrations. The next stage was probably to embellish poetic texts with portraits of the author; book-illustration in the normal sense came later. It has been plausibly argued that both Theokritos' Bucolic poems and Virgil's *Aeneid* were issued with a prefatory portrait in the first century A.D. The portrait at the beginning of the illustrated Terence manuscripts may go back to an original earlier than the archetype of the manuscripts, which seems to be datable in the third century A.D.

No illustration of a scene in a book is as early as Varro. An illustration of a comic slave has been recognised in a papyrus of the first to second century A.D., but may be illusory. The first certain illustration on papyrus is dated about A.D. 250, not necessarily earlier than the comic scenes in the archetype of the Terence manuscripts. In any case it looks as if a portrait of the author was the earliest form of book-illustration and that illustration of scenes in the book came later. Varro was a contemporary and admirer of Pasiteles, who with his world-wide knowledge of sculpture could easily have told him where to find the portraits of famous men for his *Imagines* and could have supplied him with artists to copy them.

Silver cups

One obvious source was silver cups. We have noticed the two silver cups from Bernay-Berthouville with pictures of four Early Hellenistic writers (see p. 36). They have been dated in the first century A.D., but they derive from early third-century originals, whether the originals were also silver cups or not. Pasiteles was famous as a silversmith. Nothing can be ascribed to him, but two very fine silver cups in the

FIG. 4

British Museum, which were certainly made in his lifetime, show the kind of work that he produced.

The first cup, which is one of a pair, has lost both its handles and its foot but the body with its ornament is perfectly preserved. Both sides are decorated with extraordinarily beautiful mixed floral ornament; birds and insects are shown among the vegetation. On one side an akanthos comes up from the bottom with a stalk of bearded wheat over to the right; two main stems grow out of the akanthos-sheath; the left stem bears a pear-spray high up on the left and a fig-spray below it on the right; the right stem bears a pomegranate high up on the left and a pine-spray below it on the right. The flowers at the end of the stems include periwinkle *(vinca)* and the large flower of Euphorbia type which appeared already on the Pella mosaic (see p. 24) and on the Aura Vase. The other side of the cup adds myrtle, hazel, vine, convolvulus, apple and oak. The cup has been dated with a high degree of probability in the early first century B.C. It is a late and magnificent example of the mixed floral decoration which we have traced all through our period. This late example differs chiefly in the reduction of purely formal elements (only the scrolls which hold the whole design together survive) and in the greater realism of the plants represented, which makes them considerably easier to identify: the birds and animals also help them to come alive. PLATE P. 187 PLATES PP. 22, 65

Probably we should not demand any meaning for this enchanting decoration; but if a romantic drinker wanted to give it a meaning, no one could object if he saw an allusion to the garden of the Hesperides or the cave of the Nymphs where the young Dionysos grew up. Or of course he might think of the flowers and sprays as the raw material for a garland of mixed flowers and fruits such as he might be wearing on his head while he drank. And then he might remember that Meleager had recently (about 70 B.C.) published his anthology of short poems, which he called the Garland because he equated the poets with the flowers and fruits which could be woven into a drinker's garland. Of the flowers and fruits on the cup only fig, hazel, oak and convolvulus are not identified with poets by Meleager. PLATE P. 78

The second cup, which has also lost its handles and foot, has its mixed floral ornament confined to the bottom of the bowl: it is subsidiary

PLATE 53 – Silver kantharos with scenes from an Iphigeneia tragedy. 1st century B.C. *Height 9.8 cm. British Museum. Cf. p. 189.*

to the main scene, as the floral ornament of Gnosis' mosaic is subordinate to the deer hunt (see p. 24). The owner of this cup must have been as interested in literature as the purchasers of 'Homeric bowls' (see p. 104). The story represented is known from Hyginus and the Roman tragedian Pacuvius, who wrote in the first half of the second century B.C. Orestes, Iphigeneia and Pylades, escaping from Tauris with the image of Artemis, take refuge in the precinct of Apollo on the island of Sminthe. Thoas, the king of the Taurians, pursues them to Sminthe and demands their surrender from Chryses, the ruler of the island. He was proposing

PLATE 54 – Silver kantharos with scenes from an Iphigeneia tragedy. 1st century B.C. *Height 9.8 cm. British Museum. Cf. p. 189.*

to surrender the fugitives, but his mother, Chryseis, tells him that he is not, as she has hitherto said, the son of Apollo but the son of Agamemnon, so that Orestes is his half-brother. The two half-brothers then plot to murder Thoas and take the image of Artemis back to Mykenai. The Greek original, which Pacuvius translated, was obviously designed as a sequel to Euripides' *Iphigeneia in Tauris;* but the poet was not an Athenian, as the statue is to be taken to Mykenai instead of to Brauron in Attica.

The cup has on the left the country precinct of Apollo of Sminthe. PLATE P. 190

The omphalos shows that it belongs to Apollo. Apollo's statue stands on a high base in front of the tree with a bird on its right hand. The statue is archaic, to show that the story happened long ago, or simply because it was traditional to put archaic statues in rustic precincts (see p. 69). The seated veiled woman is Iphigeneia and she has an archaic multi-breasted image of Artemis on her knees. The artist alludes to the Artemis of Ephesos; he cannot mean that this is the Artemis of Ephesos; he may have argued (or found in the text of the tragedy) that the Amazons in South Russia worshipped the same sort of Artemis as the Amazons in Ephesos. The two young men are Orestes and Pylades. It is difficult to determine which is which (and they were like enough in Pacuvius' play for Pylades to claim to be Orestes in order to save his friend). In Pacuvius' play someone prays that the gods may 'remove thy madness', so that Orestes was evidently still seeing the Furies of his mother. The seated youth has his hand to his mouth, PLATE P. 39 the gesture of one seeing a vision – like the tragic poet at Pompeii (see p. 37). Perhaps then he is Orestes, and Pylades is the energetic young man, who is ready to face the situation but has the sense to PLATE P. 191 keep one hand on Apollo's sacred tree. To the right Chryseis rushes up to tell Chryses the truth, just as he is parleying with Thoas, whose servant stands behind him.

The date of the cup is probably the same as the date of the floral cup, the first half of the first century B.C. This is given by the floral ornament and by the crowded elaboration of the rustic shrine. The whole composition may be the creation of the artist, but at this date it is more likely to be a copy of an earlier composition adapted to the scale and space available. The similarity of Pylades and Chryses to the Poseidon of Melos (see p. 149) and to the Polybios portrait suggests an origin in Pacuvius' lifetime. The Chryseis recalls the women on the PLATE P. 27 large Apulian vases like the Medeia vase (see p. 26); but this may not mean more than that the tragic heroine wore voluminous clothing, and these were naturally recorded in every medium, even when, as here, there was no reference to a stage performance. Thoas' barbarian retainer is surely unthinkable before the Pergamene Gauls (see p. 94). The most that can be said is that the scene gives the impression of a unitary composition; it is not eclectic like the second pair of Mahdia kraters, but unitary like the first pair of Mahdia kraters (see p. 168). The original, in whatever medium it was executed, may have been made in the early second century. If this is so, it is perhaps more likely that it was based on Pacuvius' Greek original rather than on Pacuvius' own Latin tragedy.

Theatres and scenery

FIG. 53

The Chryses cup is based on tragedy but makes no reference to scenery, background, costumes or masks. But we have an illustration of a tragedy as produced in a Roman theatre about 50 B.C. on a clay relief, which comes from the tomb of P. Numitorius Hilarus in Rome. The relief was set at the bottom of a little shrine consisting of a niche framed by two columns and a pediment. On each side of the shrine were two recesses in the walls for funeral urns. A great deal of colour was preserved on the relief. The main figures are a woman who holds a child by the hand and a man who comes with bad news. Both the main figures have thick red soles to their shoes (see p. 128) and therefore show that this fashion has now spread to Rome. Both wear yellow sleeves, long chitons and large himatia. The child, who is dressed in yellow, wears a Phrygian cap. The attractive interpretation that this was a scene in the *Astyanax* of Accius when Odysseus demands Astyanax from Andromache must unfortunately be rejected, as the man seems to be bringing bad news, which would not fit Odysseus. On these grounds Talthybios announcing that the Greeks have decided to kill Astyanax in Accius' *Troades* would be a better suggestion, but it is wiser not to guess. The two smaller figures on the left, of whom one is male and the other female, are probably only attendants. As this is a Roman funeral monument, the play is likely to be a Latin tragedy, and if this is accepted the relief shows that there was no distinction between Greek and Roman tragic costume.

The background is elaborate. The doors are painted blue. The outer columns are Corinthian; the inner are Ionic. Above the Corinthian columns are yellow tripods, the traditional prize in Greek athletic and choral contests. The side doors have arches, which are surmounted by herms. The columns between the doors have steep Roman pediments with red palmettes as akroteria. Over the central door is a sculptural group, a Nereid holding Achilles' helmet and riding a sea-monster, as on the marble fountain quoted in connexion with Arkesilaos (see

FIG. 53 – *Scene from a tragedy. Terracotta relief from the tomb of P. Numitorius Hilarus. Terme Museum, Rome. Cf. p. 193.*

p. 177). The cornice at the top, which in the theatre would belong to a higher storey, has yellow ox-skulls and red palmettes. The background clearly has no particular connection with tragedy, and a contemporary terracotta relief shows a scene from comedy played before a similarly rich architectural background. There the three doors each have Corinthian columns on either side; a frieze with a thick sculpted garland runs along the top. Over it a pediment, decorated with a shield and palmette akroteria, surmounts each door; between the pediments are urns. It could equally well be used for tragedy as for comedy. The dramatic poets and producers now no longer have even the modest variations permitted by Hellenistic tragic, satyric and comic sets. All plays are performed before a rich architectural background. This change can be fairly accurately dated. Rome did not have a permanent theatre until the middle of the first century, but this did not prevent the building of elaborate backgrounds and stages. It is probable that the Romans never adopted the Greek high stage. Throughout the early period the audiences stood as near the stage as they could. Polybios' rather difficult account of the performances at Anicius' triumph in 167 B.C. seems to imply easy communication between the ground level and the stage, and therefore is evidence for a low stage in Rome at a date when all Greek theatres had a high stage.

Polybios mentions a very large *skene* or background for this performance. It is just the time when the Alexandrian landscape-painter Demetrios (see p. 133) was in Rome, and when Greek theatres were being rebuilt with *thyromata*. Background with illusionistic paintings of architecture are therefore likely to have been used in Rome at this time, and they are attested for the performances at the games of Appius Claudius Pulcher in 99 B.C. A painter called Serapion, also at the beginning of the first century, 'was a most successful scene-painter but could not paint a human being'. It was this kind of scenery which was taken over for house-decoration and survives in the cubiculum of Boscoreale. But these realistic painted backgrounds did not continue in use for very much longer. In 58 B.C. Aemilius Scaurus built a three-storeyed background with marble columns in the bottom storey, glass columns in the middle storey, and columns of gilded wood in the top storey. There were 3000 bronze statues between the columns, and all the paintings from Sikyon, which had been sold to Rome to meet a debt, were exhibited. Some exaggeration may have crept into Pliny's account, but evidently this was a very elaborate architectural background for a temporary theatre; the terracotta relief reproduces on a small scale its essential elements.

FIG. 37

PLATE P. 137

FIG. 53

Pompey's theatre

A very attractive suggestion has been made that Scaurus' three-storey background was a kind of full-size model for the background of the new theatre which Pompey built as the first permanent theatre in Rome and dedicated with great magnificence to Venus Victrix in 55 B.C. Cicero remarks on the first theatre performances: 'Why 600 mules in the *Clytemnestra?* and why 3000 kraters in the *Trojan Horse?*' Tragedy seems, therefore, to be changing into a pageant. The ancient map of Rome preserves the ground-plan of Pompey's theatre and shows quite clearly the wide Roman stage, backed by a façade with columns on either side of the doors and with great columned niches at either end beyond the doors. This façade had its columns set close together like the terracotta relief, and left no space available for prospects like the Boscoreale scenery. It was richly decorated with statuary.

The main scheme is the plan advocated by Vitruvius in his description of the Roman theatre with columned façade, wide and low stage, and semicircular orchestra; presumably, as he advises, the roof of the colonnade round the top row of seats was level with the top of the stage background, so that auditorium and stage-building were connect-

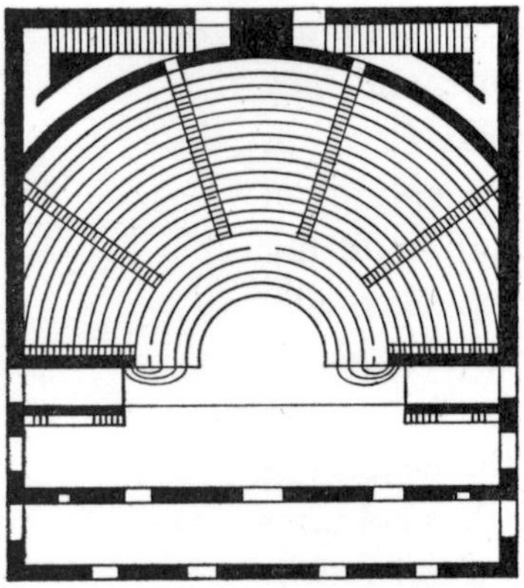

FIG. 54 – *Ground-plan of the small theatre at Pompeii. 70 B.C. Cf. p. 197.*

ed into a whole; in this type of theatre the front wall of the stage-building was bent at right angles across the side entrances (which had been spanned by a simple gateway in the theatre at Epidauros; see p. 51) and then at right angles again to form the side walls of the auditorium. Thus the sharp break between auditorium and stage-building was avoided, and the arrangement had the further advantage of roofing over the side passages.

PLATE P. 56

The theatre of Pompey had two other startling divergences from Greek practice. It was not built with the auditorium backed on a hillside but was a free-standing building with porticoes round the back to support the rising tiers of seats. Secondly, the seats enclosed a broad flight of steps leading up to the temple of Venus, which was level with the colonnade round the top row of seats.

Spectacles in Rome, including dramatic performances, were usually given on religious festival days, and were often held in front of the temple of a god or goddess; they were so arranged that the god could see them from his temple and the populace from the steps leading up to the temple. Pompey had rationalised this arrangement by including the temple in the building plan. When he proclaimed its dedication, says Tertullian, he did not name it a theatre but 'the temple of Venus under which we have placed steps for spectacles'. There is no reason to doubt Pompey's sincerity: Sulla had worshipped Venus Felix, and Caesar would soon dedicate a temple to Venus Genetrix. But architecturally the uniting of stage-building and auditorium into a single complex is a more important step.

The small theatre at Pompeii had a semicircular auditorium placed within an oblong building which was roofed. It only held about 1500 spectators and was built between 80 and 75 B.C. But there is no reason to suppose that Pompey knew it. Plutarch says that in 62 B.C. Pompey visited Mytilene and was a spectator at the traditional contest of poets: 'He was pleased with the theatre and had a copy made of its plan and elevation, because he wanted to make a similar one in Rome but larger and more imposing' Mytilene had a normal Greek theatre, but that could not have taught Pompey anything, and it is perhaps unlikely that poets (as distinct from actors) would perform in the large theatre. For this reason the suggestion that they performed in a smaller building (and a Council House is known from an inscription), and that this smaller building gave Pompey the idea for his theatre, has much to commend it. The Council House at Priene (see p. 86) had its seats rising in straight lines, but the Council House at Miletos had semicircular seating within a rectangular building; such buildings were the ancestors of the small theatre at Pompeii. Mytilene may have had a similar building, in which the poets performed for Pompey. What Pompey did essentially was to enlarge it to take 10,000 instead of 1500 spectators and to round off the external corners. A great portico ran out behind the stage-building and enclosed a rectangular court laid out as a garden. In the portico were works of art including paintings by Polygnotos, Pausias, Apelles and Antiphilos. The whole layout was a great single plan with the theatre making an apsidal end to the porticoes and garden.

FIG. 54

FIG. 16

One gets the impression that the whole of Rome was by now an art gallery, and that the artists had so many works of the past round them that they could not help being classicistic. Far away from Rome, and further away from Greece and Asia Minor, stands the monument of the Julii at St Rémy. Its date is probably subsequent to the later limit of our period, although there is some uncertainty as to whether the inscription may not have been added after the monument was complete. Its records the erection of the building by three sons in honour of their parents.

Monument of the Julii at St Rémy

FIG. 55

The tradition of such memorials can be traced back to such princely monuments as the Mausoleion of Halikarnassos in the mid-fourth century. At St Rémy the statues of the dead man and his wife stand in an open round shrine with Corinthian columns supporting a frieze of mixed floral ornament; the Corinthian capitals too have other floral elements among their akanthos-leaves. Here one may see the vegetation of the blessed fields in which the dead now exist. The next storey again has Corinthian columns at the corners and arches which are characterised as Roman by their marked keystones. The frieze above them is decorated with Tritons and with griffins ending in snaky tails. Again these monsters may symbolise the voyage of the soul across the sea to the islands of the blessed.

The base has four large reliefs: on the north-east, a cavalry battle; on the south-east, a battle which is apparently rightly interpreted as a battle of Greeks and Amazons; on the south-west a boar hunt; and on the north-west a battle between Romans and Gauls. The last two scenes belong to the life or at any rate the lifetime of the dead man; it looks rather as if the other two may have been presented as mythological parallels to them. If this is so, the sculptor is thinking in the Greek tradition; he remembers directly or through intermediaries the victory monuments which the Attalids set up over the Gauls (see p. 115). The battles are exciting compositions; the twisted foreshortened horses recall the monument of Aemilius Paulus (see p. 143); the figures at the back are incised drawings on the background; contorted figures of dead and dying fill the foreground. This is the violent style of the Pergamene Gigantomachy still alive and fruitful.

Hanging over the four battles are great, heavy garlands; their little Cupids have suspended each of them from their pegs, and on each four masks are resting. The garlands are in the tradition of the heavy mixed garland on the Pergamene base in Athens (see p. 141), and the masks on three sides show the same alternation of Papposeilenos and

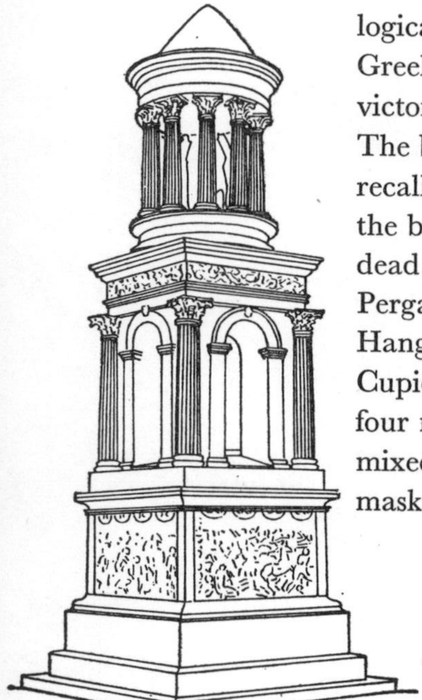

FIG. 55 – *Monument of the Julii at St Rémy, erected by Marcus Julius, Sextus and Lucius in honour of their deceased parents. Height 18m. Cf. p. 197f.*

wild-haired Satyr; but the arrangement is quite different. There the masks are on the peg which supports the garland; here they rest on the garlands themselves. The fourth side has comic masks of a girl, an old man, a slave and a young man. The garlands are thicker and the Cupids fatter and gayer than those on the Capitoline frieze (see p. 167). Again a symbolic interpretation is possible. This symposion decoration may allude to the banquets which the dead man hopes to share in the after-life, and some such interpretation must have been made of the later sarkophagi which are decorated with similar arrangements of Cupids, garlands and masks.

PLATE P. 148

FIG. 45

The symbolic interpretation can only be put forward as a possibility. We do not know the beliefs of the dead man or of his sons. Nor do we know how much the sculptor felt the symbolic meaning of what he carved. He was certainly a good artist, working in a Hellenistic tradition which was alive in his hands, so that he could adapt it to contemporary subjects. The family, whether the father was a first-generation Roman citizen or not, were certainly well-to-do and may very well have seen the relevance of the detail. But in this last phase of Hellenistic art, when Greek artists, whether they had local apprentices or not, were working for Romans or Romanised non-Greeks, we can never be certain how far to go in interpreting the decoration of any particular monument. A great official monument such as the Ara Pacis was undoubtedly planned with the greatest care, and the decoration is likely to have had a meaning; but it would be bold to suppose that all the neo-Attic maenads, wherever they occur, suggested to their owners the eternal bliss of the worshippers of Dionysos or Bacchus. We must remain content with the knowledge that some people would have felt the allusion, while others would only have admired the beauty of their poses and drapery.

Two well-known Romans may form a conclusion to this survey: one a collector and art-dealer, in whom we shall expect the commercial motive to be as strong as the aesthetic, and the other an educated man who collected in a small way and tells us what he thinks.

Verres

Verres was a Roman of noble family, who had an official position in Asia in 80–79 B.C. and in Sicily in 73–70 B.C., and used his position to plunder the provincials of their art treasures. He thought nothing of robbing the temple of Hera at Samos or of removing the paintings from the temple of Athena at Syracuse. The artists whose works he removed from temples and private collections included the fifth-century sculptors Myron and Polykleitos, the fourth-century sculptors Praxiteles and Silanion; a portrait of Stesichoros as a twisted old man holding a book was almost certainly Hellenistic. The range is what would be expected of a connoisseur at this time: it goes back to the early classical sculptor Myron but not, so far as we know, any further. He also shared the contemporary interest in vessels of precious metal. He found a hydria by Boethos, which was an heirloom; this was

FIG. 15 presumably the Boethos who made a group of a child strangling a goose, since Pliny says that this Boethos' real fame was as a silver-worker (see p. 76). Verres also acquired cups by Mentor, who was one of the most famous silversmiths and lived in the fifth or early fourth century. In all these operations in Sicily he used as his assistants two Asiatic Greeks, one a modeller in wax and the other a painter; they were expert both in discovering valuable works and in gaining possession of them.

They presumably also helped him in the workshop which he set up in the palace at Syracuse. Here he collected a large number of gold reliefs from dishes and incense-burners stolen from the Sicilians. He secured the services of a large number of engravers and vase-makers, who worked for eight months incorporating the gold reliefs in cups and drinking-vessels so skilfully that they seemed to belong there. In fact Verres set up an antique-factory in Syracuse.

Verres may not have been so completely unprincipled as Cicero made out. He is good evidence for the range of taste in first-century Rome and for the state of the market. He collected for himself, and he undoubtedly used works of art as bribes and payments, but he was clearly also a dealer on a considerable scale.

Cicero

Cicero, from whom our information about Verres comes, is himself an interesting figure. A provincial, who came to Rome as a boy and later spent two years in Athens and Rhodes studying rhetoric and philosophy, he is best known as an orator and politician. His numerous books were outstandingly successful in opening Greek philosophy and rhetorical theory to the Romans. He was also a very accomplished translator of Greek poetry. In the speeches against Verres he shows that he knows enough art history to be able to understand and point out the enormities of Verres. In the *Brutus* he sketches a history of development in art as a parallel to the history of literary development in Rome: the statues of Kanachos are rather stiff, Kalamis is softer, Myron has not yet reached verisimilitude, but Polykleitos' works are almost perfect. In painting Zeuxis, Polygnotos and Timanthes are at a less perfect stage of development than Protogenes and Apelles. He may, of course, have derived this from an art historian rather than from observation; he probably did so, but he claims to have seen in Rhodes the Ialysos by Protogenes, and in any case this recital is an indication of what the educated man is expected to know. It is interesting that his range of sculptors starts with Kanachos, who was working in the late sixth century, and reaches its peak with Polykleitos in the second half of the fifth century: it is very much the range copied by the more academic of the neo-Attic artists.

The setting of the *Brutus* is his own garden, under the statue of Plato. The discussion is presided over by the great Greek philosopher; similarly his friend Atticus has a seat under a statue of Aristotle. The Greek tradition is transferred to Rome. Cicero, in writing to Atticus in Greece, where works of art can be bought, is most concerned that he should have statues suitable for a gymnasium or palaestra, not because he wants to take exercise but because the gymnasium or wrestling school in Greece also had lecture-rooms and libraries. He is very pleased with the idea of marble herms with bronze heads, which naturally recall to us the bronze herm copying the Polykleitan Doryphoros in the Villa of Piso at Herculaneum. He is very pleased with a herm which carries the head of Athena, as the goddess of learning, and with herms of Herakles; presumably he is thinking rather of Herakles' choice of the steep path which led to virtue instead of the downhill road which led to vice – the allegory of Prodikos which he quotes in *De Officiis*. On the other hand he has no use for statues of maenads, however 'pretty' they may be; their associations are unsuitable for a library.

Conclusion

Here then is an educated Roman, who chooses his works of art entirely for the associations aroused by their subject matter. This means that the kind of interpretation given above for the St Rémy memorial is probably justifiable; it means also that for a great national work like the Ara Pacis both the patron and the artist can count on an intelligent public which will catch the allusions. Late Hellenistic art is certainly civilised art in the sense that it makes this appeal for interpretation by civilised people, who know the history of art and can understand an allusion to Greek literature. Technically the artists are highly accomplished. But maenads should not be 'pretty'; 'softly-breathing' (Virgil) may be a suitable epithet for neo-Attic work, but no one would think of applying it to an archaic kouros or to the Elgin marbles or to the Pergamene Gigantomachy. No great thoughts are being expressed now, no new aesthetic or technical problems are being solved: instead we have an academic art of great efficiency, refinement and charm.

APPENDIX OF PLATES

1 – Tyche of Antioch. Marble statue. Copy of original from circa 300 B.C. *Height 89 cm. Vatican Museum. Cf. pp. 19, 32, 62, 76, 96, 108.*

2 – 'Themis'. Marble statue from Rhamnous. 300 B.C. *Height 2.22 m. Athens, National Museum 231. Cf. p. 64.*

3 – Chrysippos. Marble statue. Copy of original from circa 210 B.C. *Paris, Louvre 80. Cf. pp. 44, 146, 181, 184.*

4 – Side panel of a chest from Amphipolis. Terracotta. 3rd century B.C. *Height 18 cm. Kavalla Museum. Cf. pp. 60, 131.*

5 – Demosthenes by Polyeuktos. Marble statue. Copy of original from circa 280 B.C. *Height 2.07 m. Vatican, Braccio Nuovo 62. Cf. pp. 44, 181, 182, 184.*

6 – Apotheosis of Homer. Marble relief from Bovillae. 150–125 B.C. *Height 1.17 m. British Museum 2191. Cf. pp. 35, 55, 59, 108, 128.*

7 – Zeus and Porphyrion. Marble relief from altar of Zeus, Pergamon. 200–175 B.C. *Height 2.30 m. Berlin, Pergamon Museum. Cf. p. 119.*

8 – Alkyoneus, Athena, Nike and Ge. Marble relief from altar of Zeus, Pergamon. 200–175 B.C. *Height 2.30 m. Berlin, Pergamon Museum. Cf. p. 119.*

9 – Fragment of robe from the marble group by Damophon at Lykosoura. 180–160 B.C. *Athens, National Museum. Cf. pp. 144, 145, 167.*

10 – Tragedy. Marble statue from Pergamon. 200 B.C. *Height 1.80 m. Berlin, Pergamon Museum. Cf. pp. 55, 128.*

11 – Portrait of a Roman. Marble statue from Tivoli. 100–75 B.C. *Height 1.93 m. Rome, Terme Museum 106513. Cf. pp. 182, 184.*

12 – Dionysos and Thiasos. Marble krater from Mahdia. *Height of statues 60 cm. Bardo, Musée National C 1204. Cf. p. 169.*

13 – Dancer. Bronze statuette. 220–200 B.C. Alexandria (?). *Height 20.7 cm. New York, Baker Collection. Cf. pp. 76, 96.*

14–16 – Theseus, Aigeus, Medeia. Marble reliefs from the Agora. *Height 1.09 m. Athens, Agora Museum S 7327. Cf. pp. 164, 166.*

17 – Maenad. Marble relief from Pergamon. 150–130 B.C. *Height 1.45 m. Istanbul, Archaeological Museum 575. Cf. p. 126.*

18–20 – Artemis, Demeter, Anytos. Marble heads from Lykosoura. 180–160 B.C. *Athens, National Museum 1734–6. Cf. pp. 144, 146.*

21 – Portrait of a Roman. Marble statue from Delos. 100 B.C. *Height 2.25 m. Athens, National Museum 1828. Cf. pp. 182, 184.*

22 – Theatre at Akrai. 250 B.C. *Cf. p. 51.*

23 – Fragment of a Centuripe vase. 3rd century B.C. *Syracuse, Museo Nazionale. Cf. pp. 31, 32, 38.*

24 – Olympieion at Athens. 170 B.C. *Cf. p. 90.*

25 – Temple of Fortune at Praeneste – Palestrina. Early 1st century B.C.

26 – 'Alexander Sarkophagos.' After 330 B.C. *Istanbul, Archaeological Museum. Cf. p. 38.*

1

2

3

4

5

7

8

9

10

11

12

1

14

15

16

17

18

1

20

22

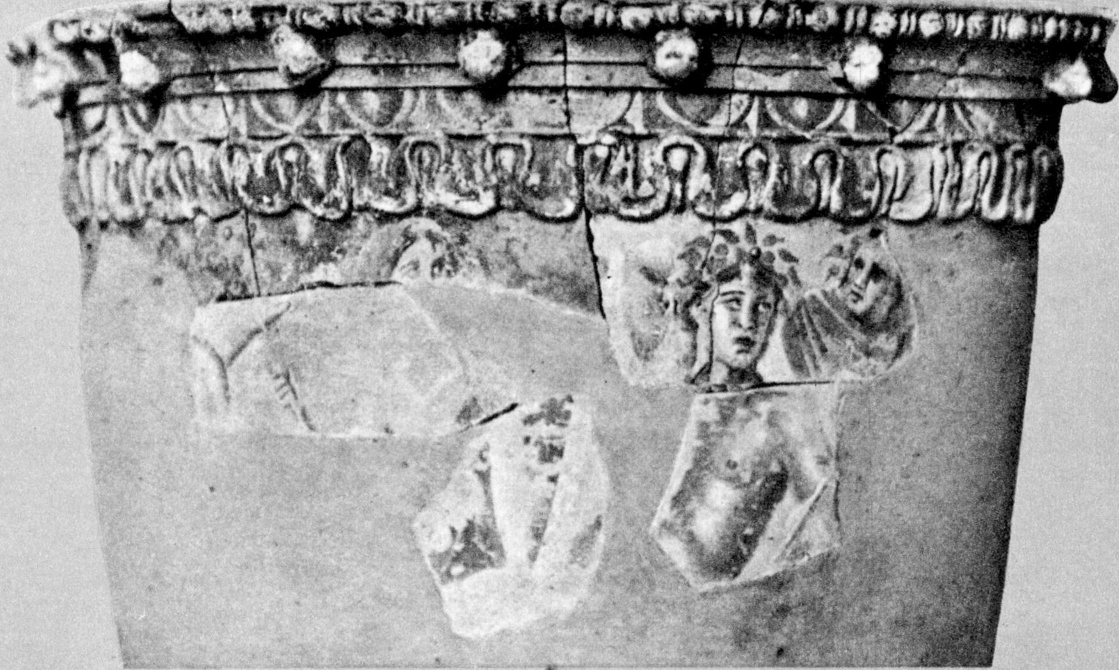

23

24

2

APPENDIX

CHRONOLOGICAL TABLE

B.C.	GREECE AND THE ISLANDS	EGYPT
350	Sculptors: Lysippos, Bryaxis, Leochares, sons of Praxiteles	
	Painters: Pausias, Nikias, Apelles	
	Plastic vase: Dionysos in Cave of Nymphs	
325		
	323 Death of Alexander	(323)–283 Ptolemy I
	322 Death of Aristotle	
	Pella mosaics	
	Dherveni krater	Protogenes, Apelles, Antiphilos painting
	Early Tanagra statuettes	
300		Portrait of tragic actor
	292 Death of Menander	
		285–246 Ptolemy II
	283–239 Antigonos II	
	280 Statue of Demosthenes	
	Themis of Rhamnous	Apollonios Rhodios, Theokritos, Kallimachos,
	Tanagra statuettes	Philikos, Lykophron writing
	Kantharos of Menokles	Portraits of Philikos, Lykophron
	Muses in Ambracia	
	Epidauros theatre	Sarapieion
	Thasos Choregic monument	Ptolemy's symposion tent
	Originals of Boscoreale fresco	Fayence oinochoai
		Delos: bronze relief
	Comic masks from Amphipolis	
	Original of Vatican Ariadne	
	Menedemos of Eretria	
	Aratos of Soli writing	
275		
	272 Death of Pyrrhos	
	251–213 Aratos of Sikyon	
250	Tragic actor as Herakles (terracotta)	Hadra hydriai
		246–221 Ptolemy III
225		
	221–179 Philip V of Macedon	221–203 Ptolemy IV
		Homereion
		Homeric bowls
		203–181 Ptolemy V
	Portrait of Chrysippos	Bronze dancer
	Vergina tomb	

CHRONOLOGICAL TABLE

ASIA MINOR	SICILY AND ITALY	B.C.
	Apulian, Paestan, Campanian, Gnathia vases	350
(323)–280 Seleukos I of Syria		325
Alexander sarkophagos		
Tyche of Antioch	Ficoroni Cista	300
280–262 Antiochos I of Syria Herondas writing Sons of Praxiteles in Kos Asklepieion in Kos Boy with goose (Boethos)	Later Gnathia vases	
	275 Defeat of Pyrrhos at Beneventum 272 Roman capture of Tarentum 265 Hiero II of Syracuse	275
	Centuripe vases	250
241–197 Attalos I of Pergamon		
	240 Livius Andronicus in Rome Akrai theatre	
		225
	212 Marcellus captures Syracuse 209 Roman capture of Tarentum	
Portrait of Antiochos III Victory monument over Gauls Relief from Tralles Drunken old woman (Myron) Menelaos and Patroklos Artemis and Iphigeneia Originals of Dioskourides mosaics Temple of Artemis at Magnesia Ekklesiasterion at Priene	Plautus writing Ennius writing	

CHRONOLOGICAL TABLE

B.C.	GREECE AND THE ISLANDS	EGYPT
200		
	197 Flamininus defeats Philip V	
		181 Ptolemy VI
175		
	174 Temple of Zeus Olympios, Athens	
	168 Aemilius Paulus defeats Perseus of Macedon	
	167 Aemilius Paulus' monument at Delphi	
	Aigeira Zeus	
	Lykosoura Group	
150		
	Athens, Stoa of Attalos	
	Portrait of Karneades	
	Oropos theatre	
	146 Mummius sacks Corinth	
	Achaea, portrait of Polybios	Apotheosis of Homer (relief)
	Melos, Aphrodite and Poseidon	
	Delos, House of the Masks	
125		
	Athens theatre, round base with masks	
	Agora, archaistic reliefs	
	Delos portraits	
	Delos, Diadoumenos	
	Thessaly, necklace with masks	
100		
	Neo-Attic reliefs from Mahdia wreck	
	86 Sulla sacks Athens	Mosaic with Erotes hunting

CHRONOLOGICAL TABLE

ASIA MINOR	SICILY AND ITALY	B.C.
		200
197–160 Eumenes II of Pergamon		
	194 Triumph of Flamininus	
	187 Triumph of Fulvius Nobilior	
Nike of Samothrace	Temple of Herculus Musarum	
Pergamon library, altar, theatre	Apollo of Falerii	
Laokoon		
Dove mosaic		
Telephos picture		
Bronze satyr (Casa del Fauno)		
175 Antiochos IV Epiphanes of Syria		
		175
	168 Pacuvius, Terence writing	
	167 Polybios in Rome. Triumph of Anicius	
	164 Demetrios topographos in Rome	
162 Demetrios I of Syria		
160–139 Attalos II of Pergamon		
Hellenistic prince (bronze)	Originals of Boscoreale cubiculum	
		150
Myrina terracottas	Originals of Esquiline landscapes	
	Head from Largo Argentino	
	Syracuse, Muses	
	146 Portico of Metellus	
139–133 Attalos III of Pergamon		
133 Rome inherits Pergamon		
129 Organisation of Roman province of Asia		
Myrina terracottas	Dionysios and Polykles in Rome	
Amisos terracotta, tragic actor as Herakles		
Pergamon, maenad relief		
		125
		100
	99 Games of Appius Claudius Pulcher	
	89 Pasiteles becomes a Roman citizen	
88 Mithradates overruns Asia Minor		
	78 Basilica Aemilia	
	Victory frieze from Capitol	
	Round temple at Tivoli; Pompeii, small theatre	
	Portrait of Roman general	
	'Arringatore'	
	'Brutus'	

CHRONOLOGICAL TABLE

B.C.	GREECE AND THE ISLANDS	EGYPT
75		
50		
	48 Propylaia at Eleusis	
	Tower of the Winds	
25		

CHRONOLOGICAL TABLE

ASIA MINOR	SICILY AND ITALY	B.C.
		75
70 Rhodes, archaistic relief	73–70 Verres in Sicily	
	67 Coins of Pomponius Musa	
	58 Games of Aemilius Scaurus	
	55 Pompey's theatre. Death of Lucretius	
	British Museum, silver cups	
	'Idolino'	
	Numitorius relief (terracotta)	
	Stephanos youth	
	Dionysos and Comic Poet (Vatican)	
	Casa del Fauno	
	Villa dei Misteri	
		50
	48 Temple of Venus Genetrix (Arkesilaos)	
	44 Death of Julius Caesar	
	39 Varro, *Imagines*	
	Monument of Julii, St Rémy, France	
	Busts of Cicero and Pompey	
	Esquiline frescoes	
	Boscoreale frescoes	
		25
	13–9 Ara Pacis	
	Arretine ware	
	Relief with portrait busts	

GLOSSARY

Akroterion
Sculptured decoration above the three corners of a pediment.

Chiton
Long or short garment of fine wool or linen worn by men and women.

Choregos
The rich man entrusted by a Greek city-state with the production of a choral or dramatic performance.

Encaustic
A technique of painting in which the colour was applied with heated wax.

Exedra
A recess, usually curved, containing seats, often large enough to be used as a lecture-room.

Herm
A square shaft surmounted by a head and equipped with genitals. In the classical period the head was a head of Hermes, and herms were placed at gateways and doorways. From the fourth century other heads were often substituted for that of Hermes.

Hetaira
Prostitute.

Himation
Woollen garment, usually heavy, worn over chiton by men and women.

Hydria
Water-jar with a vertical back handle for pouring and two horizontal side handles for lifting.

Iambos
A shortish poem written in iambic metre.

Kerameikos
The quarter at Athens where the potters worked and which contained a large burial-ground.

Krater
A wide-mouthed vessel for mixing wine and water.

Lagynos
A jug with an approximately hemispherical body, a long, narrow, straight neck, and a back handle; used for carrying wine and pouring it into cups.

Mimiambos
A shortish poem written in iambic metre, dramatic in form.

Oinochoe
Wine-jug, often with trefoil mouth and with single back handle; used for carrying wine and pouring it into cups.

Orchestra
The circular dancing-floor of the Greek theatre.

Pediment
The low gable bounding the roof of the Greek temple (and occasionally of other buildings). It was surmounted by *akroteria.*

Propylaia
A gateway protected by more or less elaborate porches on either side.

Red-figure
The technique of decorating vases so that the figures were left in the colour of the clay and the background filled in with glaze which fired black. The inner markings of the figures were done in the same black glaze and details were added in white, red, yellow, gold, and occasionally in other colours.

Symposion
A drinking-party.

Tainia
A long scarf or sash worn on festal occasions and used as decoration.

Thiasos
Any religious association, particularly the association of mythical devotees of Dionysos, satyrs and maenads.

Thyrsos
A fennel-stalk with a head made of ivy-leaves, carried by Dionysos and his *thiasos.*

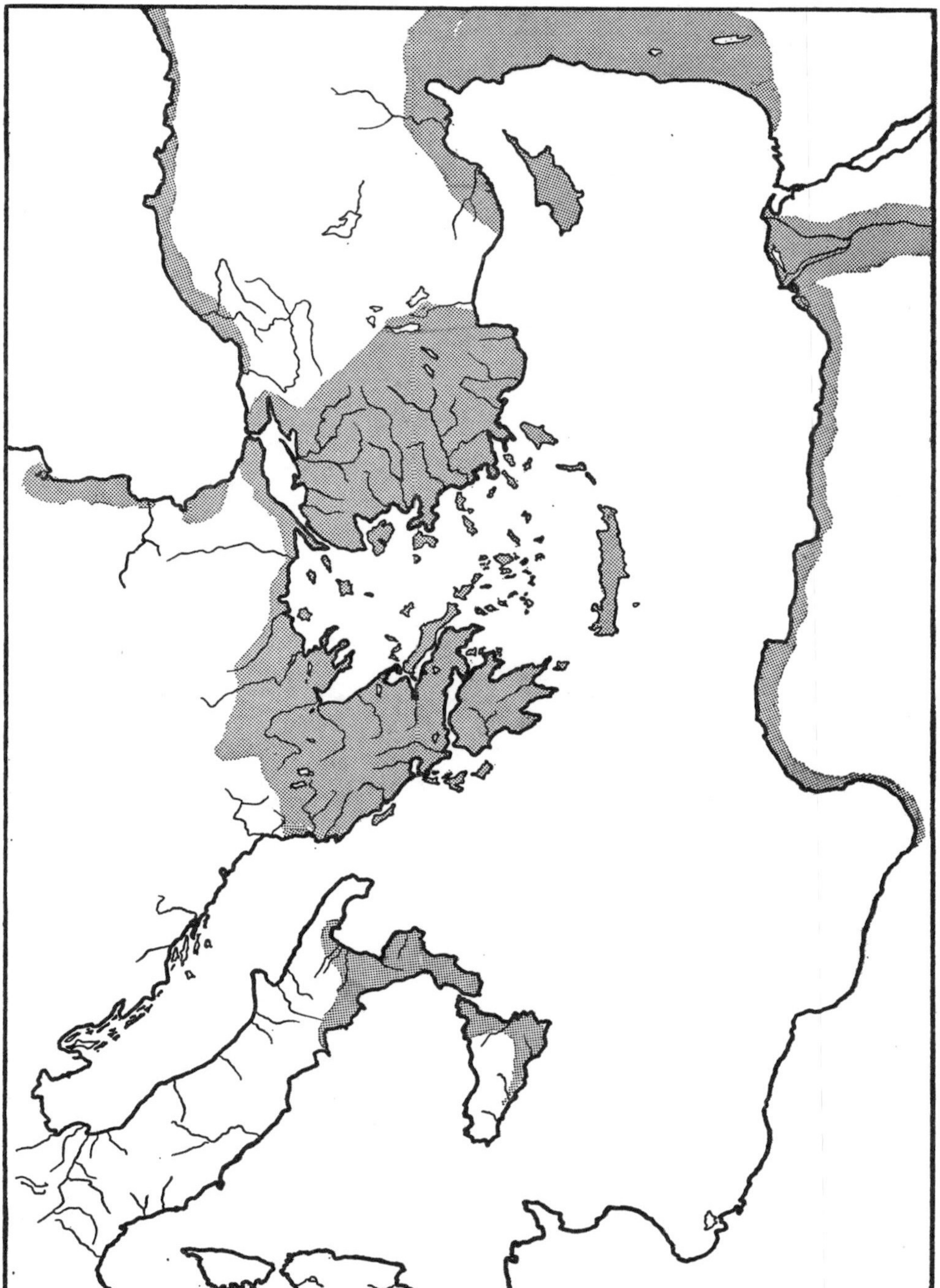

EXPANSION OF HELLENISM

GREECE AND ASIA MINOR

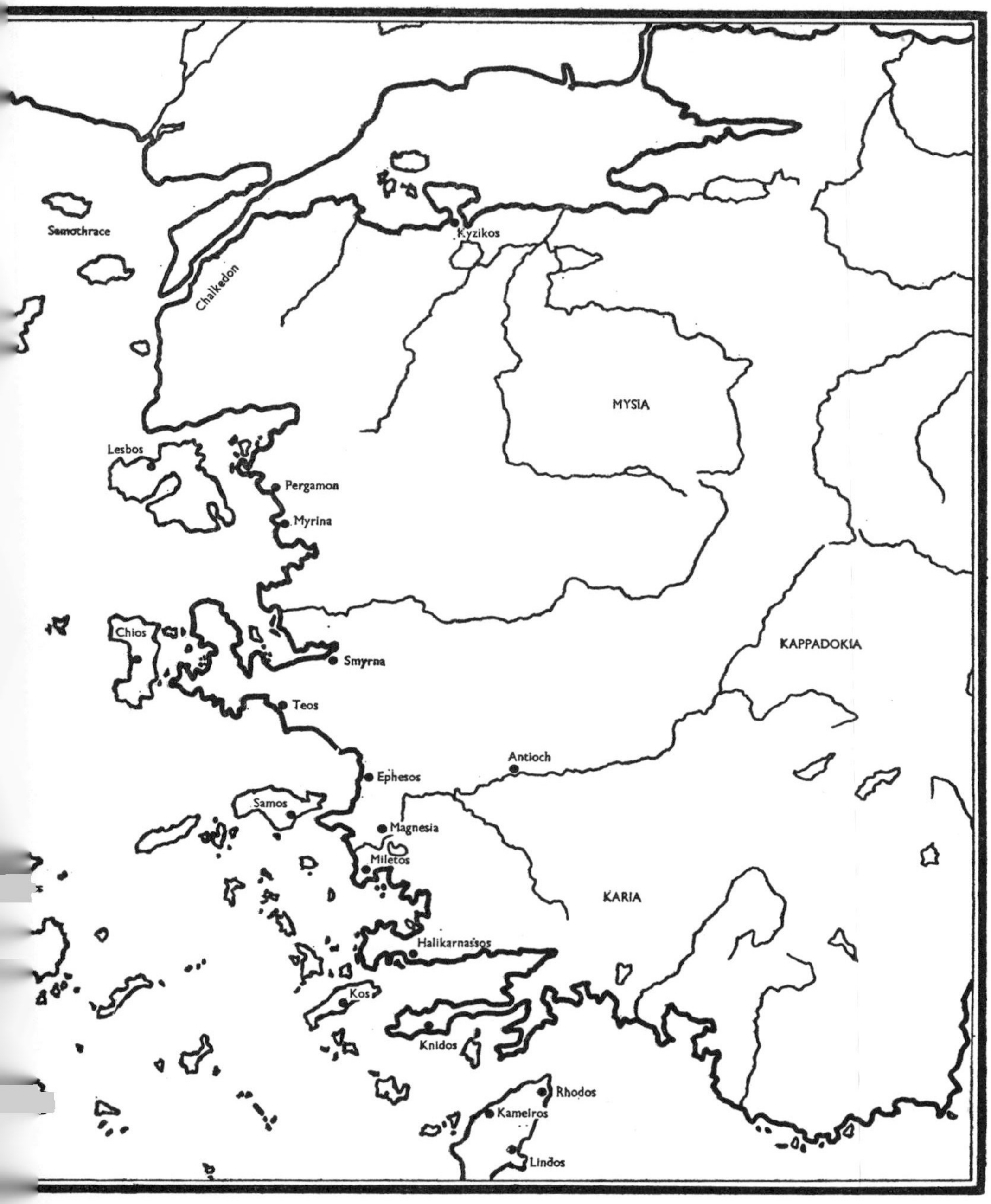
Samothrace
Chalkedon
Kyzikos
MYSIA
Lesbos
Pergamon
Myrina
Chios
Smyrna
KAPPADOKIA
Teos
Antioch
Ephesos
Samos
Magnesia
Miletos
KARIA
Halikarnassos
Kos
Knidos
Rhodos
Kameiros
Lindos

BIBLIOGRAPHY

The following abbreviations are used for journals:

AJA	American Journal of Archaeology
AM	Mitteilungen des deutschen archäologischen Instituts (Athenische Abteilung)
BCH	Bulletin de Correspondence Hellénique
BJ	Bonner Jahrbücher
BSA	Annual of the British School at Athens
JDAI	Jahrbuch des deutschen archäologischen Instituts
JHS	Journal of Hellenic Studies
JRS	Journal of Roman Studies
JWI	Journal of the Warburg and Courtauld Institutes
RM	Mitteilungen des deutschen archäologischen Instituts (Römische Abteilung)

This bibliography gives a small selection of useful general books, and then gives references for particular topics and objects discussed in the text. (I have used short titles after the first reference.)

HISTORY:

M. Rostovtzeff, Social and Economic History of the Hellenistic World, Oxford, 1941.
V. Ehrenberg, The Greek State, Oxford, 1960.

LITERATURE:

A. Lesky, History of Greek Literature, London, 1966.
T. B. L. Webster, Hellenistic Poetry and Art, London, 1964.

SCULPTURE:

G. Lippold, Die Griechische Plastik, Munich, 1950.
M. Bieber, The Sculpture of the Hellenistic Age, New York, 1961 (abbreviated *Hell. Sc.*).

PAINTING:

A. Rumpf, Malerei und Zeichnung, Munich, 1953 (abbreviated *M.u.Z.*).

ARCHITECTURE:

A. W. Lawrence, Greek Architecture, London, 1957.

See also the following recent publications:

G. M. A. Richter, The Portraits of the Greeks, London, 1965.
D. E. Strong, Greek and Roman Gold and Silver Plate, London, 1966.
L. Forti, La Ceramica di Gnathia, Naples, 1966.
B. Segall, Tradition und Neuschöpfung in der frühalexandrinischen Kleinkunst, Berlin, 1966.
B. F. Cook, 'Inscribed Hadra hydrias', Metrop. Museum Papers, 12, 1966.
D. B. Thompson, 'Origin of Tanagras', AJA, 70, 1966, 52.

INTRODUCTION

PAGE 13 HELLENISTIC KINGDOMS AND GREEK CITIES: *V. Ehrenberg*, The Greek State, part II, ch. III, 3.

PAGE 13 ETRUSCAN ART: *G. A. Mansuelli*, Etruria and Early Rome, London, 1966. (ART OF THE WORLD.)

PAGE 14 ARISTOTELIAN INFLUENCE ON HELLENISTIC ART CRITICISM: *T. B. L. Webster*, Art and Literature in Fourth-Century Athens, London, 1956, 53 f., 123 f.

PAGE 15 ART SCHOLARSHIP IN THE HELLENISTIC AGE: *K. Jex-Blake and E. Sellers*, The Elder Pliny's Chapters on the History of Art, London, 1896, xiii ff.; *E. Pernice*, Handbuch der Archäologie, II, Munich, 1938, 313 ff.

PAGE 15 KALLIMACHOS Fr. 196: *R. Pfeiffer*, JHS 61, 1941, 1. Fr. 114: *R. Pfeiffer*, JWI 15, 1952, 20.

PAGE 16 ART COLLECTIONS: *A. Rumpf*, Archäologie, I, Berlin, 1953, 12 f. Aratos: *Plutarch*, Aratos 12. Pergamon: Alterthümer von Pergamon, VIII, 46–50.

PAGE 17 TEMPLES: *Herondas*, Mimiambos IV. Mummius: *Pliny*, Nat. Hist., 35, 24. Syracuse: *Cicero*, in Verr. II, iv, 122–3.

PAGE 17 COPIES: *G. M. A. Richter*, Three Critical Periods in Greek Sculpture, Oxford, 1952, 34, 37 f. *A. Rumpf*, Archäologie, II, 81 ff. Pictures in Delphi: *S.I.G.*[3], no. 682.

I. EARLY HELLENISTIC PERIOD

PAGE 19 TYCHE OF ANTIOCH: *T. Dohrn*, Die Tyche von Antiocheia, Berlin, 1960. *Apollonios Rhodios*, 1, 549. *L. Petersen*, Zur Geschichte der Personifikation, Würzburg, 1939.

PAGE 20 DHERVENI KRATER: *Makaronas*, Archeiologikon Deltion, 18 B, 1963. On the symbolism of Dionysiac scenes in the fourth century: *H. Metzger*, Les représentations dans la céramique attique du IVe siècle, Paris, 1951, 409 ff.

PAGE 23 PELLA MOSAICS: *M. Robertson*, JHS 85 (1965); *Makaronas*, Archeiologikon Deltion, 17 B, 1961/2, 209 ff.

Mosaics and textiles: *F. von Lorentz*, RM 52, 1937, 165 ff., and with more recent references my article in the Bulletin of the John Rylands Library, 45, 1962, 263 f. Krateros' dedication: *Pliny*, Nat. Hist., 34, 64; *Plutarch*, Alexandros, 40.

PAGE 24 PAUSIAS: *Pliny*, Nat. Hist., 35, 127; 125. Nikias: *Demetrios*, de Elocutione, 76. Hellenistic epigram: *C. H. Roberts*, Journal of Juristic Papyrology, 4, 1950, 215; *T. B. L. Webster*, ibid., 5, 1951.

PAGE 24 PALACE AT VERGINA (PALATITSA): *M. Andronikos*, To anaktoro tes Verghinas, Athens, 1961. Tomb.: *A. W. Lawrence*, op. cit., 211.

PAGE 25 TOMB AT SYRACUSE (Museo Nazionale 30285): Sokrates ap. *Plato*, Respublica, 401 b. Ganymede ear-ring: *P. Jacobsthal*, Greek Pins, Oxford, 1956, 70. On the connection of immortality with this floral ornament: *K. Schauenburg*, RM 64, 1957, 148; JDAI 78, 1963, 294. Eileithyia on Apulian vases: *A. D. Trendall*, Vasi Dipinti del Vaticano, II, 1955, 104.

Euripides, Hippolytos 165. Wedding-vases: AJA 69, 1965, 64.

PAGE 26 MEDEIA VASE (Munich No. 810 J): *M. Schmidt*, Der Dareiosmaler und sein Umkreis, Münster, 1960; *L. Sechan*, Études sur la tragédie grecque, Paris, 1926, 405; *T. B. L. Webster*, Art and Literature in Fourth-Century Athens, London, 1956, 66. On connection of mythical scenes with funerals: *K. Schauenburg*, BJ, 1961, 232 f. On the Tarentine theatre: my Griechische Bühnenaltertümer, Göttingen, 1963, 53 f.; Institute of Classical Studies (London), Bulletin Supplement, no. 14, 1962, 74 f.

PAGE 28 GNATHIA and Sikyonian painting: *H. Bulle*, Eine Skenographie, Berlin, 1934. Krater: *A. H. Smith*, Corpus Vasorum Antiquorum, British Museum, 1, pl. IV Dc, 1, 17, F 550. Oenochoe: Cleveland Museum of Art, John L. Severance Collection, 52.16; Antike Kunst, 1960, 31.

PAGE 30 NIKIAS: *A. Rumpf*, M.u.Z. 143 f. Euphranor: *A. Rumpf*, M.u.Z. 131 f.

PAGE 31 CENTURIPE VASES: *A. D. Trendall*, Bull. Metr. Mus., 1955, 161 ff. Syracuse fragment and painting from Villa Farnesina: *A. Ippel*, RM 44, 1929, 45 and pl. 9.

PAGE 31 — TOMBA DELL' ORCO: *G. A. Mansuelli*, Etruria and Early Rome, London, 1966, 182. Ficoroni Cista: ibid., 148.

PAGE 32 — BOSCOREALE: *P. W. Lehmann*, Roman Wall-Paintings from Boscoreale, New York, 1953; *M. Robertson*, JRS, 45, 1955, 58 ff.; *D. B. Thompson*, Troy, Supplementary Monographs 3, Princeton, 1963, 52, n. 128.

PAGE 33 — ANTIOCHOS III: *M. Bieber*, Hell. Sc., 87.

PAGE 33 — BRYAXIS AND SARAPIS: *J. H. Jongkees*, JHS 68, 1948, 29 ff.; *J. Charbonneaux*, Monuments Piot, 52, 1962, 15; *B. Ashmole*, A Catalogue of the Ancient Marbles at Ince Blundell Hall, Oxford, 1929, nos. 38–9. Sarapieion and cult: *M. P. Nilsson*, Geschichte der griechischen Religion, II, Munich, 1950, 149; *A. Rowe*, Bulletin of the John Rylands Library, 39, 1957, 489; *Bradford Welles*, Historia, 11, 1962, 286; *V. Ehrenberg*, The Greek State, 208 (250). *Kallimachos*, Hymn IV, 228. The Homereion of Ptolemy IV: below, p. 104.

PAGE 35 — SARAPIEION AT MEMPHIS: *J. Lauer and C. Picard*, Les Statues Ptolémaïques du Sarapieion de Memphis, Paris, 1955. Demetrius of Phaleron and Egypt: *F. Wehrli*, Die Schule des Aristoteles, IV, Basle, 1949, nos. 63–71.

PAGE 35 — SARAPIEION AT ALEXANDRIA: *Kallimachos*, fr. 191. *B. Rees*, Classical Review, 75, 1961, 1.

PAGE 36 — SILVER CUPS: *K. Schefold*, Die Bildnisse der antiken Dichter, Redner, und Denker, Basle, 1943, 47, 216, 226; *C. Picard*, Monuments Piot, 44, 1950, 53 f.

PAGE 36 — BEGRAM PLASTERS: *O. Kurz* in *E. Hackin*, Nouvelles récherches à Begram, Paris, 1954, 110 ff.

PAGE 37 — PHILIKOS AND PROTOGENES: *Pliny*, Nat. Hist., 35, 106; *E. Pfuhl*, Malerei und Zeichnung der Griechen, München, 1923, 842.

PAGE 37 — TRAGIC ACTOR: *L. Curtius*, Die Wandmalerei Pompejis, Hildesheim, 1960, 276. Gorgosthenes: *Pliny*, Nat. Hist., 35, 93. Alexander mosaic and Apelles: *A. Rumpf*, AM, 77, 1962, 229.

PAGE 38 — ALEXANDER SARKOPHAGOS (Istanbul, Archaeological Museum 68): *F. Winter*, Der Alexandersarkophag von Sidon, Leipzig, 1912.

PAGE 41 — TANAGRA STATUETTES: *G. Kleiner*, JDAI, Ergänzungsheft, 15, 1942. Athenian origin of Tanagra types: *D. B. Thompson*, Hesperia, 21, 1952, 116; 23, 1954, 72; 26, 1957, 108; 28, 1959, 127; 31, 1962, 244; 32, 1963, 88.

PAGE 43 — OLD DERELICTS: *M. Bieber*, Hell. Sc., 141. The drunken old woman in Munich, ibid. 81. *Pliny*, Nat. Hist., 36, 32. *Poseidippos*, Anthologia Palatina, V, 134.

PAGE 44 — DEMOSTHENES: *K. Schefold*, Bildnisse etc., 106. On the gesture: *T. Dohrn*, JDAI, 70, 1955, 66 f.; *Aristotle*, Poetics, 1454 b 9. Aeschines: *K. Schefold*, op. cit., 102.

PAGE 44 — CHRYSIPPOS: *K. Schefold*, op. cit., 126; *M. Bieber*, Hell. Sc., 68.

PAGE 46 — THASOS: Theatre: *F. Salviat*, BCH, 84, 1960, 300. Choregic monument: *G. Daux*, BCH, 50, 1926, 234 (inscriptions); *P. Devambez*, Monuments Piot, 38, 1941, 113 (sculpture); *C. Picard*, Comptes-rendues de l'Academie des Inscriptions, 1944, 127 (interpretation of building). For another semicircular base with Dionysos and the Muses, also in the precinct of Dionysos, *F. Salviat*, BCH, 1959, 288, 302, 324.

PAGE 50 — DEVELOPMENT OF THE THEATRE: summarised in my Griechische Bühnenaltertümer, 19 f. Chorus and high stage; *G. M. Sifakis*, Bulletin of the Institute of Classical Studies (London), 10, 1963, 31 ff.

PAGE 51 — EPIDAUROS THEATRE: *A. von Gerkan and W. Müller-Wiener*, Das Theater von Epidauros, Stuttgart, 1961.

PAGE 55 — TRAGEDY AND COMEDY ON RED-FIGURED VASES: cf. my Athenian Art and Literature, 40 f. Gnathia Muse, Bowdoin College: *K. Herbert*, Ancient Art in Bowdoin College, Cambridge (Mass.), 1964, no. 228. Praxitelean base (Athens, N.M. 215–7): *G. Lippold*, Griechische Plastik, 238, pl. 85.

PAGE 57 — MUSES: *Aristophanes*, Ranae 875. Vita Sophoclis 6. Syracuse, Museo Nazionale, 695, 711, 50702. *Kallimachos*, fr. 4, 22; 43, 56. *Apollonios Rhodios* 3, 1.

PAGE 57 COINS OF POMPONIUS MUSA: *E. A. Sydenham*, Roman Republican Coinage, London, 1952, nos. 810–23. The temple: *S. B. Platner and T. Ashby*, A Topographical Dictionary of Ancient Rome, Oxford, 1929, 255; *A. Klugmann* in Comm. Phil. in hon. Th. Mommsen, Berlin, 1877, 262; *B. Tamm* in Opuscula Romana, 3, 157. Fulvius and Ennius: *O. Skutsch*, Classical Quarterly, 38, 1944, 79 ff.; 13, 1963, 89 f. Pyrrhos' ring: *Pliny*, Nat. Hist., 37, 5.

PAGE 59 AGORA TERRACOTTA (Athens, Agora Museum T 862): Hesperia, 29, 1960, 260.

PAGE 60 PLAQUE FROM AMPHIPOLIS (Kavalla Museum): BCH, 83, 1959, 711, fig. 4. Development of slave mask: JDAI, 76, 1961, 100.

PAGE 64 THEMIS OF RHAMNOUS (Athens, N.M. 231): *M. Bieber*, Hell. Sc., 65. The inscription: I.G., II/III^2, 3109.

PAGE 64 ANYTE: Anthologia Palatina XVI, 291; IX, 314.

PAGE 64 THEOKRITOS: full references and discussion in my Hellenistic Poetry and Art, 82 f., 164 f.

PAGE 65 CAVE OF THE NYMPHS: e.g. Corinthian bronze mirror, Berlin 8148, *E. Pfuhl*, Malerei und Zeichnung, fig. 625. Garden of the Hesperides, e.g. Paestan squat lekythos: Naples 2873, *A. D. Trendall*, Paestan Pottery, 1936, pl. 4.

PAGE 66 MOULDED VASE (Athens, Agora P 12822): *D. B. Thompson*, Hesperia, 23, 1954, 83.

PAGE 66 BANQUETING TENT: *F. Studniczka*, Das Symposion Ptolemaios II, Leipzig, 1914. The text of *Kallixeinos* is preserved by *Athenaeus*, v, 196 a.

PAGE 66 THEOKRITOS: Ptolemy II and Zeus, XVII, 1; tapestry of Adonis, XV, 78; Herakles, XVII, 28.

PAGE 69 MENOKLES' CUP (Athens, Agora Museum P 6898): *T. L. Shear*, Hesperia, 6, 1937, 375, fig. 39.

PAGE 70 BRONZE RELIEF IN DELOS (Delos Museum): *M. Bieber*, Hell. Sc., 153; *M. Rostovtzeff*, Social and Economic History, 796; *M. P. Nilsson*, The Dionysiac Mysteries of the Hellenistic and Roman Age, Lund, 1957, 102.

PAGE 71 FAYENCE OINOCHOE (London, British Museum, K 77): The masks: Griechische Bühnenaltertümer, 49, pl. 4. Athenian maypole: red-figure bell-krater, Copenhagen, Nat. Mus., 13817, Corpus Vasorum Antiquorum, Denmark 8, pl. 347. Altar and goat: Istanbul, *A. Adriani*, Una Coppa paesistica, Rome, 1959, 20. Add to his two examples Corpus Vasorum Antiquorum, United States 8, pl. 33, 1.

PAGE 72 TRALLES RELIEF (Istanbul 1423): *G. Lippold*, Die griechische Plastik, 343.

PAGE 72 ASKLEPIEION AT KOS: *R. Herzog*, Kos, I, Asklepieion, Berlin, 1932. HERONDAS: cf. my Hellenistic Poetry and Art, 90 ff.

PAGE 75 STATUES FROM KOS: *M. Bieber*, Hell. Sc., 20 f., figs. 32–3, 43.

PAGE 75 GIRL WITH APPLE: *N. Svoronos*, Archaiologike Ephemeris, 1917, 78 ff.; *K. Lehmann*, AJA, 49, 1945, 430. Grave-relief from Ephesos (Vienna, I, 873): *F. Winter*, Kunstgeschichte in Bildern, 371, 5.

PAGE 76 BOY WITH GOOSE (Vienna 816): *M. Bieber*, Hell. Sc., 136; *A. Rumpf*, Jahrbuch des Österreichischen Archäologischen Instituts, 39, 1952, 86 ff. *Kallimachos*, Epigram 38.

PAGE 76 BAKER DANCER: *D. B. Thompson*, AJA, 54, 1950, 371; Troy, Supplement 3, 104, n. 205.

PAGE 77 SNAKE TREASURY: *M. P. Nilsson*, Geschichte der griechischen Religion, II, 1955, 73, pl. 1, 2.

PAGE 77 PICTURE OF SACRIFICE: *S. Eitrem*, Archaiologike Ephemeris, 1953/4, I, 25 ff.; Corpus Vasorum Antiquorum, Norway I, 1965, pl. 4.

PAGE 77 HADRA HYDRIA (New York, Metropolitan Museum, 90.9.60): *B. R. Brown*, Ptolemaic Paintings and Mosaics, New York, 1957, 62 f., no. 45. Antiphilos: *Pliny*, Nat. Hist., 35, 138. *Apollonios Rhodios*, 3, 755; 4, 167.

PAGE 79 APELLES AND HERONDAS: *S. Luria*, Miscellanea di Studi Alessandrini, Turin, 1963, 394 ff. Apelles' Slander: cf. my Art and Literature in Fourth-Century Athens, 137.

II. MIDDLE HELLENISTIC PERIOD

PAGE 85 LEOCHARES: *M. Bieber*, Hell. Sc., 62 f.

PAGE 85 PRIENE: *M. Schede*, Ruinen von Priene, Berlin, 1934. *G. Kleiner*, Paulys Realencyclopädie, s.v. Priene.

PAGE 85 LINDOS: *E. Dyggve*, Lindos III, Copenhagen, 1960. Kameiros, Clara Rhodos, 6–7, 1932, 222 ff. Priene: see note on p. 85.

PAGE 87 HERMOGENES: *Vitruvius* III, ii, 6; iii, 8–9; IV, iii, 1. Temple at Magnesia: *C. Humann*, Magnesia am Maeander, Berlin, 1904. Sculpture: *M. Bieber*, Hell. Sc., 164. Reconstruction: *M. Rostovtzeff*, Social and Economic History, 820.

PAGE 88 AMAZONS: *Kallimachos*, Hymn III, 237 ff.

PAGE 90 TEMPLE OF OLYMPIAN ZEUS AT ATHENS: *Vitruvius*, VII, praef. 15. Inscription: I.G. III, 561. The artists: *O. Rubensohn*, JDAI, 50, 1935, 55 ff.

PAGE 92 PERGAMON: *E. W. Hansen*, The Attalids of Pergamon, Ithaca, 1947. Attalos I monument for victory over the Gauls: *A. Schober*, RM, 51, 1936, 104; *M. Bieber*, Hell. Sc., 107 f.

PAGE 93 ACROPOLIS DEDICATION: *Pausanias*, I, 25, 2; *Plutarch*, Vita Antoni, 60.

PAGE 96 MENELAOS AND PATROKLOS: *M. Bieber*, Hell. Sc., 78. Achilles and Penthesilea: ibid., 79.

PAGE 96 ARTEMIS AND IPHIGENEIA (Copenhagen, Ny Carlsberg 1048–9): *M. Bieber*, Hell. Sc., 77; *F. Studniczka*, Abhandlungen Sächsischer Akademie, 37, 1926. Myrina terracotta: Louvre, MYR 163.

PAGE 97 LAOKOON (Vatican 74): *M. Bieber*, Hell. Sc., 135; *F. Magi*, Atti della Pontificia Accademia, Memorie 9, 1960; *G. M. A. Richter*, Three Critical Periods in Greek Sculpture, Oxford, 1951, 66. *Pliny*, Nat. Hist., 36, 37.

PAGE 98 NIKE OF SAMOTHRACE (Paris, Louvre 2369): *M. Bieber*, Hell. Sc., 125; *K. Lehmann*, Hesperia, 21, 1952, 20; Archaeology, 6, 1953, 35. Myrina terracotta: Stanford University Museum 63.54. Replica: Boston, Fine Arts Museum 01.7706. *D. Burr*, Terracottas from Myrina in Boston, Boston, 1934, no. 70.
Mithradates, *Plutarch*, Sulla 11.

PAGE 101 MARSYAS (Rome, Conservatori etc.): *M. Bieber*, Hell. Sc., 110. Dirke (Naples, Mus. Naz. 260): ibid., 133; *Pliny*, Nat. Hist., 36, 33.

PAGE 101 MENELAOS HELMET: *B. Schweitzer*, Abhandlungen Sächsischer Akademie, 43, 1936, 17, 104.

PAGE 101 LIBRARY: *C. Callmer*, Opuscula Archaeologica, 3, 1944, 148.

PAGE 101 ATHENA PARTHENOS: *G. Lippold*, Griechische Plastik, 359. Statues of poets: Pergamon VIII, 198–203. Epigram: Anthologia Palatina, VII, 15.

PAGE 102 PORTRAIT OF HOMER (Naples etc.): *M. Bieber*, Hell. Sc., 143. Kyzikos reliefs: Anthologia Palatina, III; *A. Rumpf*, Bonner Jahrbücher, 158, 1958, 260.

PAGE 103 DOVE MOSAIC: *K. Parlasca*, JDAI, 78, 1963, 256; *Homer*, Iliad 11, 632–7.

PAGE 104 HIERO'S SHIP: *Athenaeus*, 5, 207–9. Homereion at Alexandria: *Aelian*, Varia Historia, 13, 22.

PAGE 104 HOMERIC BOWLS: *U. Hausmann*, Hellenistische Reliefbecher, Stuttgart, 1960; AM, 73, 1958, 50. Drama in Boeotia: Griechische Bühnenalterthümer, 38 f. Iphigeneia bowl: Hausmann, no. 11; cf. also no. 10. Phoinissai bowl: Hausmann, no. 2; cf. also nos. 3–4.

PAGE 108 ALEXANDRIAN POETIC COMPETITION: *Vitruvius*, VII, praef. 5.

PAGE 110 HOMER RELIEF (British Museum 2191): *M. Bieber*, Hell. Sc., 127; *A. Adriani*, Coppa Paesistica, 32; *Leiva Petersen*, Zur Geschichte der Personifikation, 63; *K. Schefold*, Bildnisse, 148.

PAGE 115 MOSAIC IN ALEXANDRIA (Alexandria Museum, Room XIX): *B. R. Brown*, Ptolemaic Paintings and Mosaics, no. 50. Hadra Hydria (Berlin 3767): *E. Pfuhl*, Malerei und Zeichnung, fig. 759.

PAGE 115 ALTAR OF ZEUS: *G. Bruns*, Der grosse Altar von Pergamon, 1949; *E. Schmidt*, The Great Altar at Pergamon, Leipzig, 1962; *H. Luschey*, 116–7 Winckelmannsprogram, Berlin, 1962; *F. Vian*, La Guerre des Géants, Paris, 1952; *M. Bieber*, Hell. Sc., 114; *G. Lippold*, Griechische Plastik, 354, 358.

PAGE 119 OTOS etc.: *Homer*, Od. 11, 305 ff. Apollo Belvedere and Artemis of Versailles: *M. Bieber*, Hell. Sc., figs. 200–1. Parthenon pediment: *P. E. Corbett*, The Sculpture of the Parthenon, London, 1959.

PAGE 120 ANCESTRY OF PERGAMENE KINGS: Nikander, fr. 104. Telephos frieze: add to the references for the Gigantomachy, *E. Simon*, JDAI, 76, 1961, 126.

PAGE 122 TELEPHOS PICTURE (Naples, Mus. Naz.): *E. Simon*, JDAI, 76, 1961, 138; *A.M.G. Little*, AJA, 68, 1964, 392. Initiates: inscription of 1st cent. A.D., Pergamon, VIII, 484-6.

PAGE 123 HELLENISTIC RULER (Rome, Terme 544): *M. Bieber*, Hell. Sc., 160.

PAGE 123 BRONZE SATYR (Naples, Mus. Naz. 814): *M. Bieber*, Hell. Sc., 39. Mask mosaic (Naples, Mus. Naz. 9994); *A. Rumpf*, M.u.Z., 152, pl. 53, 3.

PAGE 124 VILLA DEI MISTERI: *E. Simon*, JDAI, 76, 1961, 131f.; *G. Zuntz*, Proceedings of the British Academy, 49, 1963, 177 f. Myrina terracottas: *S. Mollard-Besques*, Catalogue raisonné des figurines et reliefs en terrecuite, II, Myrina, Paris, 1963. Dionysos and Ariadne: ibid., pl. 94. *D. Burr*, Terracottas from Myrina in the Museum of Fine Arts, Boston, 1934.

PAGE 124 BRONZE GROUP: *M. Bieber*, Hell. Sc., 82. Stoa of Herms and choirs: Bulletin Institute of Classical Studies, Supplement no. 14, London, 1962, 44. Herm of Alkamenes: Pergamon VII, 1, 48, no. 27. *Euripides*, Bacch. 403. Circles of Dionysos and Aphrodite: cf. my Art and Literature in Fourth-Century Athens, 16 n. 1, 40.

PAGE 126 MAENAD (Istanbul 575): *M. Bieber*, Hell. Sc., 120; *W. Fuchs*, Vorbilder der neuattischen Reliefs, Berlin, 1959, 153.

PAGE 126 DIONYSOS KATHEGEMON: *M. P. Nilsson*, Geschichte der griechischen Religion, II, 163. Kraton, the Attalistai, and the guild: *M. P. Nilsson*, ibid., 162; *A. W. Pickard-Cambridge*, Dramatic Festivals of Athens, Oxford, 1953, 299 ff.; *C. Picard*, quoted above, p. 46; Pergamon, IV, 18, pl. 13, 14, 45.

PAGE 127 THEATRE: *M. Bieber*, History of the Greek and Roman Theater, 63, 120.

PAGE 128 THE THICK-SOLED SHOE IN TRAGEDY: Halikarnassos base (London, British Museum 1106): Griechische Bühnenaltertümer, pl. 4. Amisos statuette: Paris, Louvre CA 1784.

PAGE 129 MYRINA COMIC ACTORS: cf. my Griechische Bühnenaltertümer, 46; the running slave is no. MT 27, the two young men nos. MT 1 and 15. The Dioskourides mosaics (Naples, Muz. Naz. 9985, 9987): ibid., 7, 13 f., 46 f., 63; *A. Rumpf*, M.u.Z., 153, 167. Copy at Stabiae: *S. Reinach*, Répertoire des peintures, Paris, 1922, 313, 3. The cup on the Dioskourides mosaic: *J. D. Beazley*, Etruscan Vase-painting, Oxford, 1947, 235.

PAGE 131 GOLD NECKLACE (Hamburg 1917, 193): *Küthmann-Kusel*, AM 50, 1925, 174 ff.; *R. Higgins*, Greek and Roman Jewellery, London, 1961, 169 f.

PAGE 132 OROPOS: *M. Bieber*, History of the Greek and Roman Theater², fig. 426. The inscriptions: IG VII, 423. *Vitruvius*, VII, v, 2, on house decoration; V, vi, 5, on scenery. Appius Claudius Pulcher: *Pliny*, Nat. Hist., 35, 23. Demetrios: *A. Rumpf*, M.u.Z., 158.

PAGE 133 BOSCOREALE CUBICULUM: see p. 32. Add *B. Cook*, Bulletin of the Metropolitan Museum, 1963–4, 166.

PAGE 136 GARDENS OF ADONIS: cf. *Theokritos*, XV, 110, with *A. S. F. Gow*, ad loc.

PAGE 138 ODYSSEY PICTURES: *Vitruvius*, VII, v, 2. *P. H. von Blanckenhagen*, RM, 70, 1963, 101; *A. Rumpf*, M.u.Z., 160. Homeric references: Odyssey X, 87; 100; 114–32. Hades scene: *P. Zancani-Montuoro*, Rendiconti Pontificia Accademia, 35, 1963, 67.

PAGE 141 ATHENIAN MASK RELIEF: *M. Bieber*, History of the Greek and Roman Theater², fig. 752; *T. Kraus*, Die Ranken der Ara Pacis, Berlin, 1953, 70, pl. 23. Pergamon theatre relief: Istanbul 287, Pergamon IV, 1, 13; VIII, no. 236. Reliefs from Agora: Berlin, *M. Bieber*, History of the Greek and Roman Theater², fig. 311–3, 380.

PAGE 142 STOA OF ATTALOS: *Homer A. Thompson*, The Athenian Agora, a Guide to the Excavation and Museum, Athens, 1962, 81 (with bibliography); and on the Gymnasium and Theseion, AJA, 69, 1965, 176.

PAGE 143 MONUMENT OF AEMILIUS PAULUS (Delphi): *M. Bieber*, Hell. Sc., 171, fig. 723; Fouilles de Delphes, II, Paris, 1927, 305, fig. 250; *D. E. Strong*, Roman Imperial Sculpture, London, 1961, 8, fig. 13. Text: *Plutarch*, Vita Aemilii, 28.

PAGE 144 DAMOPHON'S GROUP AT LYKOSOURA: *Pausanias*, VIII, 37, 3; *G. Dickins*, BSA, 13, 1906–7, 357, pl. 12–13. *M. Bieber*, Hell. Sc., 158; *M. P. Nilsson*, Geschichte der griechischen Religion, 1, Munich, 1951, 450. Two ladies under one cloak: *M. Guarducci*, AM, 53, 1928, 52 ff. Add Studies in Mediterranean Archaeology, 16, Lund, 1964, 17.

PAGE 146 ZEUS FROM AIGEIRA: *Pausanias*, VII, 26, 4; *M. Bieber*, Hell. Sc., 158. Fragments from Rome: *M. Bieber*, Hell. Sc., 171.

PAGE 146 PORTRAIT OF KARNEADES: *K. Schefold*, Bildnisse etc., 140. The inscription: I.G. II^2 3781.

PAGE 147 APHRODITE OF MELOS: *M. Bieber*, Hell. Sc., 159; *J. Charbonneaux*, Le Vénus de Milo, Paris, 1958.

PAGE 149 APOLLO OF KYRENE (London, British Museum 1380): *M. Bieber*, Hell. Sc., 160. Poseidon of Melos (Athens, N.M. 235): *M. Bieber*, Hell. Sc., 160.

PAGE 149 DELOS: Theatre records: cf. Griechische Bühnenaltertümer, 41. Terracottas and braziers: ibid. 42, 76. Frescoes with dramatic scenes: BCH, 87, 1963, 871. House of the Masks: *J. Chamonard*, Delos XIV, Paris, 1933; *A. Rumpf*, JDAI, 50, 1935, 1 (comparison with Vitruvius); M.u.Z., 166 (mosaics). Greek house: *Vitruvius*, VII, vii. Theatre: *O. A. W. Dilke*, BSA, 43, 1948, 136.

PAGE 154 HOUSE DECORATION: *A. Rumpf*, M.u.Z., 165. *Vitruvius*, II, viii, 9, on transferring pictures; VII, v, on house decoration.

III. LATE HELLENISTIC PERIOD

PAGE 162 ETRUSCAN ASH-CHESTS: e.g. *G. A. Mansuelli*, Etruria and Early Rome 1966, 178. Terracotta from Falerii: ibid. 135. Booty from Roman conquest and other texts for art in Rome in the Republican period: *O. Vessberg*, Studien zur Kunstgeschichte der römischen Republik, Lund, 1941, 5 ff.

PAGE 163 MARCELLUS: *Plutarch*, Vita Marcelli, 30.

CICERO on art galleries; In Verrem, II, iv, 126. For the temples and porticoes: *S. B. Platner and T. Ashby*, A Topographical Dictionary of Rome, Oxford, 1929, *sub vocibus* (with references for the works of art).

PAGE 164 ARCHAISM: Relief (Agora S 370, 7327): *Homer A. Thompson*, The Athenian Agora, 125; *C. Mitchell*, HSCP, 61, 1953, 73; AJA, 68, 1964, 47; *W. Fuchs*, Die Vorbilder der neuattischen Reliefs, JDAI, Ergänzungsheft 20, 45 f. Panathenaic amphorai: *J. D. Beazley*, Development of Attic Black-figure, Berkeley, 1951, 88. Panathenaic oinochoai: *J. R. Green*, Hesperia, 31, 1962, 92. Statues on vases: *K. Schefold*, JDAI, 52, 1937, 30; *E. Bielefeld*, Wissenschaftliche Zeitschrift Greifswald, 4, 1954/5, 379.

PAGE 165 BASIS WITH FOUR GODS (Athens, Acropolis Museum 610): bibliography as for Agora S 370 etc. Archaistic reliefs: *Fuchs*, op. cit., 27, 45 ff. Relief from Rhodes in Oxford, Ashmolean Museum: *Fuchs*, op. cit., 30; *C. A. Hutton*, JHS, 49, 1929, 243 ff., pl. 14 b. Aigeus, Theseus and Medeia: *B. B. Shefton*, AJA, 60, 1956, 159.

PAGE 166 FRIEZE FROM CAPITOLINE HILL (Rome, Conservatori, Braccio Nuovo): *G.-C. Picard*, Mélanges d'Arch. et d'Histoire, 71, 1959, 263; *D. E. Strong*, Roman Imperial Sculpture, London, 1961, 12, fig. 17–18. *Pliny*, Nat. Hist. 35, 13. The monument of Mithradates in Delos: *A. W. Lawrence*, Greek Architecture, 219, fig. 122. Portraits on shields in Athens, *R. E. Wycherley*, The Athenian Agora, III, Princeton, 1957, nos. 102, 417, 462. Weapons in a frieze, Stoa at Pergamon; *A. W. Lawrence*, 209, fig. 115.

PAGE 168 NEO-ATTIC RELIEFS: *W. Fuchs*, op. cit.; *G. M. A. Richter*, Three Critical Periods, 50 f. Mahdia kraters: 1) Dionysos and Ariadne (Tunis, Musée Alaoui, C 1202-3): *W. Fuchs*, op. cit., 108 ff., pl. 22, 24, 25, 26; Schiffsfund von Mahdia, Tübingen, 1963, pl. 68–73. Louvre, Borghese krater: *M. Bieber*, Hell. Sc., 166, 184, fig. 795. 2) Dionysos and thiasos (Tunis, Musée Alaoui, C 1204–5): *W. Fuchs*, Schiffsfund von Mahdia, Tübingen, 1963, pl. 74–79.

PAGE 169 THE MAENADS: *W. Fuchs*, Vorbilder der neuattischen Reliefs, 72 ff.

PAGE 169 THE BEARDED DIONYSOS: *G. Lippold*, Griechische Plastik, 242; *C. Picard*, La Sculpture, IV, 1, Paris 1954, 321. Dionysos visits a comic poet (Vatican): *W. Amelung*, Die Skulpturen des Vatikanischen Museums, II, 509; *D. E. Strong*, Roman Imperial Sculpture, fig. 24; (British Museum etc.); *M. Bieber*, Hell. Sc., 154, fig. 656–7; *C. Watzinger*, JDAI, 61–2, 1946–7, 76 ff.

PAGE 170 PAESTAN BELL-KRATER (Vatican AD 1); *A. D. Trendall*, Paestan Pottery, London, 1936, pl. 18. Relief in the Louvre: *M. Bieber*, ibid., fig. 655.

PAGE 171 DIONYSOS AND ARIADNE: *E. Simon*, Antike Kunst, 6, 1963, 12 ff. South Italian vase: *A. D. Trendall*, Frühitaliotische Vasenmaler, pl. 23a. Vatican Ariadne: *G. Lippold*, Griechische Plastik, 304, pl. 109/3. *Pausanias*, I, 20, 3, with *A. D. Trendall*, Archaeological Reports, 1955, 62, pl. 5.

PAGE 172 DIADOUMENOS OF DELOS: *G. M. A. Richter*, Three Periods, 42; Catalogue of Greek Sculptures in the Metropolitan Museum New York, Oxford, 1954, no. 38.

PAGE 172 GANOSIS: *Vitruvius*, VII, ix, 3.

PAGE 173 COPIES OF PAINTING: Sulla, *Lucian*, Zeuxis 3. Lucullus, *Pliny*, Nat. Hist., 35, 135.

PAGE 173 IDOLINO (Florence, Museo Archeologico, 143): *A. Rumpf*, Critica d'Arte 19/20, 1939, 17 ff.; Archäologie, II, 101; *T. Dohrn*, Festschrift Andreas Rumpf, Krefeld, 1952, 59 ff. Other examples: ibid. and *D. van Buren*, AJA, 67, 1963, 33; *F. Chamoux*, BCH, 74, 1951, 70 ff. *Lucretius*, II, 24. *Homer*, Odyssey, 7, 100.

PAGE 174 STEPHANOS AND MENELAOS: bibliography as for Idolino. *M. Bieber*, Hell. Sc., 181, figs. 784–7. Kolotes: *P. Mingazzini*, AM, 77, 1962, 293. Pausanias V, 20; *Pliny*, Nat. Hist., 35, 54.

PAGE 174 PASITELES: *G. M. A. Richter*, Three Periods, 44; *Pliny*, Nat. Hist., 33, 156; 36, 39–40; 35, 156. Chronology of bronze-makers: *Pliny*, Nat. Hist., 34, 49–52.

PAGE 176 ARKESILAOS: *M. Bieber*, Hell. Sc., 181, 184. *Pliny*, Nat. Hist., 35, 155; 36, 33, 41. Venus Genetrix: *G. Lippold*, Griechische Plastik, pl. 60/4; *Rhys Carpenter*, Sculpture of the Nike Temple Parapet, Cambridge (Mass.), 1929, 61. Erotes and panther-chariot (Naples 81007): Corpus Vasorum Antiquorum, Naples, III, iv E, pl. 54. Marble fountain: *D. E. Strong*, Roman Imperial Sculpture, 15.

PAGE 177 BEGRAM PLASTERS: *O. Kurz* in *E. Hackin*, Nouvelles récherches à Begram, Paris, 1954, 110 ff.

PAGE 177 LACONIAN DANCERS AND ARRETINE: *G. M. A. Richter*, Three Periods, 51.

PAGE 180 TIVOLI, Round temple: *D. S. Robertson*, Handbook of Greek and Roman Architecture, Cambridge, 1929, 210.

PAGE 180 ELEUSIS: *A. W. Lawrence*, Greek Architecture, 211 f.; *L. Budde and R. Nicholls*, Greek and Roman Sculpture in the Fitzwilliam Museum Cambridge, Cambridge, 1964, no. 81; *T. Kraus*, Die Ranken der Ara Pacis, Berlin, 1953, 38, pl. 8.

PAGE 180 TOWER OF THE WINDS: *A. W. Lawrence*, Greek Architecture, 237; *F. Winter*, Kunstgeschichte in Bildern, 375, 5–6; *Vitruvius*, I, vi, 4.

PAGE 181 DELOS PORTRAITS: *Michalowski*, Delos XIII; *M. Bieber*, Hell. Sc., 172 f.; *G. M. A. Richter*, Three Critical Periods, 54.

PAGE 182 FLAMININUS: *Plutarch*, Vita Flaminini, 1, 16. Scipio: *Cicero*, Rab. Post. 10, 27.

PAGE 182 TIVOLI STATUE (Rome, Terme 106513): *M. Bieber*, Hell. Sc., 173, fig. 732; *O. Vessberg*, Studien zur Kunstgeschichte der römischen Republik, Lund, 1941, 209. Poseidon of Melos; *M. Bieber*, Hell. Sc., fig. 684.

PAGE 182 ARRINGATORE: *G. A. Mansuelli*, Etruria and Early Rome, 1966, 172; *M. Bieber*, Hell. Sc., 169, fig. 717; *O. Vessberg*, op. cit., 171, pl. 19; *P. J. Riis*, Den Etruskiske Kunst, Copenhagen, 1962, 210. 'Brutus': *G. A. Mansuelli*, op. cit., 166; *O. Vessberg*, op. cit., 124, pl. 15; *P. J. Riis*, op. cit., 245. Poseidonios and Cicero: *M. Bieber*, Hell. Sc., 163, 169, fig. 696–7, 733; *K. Schefold*, Bildnisse, 150, 174.

PAGE 183 DAUGHTER OF BALBUS: *M. Bieber*, Hell. Sc., 177, fig. 753. Portrait of Polybios: *M. Bieber*,

Hell. Sc., 161, fig. 691; *K. Schefold*, Bildnisse, 146, 5; *Pausanias*, VIII, 30, 8; 37, 2; 48, 8.

PAGE 183 ROMAN PORTRAITS: *Polybius*, 6, 53, with *F. W. Walbank*, Oxford, 1957, ad loc.; *Pliny*, Nat. Hist., 35, 6; *O. Vessberg*, op. cit., 100. Lysistratos, *Pliny*, Nat. Hist. 35, 153. Greek Hellenistic grave-reliefs: *M. Bieber*, Hell. Sc., figs. 523, 538–9, 646–7; *H. Kenner*, Jahreshefte des Öst. Arch. Inst. 46, 1961, 5. Delos: *Michalowski*, Delos XIII, pls. 14, 21, 43. Cf. also *O. Vessberg*, op. cit., pl. 46, 4; 47, 1–2 (Smyrna), 31–4 (Athens). Roman funerary portraits: a very good selection in *O. Vessberg*, op. cit. On the nationality of the artists: *G. M. A. Richter*, Three Critical Periods, 53 f.

PAGE 184 ROMAN RELIEF: *O. Vessberg*, op. cit., 204. *Pliny*, Nat. Hist., 35, 13.

PAGE 186 ASKLEPIEION AT PERGAMON (Bergama 51); *T. Kraus*, Die Ranken der Ara Pacis, 70, pl. 21, 2. Frieze from temple of Divus Julius (Rome, Antiquario Forense): *T. Kraus*, op. cit., pl. 9; *D. E. Strong*, Roman Imperial Sculpture, fig. 26.

PAGE 186 ARA PACIS: *H. Kähler*, Rome and her Empire, 66 f.; *H. P. L'Orange*, Acta Inst. Rom. Norv., 1, 1962, 7; *Virgil*, Ecl. 4, 18 f.

PAGE 186 PORTRAITS IN LIBRARIES: *Pliny*, 35, 9. Piso's Villa; *M. Bieber*, Hell. Sc., figs. 141, 159, 175, 192, 214, 342, 418; *K. Schefold*, Bildnisse, 80, 100, 104, 108, 134.

PAGE 188 VARRO'S IMAGINES: *Pliny*, 35, 9; *Aulus Gellius*, 3, 10. Earliest book illustration: Papyri Societa Italiana, no. 847; *A. Bartoletti*, Studi Italiani di Filologia Classica, 34, 1962, 21. P. Oxy. 2331; *P. Maas*, Greece and Rome, 5, 1958, 171. Terence portrait: Vatican Lat. 3868, *K. Schefold*, Bildnisse, 169; *D. M. Gaunt*, C.R. 14, 1964, 135. Dating of archetype: *T. B. L. Webster*, AJA, 76, 1961, 109, further supported now by the Menander mosaics from Mytilene, BCH, 86, 1962, 874; 87, 1963, 822. Possible Theokritos portrait over his Epigram 27; *A. S. F. Gow*, ad loc.; *Virgil*, Aen. 1a-d are a similar epigram, implying a portrait.

PAGE 189 BRITISH MUSEUM SILVER CUPS: Floral cup 1960.2–1.3 (the other floral cup is 1960.2–1.2); Chryses cup 1960.2–1.1. *P. E. Corbett and D. E. Strong*, British Museum Quarterly, 33, 1962, 69. On Pacuvius' play see also my Hellenistic Poetry and Art, 284 ff.

PAGE 193 TERRACOTTA RELIEF OF TRAGEDY (Rome, Terme): *M. Bieber*, History of the Greek and Roman Theater², 162, fig. 588; *G. Rizzo*, Jahreshefte des Österreichischen Archäologischen Instituts, 8, 1905, 203; my Griechische Bühnenaltertümer, 57, 59.

PAGE 194 TERRACOTTA RELIEF OF COMEDY: *M. Bieber*, op. cit., fig. 587; *G. Rizzo*, op. cit., 210; Griechische Bühnenaltertümer, loc. cit.

PAGE 194 POLYBIOS ON ANICIUS TRIUMPH: *Athenaeus* 615b. Sarapion: *Pliny*, Nat. Hist., 35, 113.

PAGE 195 AEMILIUS SCAURUS: *Pliny*, Nat. Hist., 36, 113. On the whole development see *A. Rumpf*, 'Die Entstehung des römischen Theaters', Mitteilungen des deutschen archaeologischen Instituts, 1950, 40 ff.; *J. A. Hanson*, Roman Theater-Temples, Princeton, 1959, particularly 43 ff.; *M. Bieber*, op. cit., 181. *Cicero*, ad Fam. 7, 1. *Vitruvius*, V, 6. *Plutarch*, Vita Pompei, 42.

PAGE 197 PORTICUS POMPEI and its paintings: *Pliny*, Nat. Hist., 36, 1.

PAGE 197 MEMORIAL OF THE JULII: Antike Denkmäler, I, 7 ff.; *Hübner*, JDAI, 3, 1888, 10; *E. Garger*, RM, 52, 1937, 1 ff.; *G.-C. Picard*, Gallia, 21, 1963, 111; 22, 1964, 8; *D. E. Strong*, Roman Imperial Sculpture, fig. 55; *F. Winter*, Kunstgeschichte in Bildern, 163, 2–3; 404, 1. Garland sarcophagi: *J. M. C. Toynbee*, The Hadrianic School, Cambridge, 1934, 205 ff. On eschatological beliefs in Rome and the provinces, cf. *M. P. Nilsson*, The Dionysiac Mysteries of the Hellenistic and Roman Age, Lund, 1957, 66 ff., 131.

PAGE 199 VERRES: *Cicero*, In Verrem, II, 1, 49–51 (Asia Minor); 2, 87; 4, 4–5, 93, 126–7 (sculpture); 4, 30–31, 32, 38–41 (his helpers; precious vessels); 4, 54 (his factory).

PAGE 200 CICERO: Art history: Brutus 70; cf. de Oratore, III, vii, 26; Orator, 5. Statue of Plato: Brutus 24. Aristotle: ad Att. IV, 10, 1. Marble herms with bronze heads: ad Att., I, 8, 2. Doryphoros herm: *M. Bieber*, Hell. Sc., fig. 755. Hermathena: Ad Att., I, 4, 3. Hermeraclae: Ad Att. I, 10, 3. Prodikos: De Officiis, I, 118. Maenads: Ad Fam., VII, 23, 2.

INDEX

The numerals in italics refer to the plates and figures. The letter (G) denotes Glossary